Giving a Life Away: Suicides, Self-Harm, Prevention, and Intervention

Beatriz Scaglia

The role of the book within our culture is changing. The change is brought on by new ways to acquire & use content, the rapid dissemination of information and real-time peer collaboration on a global scale. Despite these changes one thing is clear--"the book" in it's traditional form continues to play an important role in learning and communication. The book you are holding in your hands utilizes the unique characteristics of the Internet -- relying on web infrastructure and collaborative tools to share and use resources in keeping with the characteristics of the medium (user-created, defying control, etc.)--while maintaining all the convenience and utility of a real book.

Contents

Articles

Suicide — 1
- Suicide — 1

Self-Harm — 17
- Self-harm — 17
- Self-inflicted wound — 30
- Attention seeking — 31
- Psychological pain — 33
- Self-injury Awareness Day — 34
- Enucleation of the eye — 35
- Major depressive disorder — 38

Euthanasia — 64
- Euthanasia — 64
- Voluntary euthanasia — 68
- Non-voluntary euthanasia — 81
- Involuntary euthanasia — 84
- Legality of euthanasia — 85

Murder–Suicide — 93
- Murder–suicide — 93
- Suicide pact — 97
- School shooting — 99
- Cult suicide — 110
- Crime of passion — 114

Suicide Attack — 117
- Suicide attack — 117
- Kamikaze — 138
- Shinyo (suicide boat) — 157
- Suicide weapon — 158

Mass Suicide — 160
- Mass suicide — 160
- Suicide mission — 163
- Suicide epidemic — 165
- Peer pressure — 166

Metaphorical Suicide — 169
- Political suicide — 169

Suicide Methods — 170
- Suicide methods — 170

Prevention and Intervention — 184
- Suicide prevention — 184
- Suicide intervention — 189

Epidemiology of Suicide — 193
- Epidemiology of suicide — 193
- List of countries by suicide rate — 198
- Gender and suicide — 203
- Homosexuality and psychology — 205
- Copycat suicide — 213

References

| Article Sources and Contributors | 218 |
| Image Sources, Licenses and Contributors | 219 |

Suicide

Suicide

Suicide	
Classification and external resources	
 A painting of the English romantic poet Thomas Chatterton, believed to have killed himself with arsenic in 1770	
ICD-10	X 60.[1]–X 84.[2]
ICD-9	E950[3]
MedlinePlus	001554[4]
eMedicine	article/288598[5]
MeSH	F01.145.126.980.875[6]

Suicide

Social aspects
Legislation · Philosophy Religious views · Euthanasia Assisted suicide · Right to die Benevolent suicide

Suicide crisis
Assessment of risk · Crisis hotline · Intervention · Prevention · Suicide watch
Suicide types
Copycat · Cult · Euthanasia · Familicide · Forced · Honor · Internet · Mass · Murder–suicide · Parasuicide · Suicide attack · By cop · Pact
Epidemiology
Gender · Suicide rate
History
List of suicides · Suicide methods
Related phenomena
Ideation · Self-harm · Suicide note · Locations · Failed suicide attempt
By country
China · Japan · South Korea · United States

Suicide (Latin *suicidium*, from *sui caedere*, "to kill oneself") is the act of a human being intentionally causing his or her own death. Suicide is often committed out of despair, or attributed to some underlying mental disorder which includes depression, bipolar disorder, schizophrenia, alcoholism and drug abuse. Financial difficulties, interpersonal relationships and other undesirable situations play a significant role.

Over one million people commit suicide every year. The World Health Organization estimates that it is the thirteenth-leading cause of death worldwide. It is a leading cause of death among teenagers and adults under 35. There are an estimated 10 to 20 million non-fatal attempted suicides every year worldwide.

Views on suicide have been influenced by broader cultural views on existential themes such as religion, honor, and the meaning of life. The Abrahamic religions consider suicide an offense towards God due to religious belief in the sanctity of life. In the West it was often regarded as a serious crime. Conversely, during the samurai era in Japan, seppuku was respected as a means of atonement for failure or as a form of protest. In the 20th century, suicide in the form of self-immolation has been used as a form of protest, and in the form of kamikaze and suicide bombing as a military or terrorist tactic. Sati is a Hindu funeral practice in which the widow would immolate herself on her husband's funeral pyre, either willingly, or under pressure from the family and in-laws.

Medically assisted suicide (euthanasia, or the right to die) is currently a controversial ethical issue involving people who are terminally ill, in extreme pain, or have (perceived or construed) minimal quality of life through injury or illness. Self-sacrifice for others is not always considered suicide, as the goal is not to kill oneself but to save another; however, Émile Durkheim's theory termed such acts "altruistic suicide."

Classification

Self-harm

Main article: Self-harm

Self-harm is not a suicide attempt; however, initially self-harm was erroneously classified as a suicide attempt. There is a non-causal correlation between self-harm and suicide; both are most commonly a joint effect of depression.

Euthanasia and assisted suicide

Main article: Euthanasia

Individuals who wish to end their own lives may enlist the assistance of another person to achieve death. The other person, usually a family member or physician, may help carry out the act if the individual lacks the physical capacity to do so even with the supplied means. Assisted suicide is a contentious moral and political issue in many countries, as seen in the scandal surrounding Dr. Jack Kevorkian, a medical practitioner who supported euthanasia, was found to have helped patients end their own lives, and was sentenced to prison time.

Euthanasia machine invented by Dr. Philip Nitschke, on display at Science Museum, London.

Murder–suicide

Main article: Murder–suicide

A murder–suicide is an act in which an individual kills one or more other persons immediately before or at the same time as him or herself.

The motivation for the murder in murder–suicide can be purely criminal in nature or be perceived by the perpetrator as an act of care for loved ones in the context of severe depression.

Suicide attack

Main article: Suicide attack

A suicide attack is when an attacker perpetrates an act of violence against others, typically to achieve a military or political goal, that results in his or her own death as well. Suicide bombings are often regarded as an act of terrorism. Historical examples include the assassination of Czar Alexander II and the in-part successful kamikaze attacks by Japanese air pilots during the Second World War.

Mass suicide

Main article: Mass suicide

Some suicides are done under peer pressure or as a group. Mass suicides can take place with as few as two people, in a "suicide pact", or with a larger number of people. An example is the mass suicide that took place by members of the Peoples Temple, an American cult led by Jim Jones in Guyana in 1978.

Suicide pact

Main article: Suicide pact

A suicide pact describes the suicides of two or more individuals in an agreed-upon plan. The plan may be to die together, or separately and closely timed. Suicide pacts are generally distinct from mass suicide. The latter refers to incidents in which a larger number of people kill themselves together for the same ideological reason, often within a religious, political, military or paramilitary context. Suicide pacts, on the other hand, usually involve small groups of people (such as married or romantic partners, family members, or friends) whose motivations are intensely personal and individual.

Metaphorical suicide

The metaphorical sense of "willful destruction of one's self-interest", for example political suicide.

Causes

A number of factors are associated with the risk of suicide including: mental illness, drug addiction, and socio-economic factors. While external circumstances, such as a traumatic event, may trigger suicide it does not seem to be an independent cause. Thus suicides are more likely to occur during periods of socioeconomic, familial and individual crisis.

Mental illness

See also: Depression (differential diagnoses)

Mental disorders are frequently present at the time of suicide with estimates from 87% to 98%. When broken down into type mood disorders are present in 30%, substance abuse in 18%, schizophrenia in 14%, and personality disorders in 13.0% of suicides. About 5% of people with schizophrenia die of suicide. Depression, one of the most commonly diagnosed psychiatric disorders is being diagnosed in increasing numbers in various segments of the population worldwide, and is often a precipitating factor in suicide. Depression in the United States alone affects 17.6 million Americans each year or 1 in 6 people. Within the next twenty years depression is expected to become the second leading cause of disability worldwide and the leading cause in high-income nations, including the United States.

In approximately 75% of completed suicides the individuals had seen a physician within the prior year before their death, 45%-66% within the prior month. Approximately 33% - 41% of those who completed suicide had contact with mental health services in the prior year, 20% within the prior month.

Conservative estimates are, that 10% of all psychological symptoms may be due to medical reasons, with the results of one study, suggesting that about 50% of individuals with a serious mental illness *have general medical conditions that are largely undiagnosed and untreated and may cause or exacerbate psychiatric symptoms* (Rothbard AB,*et al.* 2009)

Substance abuse

See also: Long-term effects of alcohol and Long-term effects of benzodiazepines

Substance abuse is the second most common cause of suicide after mood disorders. Both chronic substance misuse as well as acute substance abuse is associated with an increased risk of suicide. This is attributed to the intoxicating and disinhibiting effects of many psychoactive substances; when combined with personal grief such as bereavement the risk of suicide is greatly increased. More than 50% of suicides are related to alcohol or drug use. Up to 25% of drug addicts and alcoholics commit suicide. In adolescents the figure is higher with alcohol or drug misuse playing a role in up to 70% of suicides. It has been recommended that all drug addicts or alcoholics are investigated for suicidal thoughts due to the high risk of suicide.

Misuse of drugs such as cocaine have a high correlation with suicide. Suicide is most likely to occur during the "crash" or withdrawal phase of cocaine in chronic abusers. Polysubstance misuse has been found to more often result in suicide in younger adults whereas suicide from alcoholism is more common in older adults. In San Diego it was found that 30% of suicides in people under the age of 30 had used cocaine. In New York City during a crack epidemic one in five people who committed suicide were found to have recently consumed cocaine. The "come down" or withdrawal phase from cocaine can result in intense depressive symptoms coupled with other distressing mental effects which serve to increase the risk of suicide. It has been found that drinking 6 drinks or more per day results in a sixfold increased risk of suicide.

Alcohol misuse is associated with a number of mental health disorders, and alcoholics have a very high suicide rate. High rates of major depressive disorder occur in heavy drinkers and those who abuse alcohol. Controversy has previously surrounded whether those who abused alcohol who developed major depressive disorder were self medicating (which may be true in some cases) but recent research has now concluded that chronic excessive alcohol intake itself directly causes the development of major depressive disorder in a significant number of alcohol abusers.

Chronic prescribed benzodiazepine use or chronic misuse is associated with depression as well as suicide. Care should be taken when prescribing especially to at risk patients. Depressed adolescents who were taking benzodiazepines were found to have a greatly increased risk of self harm or suicide, although the sample size was small. The effects of benzodiazepines in individuals under the age of 18 requires further research. Additional caution is required in using benzodiazepines in depressed adolescents. Benzodiazepine dependence often results in an increasingly deteriorating clinical picture which includes social deterioration leading to comorbid alcoholism and drug abuse. Suicide is a common outcome of chronic benzodiazepine dependence. Benzodiazepine misuse or misuse of other CNS depressants increases the risk of suicide in drug misusers. 11% of males and 23% of females with a sedative hypnotic misuse habit commit suicide.

Cigarette smoking

There have been various studies done showing a positive link between smoking, suicidal ideation and suicide attempts. In a study conducted among nurses, those smoking between 1-24 cigarettes per day had twice the suicide risk; 25 cigarettes or more, 4 times the suicide risk, than those who had never smoked. In a study of 300,000 male U.S. Army soldiers, a definitive link between suicide and smoking was observed with those smoking over a pack a day having twice the suicide rate of non-smokers.

Problem gambling

Main article: Problem gambling

Problem gambling is often associated with increased suicidal ideation and attempts compared to the general population.

Early onset of problem gambling increases the lifetime risk of suicide. However, gambling-related suicide attempts are usually made by older people with problem gambling. Both comorbid substance use and comorbid mental disorders increase the risk of suicide in people with problem gambling.

A 2010 Australian hospital study found that 17% of suicidal patients admitted to the Alfred Hospital's emergency department was a problem gambler.

Biological

Genetics has an effect on suicide risk accounting for 30–50% of the variance. Much of this relationship acts through the heritability of mental illness.

Social

As a form of defiance or protest

In Ireland protesting via hunger strike to the death has been used as a tactic in recent times for political causes. During The Troubles in Northern Ireland a hunger strike was launched by the provisional IRA to demand that their prisoners be reclassified as prisoners of war rather than as terrorists, during the infamous 1981 hunger strikes, led by Bobby Sands; this protest resulted in 10 deaths. The cause of death was recorded as "starvation, self-imposed" rather than suicide by the coroner, modified to simply "starvation" on the death certificates after protests from the striker's families.

Judicial suicide

See also: murder–suicide

A person who has committed a crime may commit suicide to avoid prosecution and disgrace, such as in murder–suicides. Nazi leader Hermann Göring, a high-ranked Nazi and head of the Luftwaffe, committed suicide with cyanide capsules rather than be hanged after his conviction at the Nuremberg Trials. Some school shootings, including the Virginia Tech massacre, concluded with the perpetrator committing suicide.

Military suicide

Main articles: Suicide attack and :Category:Military personnel who committed suicide

In the final days of World War II, some Japanese pilots volunteered for kamikaze missions in an attempt to forestall defeat for the Empire of Japan, while Japanese ground forces initiated banzai charges. Near the end of WWII the Japanese designed a small aircraft whose only purpose was kamikaze missions. Similarly, units of the Luftwaffe flew Selbstopfereinsatz (self-sacrifice missions) against Soviet bridges. In Nazi Germany, many soldiers and government officialsWikipedia:Avoid weasel words (including Adolf Hitler) killed themselves rather than surrender to Allied forces. The Japanese also built one-man "human torpedo" suicide submarines called Kaitens.

A kamikaze attack on the escort carrier USS *White Plains*

Dutiful suicide

Dutiful suicide is an act, or non-fatal attempt at the act, of fatal self-violence at one's own hands done in the belief that it will secure a greater good, rather than to escape harsh or impossible conditions. It can be voluntary, to relieve some dishonor or punishment, or imposed by threats of death or reprisals on one's family or reputation (a kind of murder by remote control). It can be culturally traditional or generally abhorred; it can be heavily ritualized as in seppuku or purely functional. Dutiful suicide can be distinguished from a kamikaze or suicide bomb attack, in which a fighter consumes his own life in delivering a weapon to the enemy.

Disgraced Roman aristocrats were sometimes allowed to commit suicide to spare themselves a trial and penalties against their families. An example of this was Emperor Nero who reportedly committed forced suicide facing a revolt and execution. A more modern case is Erwin Rommel, who was found to have foreknowledge of the July 20 Plot on Hitler's life. Rommel was threatened with public trial, execution and reprisals on his family unless he killed himself, which he did.

Suicide as an escape

In situations where continuing to live is intolerable, some people use suicide as a means of escape. Some inmates in Nazi concentration camps are known to have killed themselves by delibertely touching the electrified fences.

According to a report by Tata Institute of Social Sciences in Mumbai, 150,000 debt-ridden farmers in India have committed suicide in the past decade.

Other factors

Socio-economic factors such as unemployment, poverty, homelessness, and discrimination may trigger suicidal thoughts. Poverty may not be a direct cause but it can increase the risk of suicide, as it is a major risk group for depression. Advocacy of suicide has sometimes been cited as a contributing factor.[citation needed]

Suicide methods

Main article: Suicide methods

The leading method of suicide varies dramatically between countries. The leading methods in different regions include hanging, pesticide poisoning, and firearms. Worldwide 30% of suicides are from pesticides. The use of this method however varies markedly from 4% in Europe to more than 50% in the Pacific region. In the United States 52% of suicides involve the use of firearms. Asphyxiation and poisoning are fairly common as well. Together they comprised about 40% of U.S. suicides. Other methods of suicide include blunt force trauma (jumping from a building or bridge, self-defenestrating, stepping in front of a train, or car collision, for example). Exsanguination or bloodletting

Percent of suicides that are by firearm in the United States, by gender and age, 1999–2005. Data from the CDC.

(slitting one's wrist or throat), intentional drowning, self-immolation, electrocution, and intentional starvation are other suicide methods. Individuals may also intentionally provoke another person into administering lethal action against them, as in suicide by cop.

Whether or not exposure to suicide is a risk factor for suicide is controversial. A 1996 study was unable to find a relationship between suicides among friends, while a 1986 study found increased rates of suicide following the televisation of news stories regarding suicide.

Prevention

Main article: Suicide prevention

Suicide prevention is an umbrella term for the collective efforts of local citizen organizations, mental health practitioners and related professionals to reduce the incidence of suicide through prevention and proactive measures. One of the first exclusively professional research centers was established in 1958 in Los Angeles. The first crisis hotline service in the U.S. run by selected, trained citizen volunteers was established 1961 in San Francisco.

Epidemiology

Main article: Epidemiology of suicide

Suicide is the tenth leading cause of death worldwide with about a million people dying by suicide annually. According to 2005 data, suicides in the U.S. outnumber homicides by nearly 2 to 1 and ranks as the 11th leading cause of death in the country, ahead of liver disease and Parkinson's. Worldwide suicide rates have increased by 60% in the past 50 years, mainly in the developing countries.

A disproportionate amount of suicides in the world occur in Asia, which is estimated to account for up to 60% of all suicides. According to the World Health Organization, China, India and Japan may account for 40% of all world suicides.

In the U.S., the rate of suicide is increasing for the first time in a decade. The increase in the overall suicide rate between 1999 and 2005 has been due primarily to an increase in suicides among whites aged 40–64, with white middle-aged women experiencing the largest annual increase.

Deaths for self inflicted injuries per 100,000 inhabitants in 2004. "Mortality and Burden of Disease Estimates for WHO Member States in 2002" (xls). World Health Organization. 2002. . Retrieved 2009-12-13.   no data   less than 3   3–6   6–9   9–12   12–15   15–18   18–21   21–24   24–27   27–30   30–33   more than 33

Gender

Main article: Gender and suicide

In the Western world, males die much more often by means of suicide than do females, although females attempt suicide more often. Some medical professionals believe this stems from the fact that males are more likely to end their lives through effective violent means, while women primarily use less severe methods such as overdosing on medications.

Suicide rate per 100,000 males (left) and female (right) (data from 1978–2008).

no data	< 1	5–5.8	5.8–8.5	12–19	19–22.5	26–29.5	33–36.5
1–5			8.5–12	22.5–26		29.5–33	>36.5

In *The Eclipse: A Memoir of Suicide*, author Antonella Gambotto-Burke reports that in the West, middle-aged men now lead "the self-annihilation stakes (40% of total suicides)." She continues: "Triggers of choice are generally separation, unemployment, debt. Male gender identity is defined by (active) conquest ... In externalizing the source of their self-esteem, they surrender all emotional independence. (Conquest requires two parties, after all.) A man cannot feel like a man without a partner, corporation, team. Manhood is a game played on the terrain of opposites. It thus follows that male sense of self disintegrates when the Other is absent."

Alcohol and drug use

In the United States 16.5% of suicides are related to alcohol. Alcoholics are 5 to 20 times more likely to kill themselves while the misuse of other drugs increases the risk 10 to 20 times. About 15% of alcoholics commit suicide, and about 33% of suicides in the under 35's have a primary diagnosis of alcohol or other substance misuse; over 50% of all suicides are related to alcohol or drug dependence. In adolescents alcohol or drug misuse plays a role in up to 70% of suicides.

Ethnicity

See also: Finno-Ugrian suicide hypothesis

National suicide rates differ significantly between countries and amongst ethnic groups within countries. For example, in the U.S., non-Hispanic Caucasians are nearly 2.5 times more likely to kill themselves than African Americans or Hispanics. In the United Kingdom suicide rates vary significantly between different parts of the country. In Scotland, for example the suicide rate is approximately double that of England.

Social aspects

Intervention

Main article: Suicide intervention

The predominant view of modern medicine is that suicide is a mental health concern, associated with psychological factors such as the difficulty of coping with depression, inescapable suffering or fear, or other mental disorders and pressures. A suicide attempt is sometimes interpreted as a "cry for help" and attention, or to express despair and the wish to escape, rather than a genuine intent to die. Most people who attempt suicide do not complete suicide on a first attempt; those who later gain a history of repetitions have a significantly higher probability of eventual completion of suicide.

In the United States, individuals who express the intent to harm themselves may be automatically determined to lack the *present mental capacity* to refuse treatment, and can be transported to the emergency department against their will. An emergency physician will determine whether inpatient care at a mental health care facility is warranted. This is sometimes referred to as being "committed". A court hearing may be held to determine the individual's *competence*. In most states, a psychiatrist may hold the person for a specific time period without a judicial order. If the psychiatrist determines the person to be a threat to himself or others, the person may be admitted involuntarily to a psychiatric treatment facility. This period is usually of three days duration. After this time the person must be discharged or appear in front of a judge. As in any judicial proceeding this person has a right to legal counsel.

Switzerland has recently taken steps to legalize assisted suicide for the chronically mentally ill. The high court in Lausanne, in a 2006 ruling, granted an anonymous individual with longstanding psychiatric difficulties the right to end his own life. At least one leading American bioethicist, Jacob Appel of Brown University, has argued that the American medical community ought to condone suicide in certain individuals with mental illness.

Legislation

Main article: Suicide legislation

In some jurisdictions, an act or incomplete act of suicide is considered to be a crime. More commonly, a surviving party member who assisted in the suicide attempt will face criminal charges.

In Brazil, if the help is directed to a minor, the penalty is applied in its double and not considered as homicide. In Italy and Canada, instigating another to suicide is also a criminal offense. In Singapore, assisting in the suicide of a mentally handicapped person is a capital offense. In India, abetting suicide of a minor or a mentally challenged person can result in a maximum 1 year prison term with a possible fine.

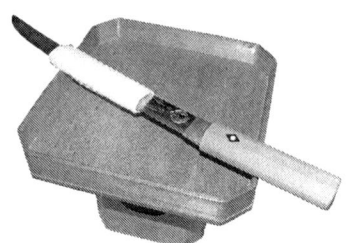

A *tantō* knife prepared for *seppuku*.

In Germany, the following laws apply to cases of suicide:

- Active euthanasia (killing on request) is prohibited by article 216 of the StGB (Strafgesetzbuch, German Criminal Code), punishable with six months to five years in jail
- German law interprets suicide as an accident and anyone present during suicide may be prosecuted for failure to render aid in an emergency. A suicide legally becomes emergency when a suicidal person loses consciousness. Failure to render aid is punishable under article 323c of the StGB, with

a maximum one year jail sentence.

Religious views

Main article: Religious views on suicide

In most forms of Christianity, suicide is considered a sin, based mainly on the writings of influential Christian thinkers of the Middle Ages, such as St. Augustine and St. Thomas Aquinas; suicide was not considered a sin under the Byzantine Christian code of Justinian, for instance. In Catholic doctrine, the argument is based on the commandment "Thou shalt not kill" (made applicable under the New Covenant by Jesus in Matthew 19:18), as well as the idea that life is a gift given by God which should not be spurned, and that suicide is against the "natural order" and thus interferes with God's master plan for the world. However, it is believed that mental illness or grave fear of suffering diminishes the responsibility of the one completing suicide. Counter-arguments include the following: that the sixth commandment is more accurately translated as "thou shalt not murder", not necessarily applying to the self; that taking one's own life no more violates God's Law than does curing a disease; and that a number of suicides by followers of God are recorded in the Bible with no dire condemnation.

Judaism focuses on the importance of valuing this life, and as such, suicide is tantamount to denying God's goodness in the world. Despite this, under extreme circumstances when there has seemed no choice but to either be killed or forced to betray their religion, Jews have committed individual suicide or mass suicide (see Masada, First French persecution of the Jews, and York Castle for examples) and as a grim reminder there is even a prayer in the Jewish liturgy for "when the knife is at the throat", for those dying "to sanctify God's Name". (See: *Martyrdom*). These acts have received mixed responses by Jewish authorities, regarded both as examples of heroic martyrdom, whilst others state that it was wrong for them to take their own lives in anticipation of martyrdom.

Suicide is not allowed in Islam; however, martyring oneself for Allah (during combat) is not considered the same as completing suicide. Suicide in Islam is seen as a sign of disbelief in God.

In Hinduism, suicide is generally frowned upon and is considered equally sinful as murdering another in contemporary Hindu society. Hindu Scriptures state that one who commits suicide will become part of the spirit world, wandering earth until the time one would have otherwise died, had one not committed suicide. However, Hinduism accept a man's right to end one's life through the non-violent practice of fasting to death, termed *Prayopavesa*. But Prayopavesa is strictly restricted to people who have no desire or ambition left, and no responsibilities remaining in this life. Jainism has a similar practice named *Santhara*. Sati, or self-immolation by widows was prevalent in Hindu society during the Middle Ages.

Philosophy

Main article: Philosophy of suicide

Some see suicide as a legitimate matter of personal choice and a human right (colloquially known as the right to die movement), and maintain that no one should be forced to suffer against their will, particularly from conditions such as incurable disease, mental illness, and old age that have no possibility of improvement. Proponents of this view reject the belief that suicide is always irrational, arguing instead that it can be a valid last resort for those enduring major pain or trauma. This perspective is most popular in continental Europe, where euthanasia and other such topics are commonly discussed in parliament and has a good deal of support.

The Way Out, or Suicidal Ideation: George Grie, 2007.

A narrower segment of this group considers suicide something between a grave but condonable choice in some circumstances and a sacrosanct right for anyone (even a young and healthy person) who believes they have rationally and conscientiously come to the decision to end their own lives. Notable supporters of this school of thought include German pessimist philosopher Arthur Schopenhauer, Friedrich Nietzsche, and Scottish empiricist David Hume. Bioethicist Jacob Appel has become the leading advocate for this position in the United States. Adherents of this view often advocate the abrogation of statutes that restrict the liberties of people known to be suicidal, such as laws permitting their involuntary commitment to mental hospitals.

Locations

Some landmarks have become known for high levels of suicide attempts. The four most popular locations in the world are reportedly San Francisco's Golden Gate Bridge, Toronto's Bloor Street Viaduct (before the construction of the Luminous Veil), Japan's Aokigahara Forest and England's Beachy Head. In 2005 the Golden Gate Bridge had a count exceeding 1,200 jumpers since its construction in 1937, in 1997 the Bloor Street Viaduct had one suicide every 22 days, and in 2002 Aokigahara had a record of 78 bodies found within the forest, replacing the previous record of 73 in 1998. The suicide rate of these places is so high that numerous signs, urging potential victims of suicide to seek help, have been posted.

Animal and bacteria suicide

Suicide has been observed in salmonella seeking to overcome competing bacteria by triggering an immune system response against them. Suicidal defences by workers are also noted in a Brazilian ant *Forelius pusillus* where a small group of ants leaves the security of the nest after sealing the entrance from the outside each evening. Pea aphids, when threatened by a ladybug, can explode themselves, scattering and protecting their brethren and sometimes even killing the lady bug. Some species of termites have soldiers that explode, covering their enemies with sticky goo. There have been anecdotal reports of dogs, horses, and dolphins committing suicide, but little hard evidence. There has been little scientific study of animal suicide.

Representations of suicide in popular culture

Film

- In *The Godfather Part II* (1974), Corleone Family consiglieri, Tom Hagen, and caporegime, Frank Pentangeli, make a deal. The Family will take care of Frank's dependents if Frank - who entered the Witness Protection Program and intended to testify about the Corleone Family's criminal activities in court, but ultimately did not - will pay penance for the intended disloyalty by slitting his wrists, Roman style, while taking a bath.
- The war drama, *The Deer Hunter* (1978), deals with such controversial issues as suicide, post-traumatic stress disorder, infidelity and mental illness.
- *Heathers* (1989) deals with the themes of individual and mass suicide by teenagers.
- The 1993 novel, *The Virgin Suicides*, and the 1999 film based on the book center on the suicides of five sisters in Grosse Pointe, Michigan during the 1970s. The Lisbon girls' suicides fascinate their community as their neighbors struggle to find an explanation for the acts.

Television

- HBO's series, *The Sopranos*, frequently addresses the theme of suicide.
  - Three characters successfully kill themselves: mobster Eugene Pontecorvo (in "Members Only") and Tony Soprano's emotionally unstable comare, Gloria Trillo (as we learn in "Everybody Hurts"), both hang themselves when they feel trapped by their lives, and corrupt, heavily indebted policeman, Vin Makazian, jumps off a bridge (in "Nobody Knows Anything") after he has been arrested and must turn in his gun and badge.
  - At least two successful suicides by characters' acquaintances are cited: Tony's sister, Janice Soprano, tells Tony (in "Everybody Hurts") that her neighbor in Seattle killed himself by "sucking down the end of a deer rifle", and Dr. Jennifer Melfi tells Tony that one of her patients committed suicide while Melfi was on the lam (in "Guy Walks Into a Psychiatrist's Office...".

- Several other characters contemplate, threaten, or bungle suicide attempts: Tony Soprano's ex-comare, Irina, threatens to kills herself (in "The Knight in White Satin Armor"), Artie Bucco - perhaps Tony's best friend - attempts suicide by mixing pills and liquor (in "Everybody Hurts"), A.J. Soprano unsuccesfully attempts suicide by drowning (in "The Second Coming") - which is fortunate, since he ultimately wants to live - and Tony's sister, Janice Soprano, confides to Bobby Baccalieri (in "Pie-O-My") that she came close to shooting herself when her husband left her, but was saved by thoughts of her son, Harpo.
- Tony Soprano dreams about self-immolation (in "Funhouse"), but denies his suicidal ideations in "The Legend of Tennessee Moltisanti", when he asks whether or not Christopher has ever contemplated suicide and Chris responds: "Suicide is for the weak".

See also

- American Foundation for Suicide Prevention
- CALM, Campaign Against Living Miserably
- Cult suicide
- National Suicide Prevention Lifeline
- Jack Kevorkian
- Organ donation#In suicides
- Parasuicide
- Quantum suicide
- Samaritans (charity)
- Senicide
- Suicide Act 1961
- Suicide bridge
- Suicide note
- Suicide Prevention Action Network USA
- Suicide tree
- Suicide watch
- Rational suicide

Books

- The Complete Manual of Suicide
- The Peaceful Pill Handbook
- Final Exit
- Suicide

Film

- The Bridge

Lists
- List of suicides
- List of countries by suicide rate
- List of suicide sites

Further reading

- Berrios G E & Mohanna M (1990) Durkheim and French Psychiatric Views on Suicide during the 19th century: a conceptual history. *British Journal of Psychiatry* 156: 1–9
- Gambotto, Antonella (2004). *The Eclipse: A Memoir of Suicide*. Australia: Broken Ankle Books. ISBN 0-975-1075-1-8.
- Jamison, Kay Redfield (2000). *Night Falls Fast: Understanding Suicide*. New York: Vintage. ISBN 0375401458.
- Simpson, George Gaylord; Durkheim, Emile (1997). *Suicide: a study in sociology*. New York: Free Press. ISBN 0-684-83632-7.
- McDowell, Eugene E.; Stillion, Judith M. (1996). *Suicide across the life span: premature exits*. Washington, DC: Taylor & Francis. ISBN 1-56032-304-3.
- Stone, Geo (2001). *Suicide and attempted suicide*. New York, NY: Carroll & Graf. ISBN 0-7867-0940-5.
- Hakim, David (2008). *Man Down CineSource Magazine* [7].

External links

- Suicide [8] at the Open Directory Project
- Stamp Out Suicide! [9] website that promotes suicide awareness and supports suicide prevention
- American Foundation for Suicide Prevention [10]
- Samaritans [11], a charity in the United Kingdom for suicide prevention
- Welcome to Befrienders Worldwide [12], a worldwide support organization helping those considering suicide or coping with its impact
- Council of Europe, *Child and teenage suicide in Europe: A serious public-health issue* [13], 27 March 2008.

pnb:خودکشی

Self-Harm

Self-harm

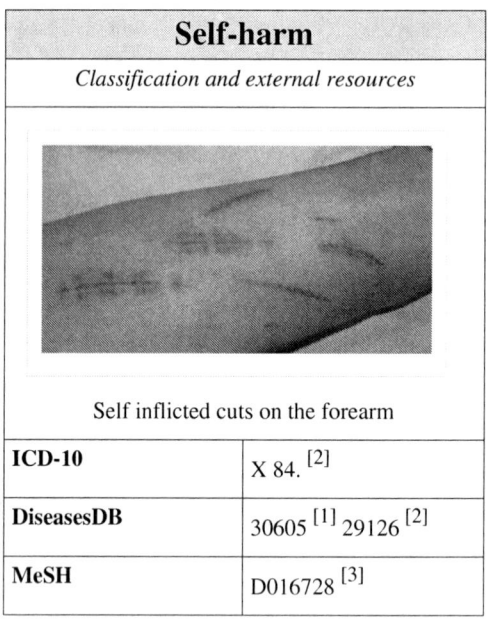

Self-harm	
Classification and external resources	
Self inflicted cuts on the forearm	
ICD-10	X 84. [2]
DiseasesDB	30605 [1] 29126 [2]
MeSH	D016728 [3]

Self-harm (SH) or **deliberate self-harm** (DSH) includes **self-injury** (SI) and **self-poisoning** and is defined as the intentional, direct injuring of body tissue without suicidal intent. These terms are used in the more recent literature in an attempt to reach a more neutral terminology. The older literature, especially that which predates the DSM-IV-TR, almost exclusively refers to **self-mutilation**. The term is synonymous with "self-injury." The most common form of self-harm is skin cutting but self-harm also covers a wide range of behaviours including, but not limited to, burning, scratching, banging or hitting body parts, interfering with wound healing, hair pulling (trichotillomania) and the ingestion of toxic substances or objects. Behaviours associated with substance abuse and eating disorders are usually not considered self-harm because the resulting tissue damage is ordinarily an unintentional side effect. However, the boundaries are not always clear-cut and in some cases behaviours that usually fall outside the boundaries of self-harm may indeed represent self-harm if performed with explicit intent to cause tissue damage. Although suicide is not the intention of self-harm, the relationship between self-harm and suicide is complex, as self-harming behaviour may be potentially life-threatening. There is also an increased risk of suicide in individuals who self-harm to the extent that self-harm is found in 40–60% of suicides. However, generalising self-harmers to be suicidal is, in the majority of cases, inaccurate.

Self-harm is listed in the Diagnostic and Statistical Manual of Mental Disorders (DSM-IV-TR) as a symptom of borderline personality disorder. However patients with other diagnoses may also self-harm, including those with depression, anxiety disorders, substance abuse, eating disorders, post-traumatic stress disorder, schizophrenia, and several personality disorders. Self-harm is also apparent in high-functioning individuals who have no underlying clinical diagnosis. The motivations for self-harm vary and may be used to fulfill a number of different functions. These functions include self-harm being used as a coping mechanism which provides temporary relief of intense feelings such as anxiety, depression, stress, emotional numbness and a sense of failure or self-loathing. Self-harm is often associated with a history of trauma and abuse including emotional abuse, sexual abuse, drug dependence, eating disorders, or mental traits such as low self-esteem or perfectionism. There is also a positive statistical correlation between self-harm and emotional abuse. There are a number of different methods that can be used to treat self-harm and which concentrate on either treating the underlying causes or on treating the behaviour itself. When self-harm is associated with depression, antidepressant drugs and treatments may be effective. Other approaches involve avoidance techniques, which focus on keeping the individual occupied with other activities, or replacing the act of self-harm with safer methods that do not lead to permanent damage.

Self-harm is most common in adolescence and young adulthood, usually first appearing between the ages of 14 and 24. However, self-harm can occur at any age, including in the elderly population. The risk of serious injury and suicide is higher in older people who self-harm. Self harm is not limited to humans. Captive non-human animals are also known to participate in self-mutilation, such as captive birds and monkeys.

Classification

Self-harm (SH), also referred to as *self-injury* (SI), *self-inflicted violence* (SIV) or *self-injurious behaviour* (SIB), refers to a spectrum of behaviours where demonstrable injury is self-inflicted. The term *self-mutilation* is also sometimes used, although this phrase evokes connotations that some find worrisome, inaccurate, or offensive. *Self-inflicted wounds* is a specific term associated with soldiers to describe non-lethal injuries inflicted in order to obtain early dismissal from combat. This differs from the common definition of self-harm, as damage is inflicted for a specific secondary purpose. A broader definition of self-harm might also include those who inflict harm on their bodies by means of disordered eating.

Intentional drug abuse or overdose is a form of self-harm often committed with suicidal undertones.

A common belief regarding self-harm is that it is an attention-seeking behaviour; however, in most cases, this is inaccurate. Many self-harmers are very self-conscious of their wounds and scars and feel guilty about their behaviour leading them to go to great lengths to conceal their behaviour from others. They may offer alternative explanations for their injuries, or conceal their scars with clothing. Self-harm in such individuals is not associated with suicidal or para-suicidal behaviour. A person who self-harms is not usually seeking to end their own life; it has been suggested instead that they are using self-harm as a coping mechanism to relieve emotional pain or discomfort. Studies of individuals with developmental disabilities (such as mental retardation) have shown self-harm being dependent on environmental factors such as obtaining attention or escape from demands. Though this is not always the case, some individuals suffer from dissociation and they harbor a desire to feel real and/or to fit in to society's rules.

Signs and symptoms

80% of self-harm involves stabbing or cutting the skin with a sharp object. However, the number of self-harm methods are only limited by an individual's inventiveness and their determination to harm themselves; this includes, but is not limited to burning, self poisoning, alcohol abuse, self-embedding of objects and forms of self-harm related to anorexia and bulimia. The locations of self-harm are often areas of the body that are easily hidden and concealed from the detection of others. As well as defining self-harm in terms of the act of damaging one's own body, it may be more accurate to define self-harm in terms of the intent, and the emotional distress that the person is attempting to deal with. Neither the

DSM-IV-TR nor the ICD-10 provide diagnostic criteria for self-harm. It is often seen as only a symptom of an underlying disorder, though many people who self-harm would like this to be addressed. A formal proposal is currently under review (2010) to include Non-Suicidal Self Injury as a distinct diagnosis in the forthcoming 5th edition of the Diagnostic and Statistical Manual of Mental Disorders (DSM-5).

Cause

Mental illness

Although some people who self-harm do not suffer from any forms of recognised mental illness, many people experiencing various forms of mental ill-health do have a higher risk of self-harm. The key areas of illness which exhibit an increased risk include borderline personality disorder, depression, phobias, and conduct disorders. Substance abuse is also considered a risk factor as are some personal characteristics such as poor problem solving skills and impulsivity. There are parallels between self-harm and Munchausen syndrome, a psychiatric disorder where those affected feign illness or trauma. There may be a common ground of inner distress culminating in self-directed harm in a Munchausen patient. However, a desire to deceive medical personnel in order to gain treatment and attention is more important in Munchausen's than in self-harm.

Psychological factors

Emotionally invalidating environments where parents punish children for expressing sadness or hurt can contribute to a difficulty experiencing emotions and increased rates of self harm. Abuse during childhood is accepted as a primary social factor, as is bereavement, and troubled parental or partner relationships. Factors such as war, poverty, and unemployment may also contribute. In addition, some individuals with pervasive developmental disabilities such as autism engage in self-harm, although whether this is a form of self-stimulation or for the purpose of harming oneself is a matter of debate.

Genetics

The most distinctive characteristic of the rare genetic condition Lesch-Nyhan syndrome is self-harm and may include biting and head banging. Genetics may contribute to the risk of developing other psychological conditions, such as anxiety or depression, which could in turn lead to self-harming behaviour. However, the link between genetics and self-harm in otherwise healthy patients is largely inconclusive.

Drugs and alcohol

Substance misuse, dependence and withdrawal is associated with self-harm. Benzodiazepine dependence as well as benzodiazepine withdrawal is associated with self-harming behaviour in young people. Alcohol is a major risk factor for self harm. A study which analysed self-harm presentations to emergency rooms in Northern Ireland found that alcohol was a major contributing factor and involved in 63.8 percent of self-harm presentations.

Pathophysiology

Self-harm is not typically suicidal behaviour, although there is the possibility that a self-inflicted injury may result in life-threatening damage. Although the person may not recognise the connection, self-harm often becomes a response to profound and overwhelming emotional pain that cannot be resolved in a more functional way.

The motivations for self-harm vary as it may be used to fulfill a number of different functions. These functions include self-harm being used as a coping mechanism which provides temporary relief of intense feelings such as anxiety, depression, stress, emotional numbness and a sense of failure or self-loathing. There is also a positive statistical correlation between self-harm and emotional abuse. Self-harm may become a means to manage pain, in contrast to the pain that may have been experienced earlier in the sufferers life (e.g. through abuse) over which they had no control.

Other motives for self-harm do not fit into medicalised models of behaviour and may seem incomprehensible to others, as demonstrated by this example:

> My motivations for self-harming were diverse, but included examining the interior of my arms for hydraulic lines. This may sound strange.

Assessment of motives in a medical setting is usually based on precursors to the incident, circumstances and information from the patient. However, limited studies show that professional assessments tend to suggest more manipulative or punitive motives than personal assessments.

The UK ONS study reported only two motives: "to draw attention" and "because of anger". For some people harming oneself can be a way to draw attention to the need for help and to ask for assistance in an indirect way but may also be an attempt to affect others and to manipulate them in some way emotionally. However, those with chronic, repetitive self-harm often do not want attention and hide their scars carefully.

Many people who self-harm state that it allows them to "go away" or dissociate, separating the mind from feelings that are causing anguish. This may be achieved by tricking the mind into believing that the present suffering being felt is caused by the self-harm instead of the issues they were facing previously: the physical pain therefore acts as a distraction from the original emotional pain. To complement this theory, one can consider the need to 'stop' feeling emotional pain and mental agitation.

"A person may be hyper-sensitive and overwhelmed; a great many thoughts may be revolving within their mind, and they may either become triggered or could make a decision to stop the overwhelming feelings." The sexual organs may be deliberately hurt as a way to deal with unwanted feelings of sexuality, or as a means of punishing sexual organs that may be perceived as having responded in contravention to the person's wellbeing. (e.g., responses to childhood sexual abuse).

Those who engage in self-harm face the contradictory reality of harming themselves whilst at the same time obtaining relief from this act. It may even be hard for some to actually initiate cutting, but they often do because they know the relief that will follow. For some self-harmers this relief is primarily psychological whilst for others this feeling of relief comes from the beta endorphins released in the brain. Endorphins are endogenous opioids that are released in response to physical injury, act as natural painkillers, and induce pleasant feelings and would act to reduce tension and emotional distress. Many self-harmers report feeling very little to no pain while self-harming and, for some, deliberate self-harm may become a means of seeking pleasure.

Alternatively, self-harm may be a means of feeling *something*, even if the sensation is unpleasant and painful. Those who self-harm sometimes describe feelings of emptiness or numbness (anhedonia), and physical pain may be a relief from these feelings. "A person may be detached from himself or herself, detached from life, numb and unfeeling. They may then recognise the need to function more, or have a desire to feel real again, and a decision is made to create sensation and 'wake up'."

As a coping mechanism, self-harm can become psychologically addictive because, to the self-harmer, it works; it enables him/her to deal with intense stress in the current moment. The patterns sometimes created by it, such as specific time intervals between acts of self-harm, can also create a behavioural pattern that can result in a wanting or craving to fulfill thoughts of self-harm.

Prevention

Self-harm awareness

There are many movements among the general self-harm community to make self-harm itself and treatment better known to mental health professionals as well as the general public. For example, Self-injury Awareness Day (SIAD) is set for March 1 of every year, where on this day, some people choose to be more open about their own self-harm, and awareness organisations make special efforts to raise awareness about self-harm. Some people wear an orange awareness ribbon or wristband to encourage awareness of self-harm.

The orange ribbon of self harm awareness.

Treatment

There is considerable uncertainty about which forms of psychosocial and physical treatments of patients who harm themselves are most effective and as such further clinical studies are required. Psychiatric and personality disorders are common in individuals who self-harm and as a result self-harm may be an indicator of depression and/or other psychological problems. Many people who self-harm suffer from moderate or severe clinical depression and therefore treatment with antidepressant drugs may often be effective in treating these patients. Cognitive Behavioural Therapy may also be used (where the resources are available) to assist those with axis 1 diagnoses, such as depression, schizophrenia, and bipolar disorder. Dialectical behavioural therapy (DBT) can be very successful for those individuals exhibiting a personality disorder, and could potentially be used for those with other mental illnesses who exhibit self-harming behaviour. Diagnosis and treatment of the causes of self-harm is thought by many to be the best approach to treating self-harm. But in some cases, particularly in clients with a personality disorder, this is not very effective, so more clinicians are starting to take a DBT approach in order to reduce the behaviour itself. People who rely on habitual self-harm are sometimes psychiatrically hospitalised, based on their stability, and their ability and especially their willingness to get help.

In individuals with developmental disabilities, occurrence of self-harm is often demonstrated to be related to its effects on the environment, such as obtaining attention or desired materials or escaping demands. As developmentally disabled individuals often have communication or social deficits, self-harm may be their way of obtaining these things which they are otherwise unable to obtain in a socially appropriate way (such as by asking). One approach for treating self-harm thus is to teach an alternative, appropriate response which obtains the same result as the self-harm.

Avoidance techniques

Generating alternative behaviours that the sufferer can engage in instead of self-harm is one successful behavioural method that is employed to avoid self-harm. Techniques, aimed at keeping busy, may include journaling, taking a walk, participating in sports or exercise or being around friends when the sufferer has the urge to harm themselves. The removal of objects used for self-harm from easy reach is also helpful for resisting self-harming urges. The provision of a card that allows sufferers to make emergency contact with counselling services should the urge to self-harm arise may also help prevent the act of self-harm. Alternative and safer methods of self-harm that do not lead to permanent damage, for example the snapping of a rubber band on the wrist, may also help calm the urge to self-harm. Using biofeedback may help raise self-awareness in the suffer of certain pre-occupations or particular mental state or mood that precede bouts of self-harming behavior, and help the sufferer identify techniques to avoid those pre-occupations before they lead to self-harm. Any avoidance or coping strategy must be appropriate to the individual's motivation and reason for harming.

Epidemiology

It is difficult to gain an accurate picture of incidence and prevalence of self-harm. This is due in a part to a lack of sufficient numbers of dedicated research centers to provide a continuous monitoring system. However, even with sufficient resources, statistical estimates are crude since most incidences of self-harm are undisclosed to the medical profession as acts of self-harm are frequently carried out in secret, and wounds may be superficial and easily treated by the individual. Recorded figures can be based on three sources: psychiatric samples, hospital admissions and general population surveys. About 10% of admissions to medical wards in the UK are as a result of self-harm, the majority of which are drug overdoses. However, studies based only on hospital admissions may hide the larger group of self-harmers who do not need or seek hospital treatment for their injuries, instead treating themselves. Many adolescents who present to general hospitals with deliberate self-harm report previous episodes for which they did not receive medical attention.

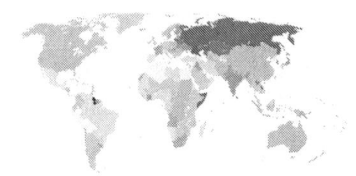

World-map showing the disability-adjusted life year, which is a measure of each country's disease burden, for self inflicted injuries per 100,000 inhabitants in 2004. "Mortality and Burden of Disease Estimates for WHO Member States in 2002" (xls), World Health Organization, 2002, , retrieved 2009-12-13   no data   less than 80   80–160   160–240   240–320   320–400   400–480   480–560   560–640   640–720   720–800   800–850   more than 850

The best available research indicates that in the United States up to 4% of adults self-harm with approximately 1% of the population engaging in chronic or severe self-harm. Current research suggests that the rates of self-harm are much higher among young people with the average age of onset between 14 and 24. The earliest reported incidents of self-harm are in children between five and seven years old. In the UK in 2008 rates of self-harm in young people could be as high as 33%. In addition there appears to be an increased risk of self-harm in college students than among the general population. In a study of undergraduate students in the United States, 9.8% of the students surveyed indicated that they had purposefully cut or burned themselves on at least one occasion in the past. When the definition of self-harm was expanded to include head-banging, scratching oneself, and hitting oneself along with cutting and burning, 32% of the sample said they had done this.

Gender differences

The latest aggregated research has found generally similar rates of self-harm between men and women. However, much of the past research has indicated that up to four times as many females as males have direct experience of self-harm. Nevertheless, caution is needed in seeing self-harm as a greater problem for females, since males may engage in different forms of self-harm which could be easier to hide or explained as the result of different circumstances. For example, men more frequently report burning and hitting themselves, whereas women are more likely to report cutting and burning themselves.

Hence, there remain widely opposing views as to whether the gender paradox is a real phenomenon, or merely the artifact of bias in data collection.

The WHO/EURO Multicentre Study of Suicide, established in 1989 demonstrated that, for each age group, the female rate of self-harm exceeded that of the males, with the highest rate among females in the 13–24 age group and the highest rate among males in the 12–34 age group. However, this discrepancy has been known to vary significantly depending upon population and methodological criteria, consistent with wide-ranging uncertainties in gathering and interpreting data regarding rates of self-harm in general. Such problems have sometimes been the focus of criticism in the context of broader psychosocial interpretation. For example, feminist author Barbara Brickman has speculated that reported gender differences in rates of self-harm are due to deliberate socially biased methodological and sampling errors, directly blaming medical discourse for pathologising the female.

This gender discrepancy is often distorted in specific populations where rates of self-harm are inordinately high, which may have implications on the significance and interpretation of psychosocial factors other than gender. A study in 2003 found an extremely high prevalence of self-harm among 428 homeless and runaway youth (age 16 to 19) with 72% of males and 66% of females reporting a past history of self-harm. However, in 2008, a study of young people and self-harm saw the gender gap close, with 32% of young females, and 22% of young males admitting to self-harm. Studies also indicate that males who self-harm may also be at a greater risk of completing suicide.

There does not appear to be a difference in motivation for self-harm in adolescent males and females. For example, for both genders there is an incremental increase in deliberate self-harm associated with an increase in consumption of cigarettes, drugs and alcohol. Triggering factors such as low self-esteem and having friends and family members who self-harm are also common between both males and females. One limited study found that, among those young individuals who do self-harm, both genders are just as equally likely to use the method of skin-cutting. However, females who self-cut are more likely than males to explain their self-harm episode by saying that they had wanted to punish themselves. In New Zealand, more females are hospitalised for intentional self-harm than males. Females more commonly choose methods such as self-poisoning that generally are not fatal, but still serious enough to require hospitalisation.

Elderly

In a study of a district general hospital in the UK, 5.4% of all the hospital's self-harm cases were aged over 65. The male to female ratio was 2:3 although the self-harm rates for males and females over 65 in the local population were identical. Over 90% had depressive conditions, and 63% had significant physical illness. Under 10% of the patients gave a history of earlier self-harm, while both the repetition and suicide rates were very low, which could be explained due to the absence of factors known to be associated with repetition, such as personality disorder and alcohol abuse. However, NICE Guidance on Self-harm in the UK suggests that older people who self-harm are at a greater risk of completing suicide, with 1 in 5 older people who self-harm going on to end their life.

Developing world

Only recently have attempts to improve health in the developing world concentrated on not only physical illness but mental health also. Deliberate self-harm is common in the developing world. Research into self-harm in the developing world is however still very limited although an important case study is that of Sri-Lanka, which is a country exhibiting a high incidence of suicide and self-poisoning with agricultural pesticides or natural poisons. Many people admitted for deliberate self-poisoning during a study by Eddleston *et al.* were young and few expressed a desire to die, but death was relatively common in the young in these cases. The improvement of medical management of acute poisoning in the developing world is poor and improvements are required in order to reduce mortality.

Some of the causes of deliberate self-poisoning in Sri Lankan adolescents included bereavement and harsh discipline by parents. The coping mechanisms are being spread in local communities as people are surrounded by others who have previously deliberately harmed themselves or attempted suicide. One way of reducing self-harm would be to limit access to poisons; however many cases involve pesticides or yellow oleander seeds, and the reduction of access to these agents would be difficult. Great potential for the reduction of self-harm lies in education and prevention, but limited resources in the developing world make these methods challenging.

Prison inmates

Deliberate self-harm is especially prevalent in prison populations. A proposed explanation for this is that prisons are often violent places, and prisoners who wish to avoid physical confrontations may resort to self-harm as a ruse, either to convince other prisoners that they are dangerously insane and resilient to pain or to obtain protection from the prison authorities.

History

The term "*Self-mutilation*" occurred in a study by L. E. Emerson in 1913 where he considered self-cutting a symbolic substitution for masturbation. The term reappeared in an article in 1935 and a book in 1938 when Karl Menninger refined his conceptual definitions of self-mutilation. His study on self-destructiveness differentiated between suicidal behaviors and self-mutilation. For Menninger, self-mutilation was a non-fatal expression of an attenuated death wish and thus coined the term *partial suicide*. He began a classification system of six types:

1. neurotic – nail biters, pickers, extreme hair removal and unnecessary cosmetic surgery.
2. religious – self-flagellants and others.
3. puberty rites – hymen removal, circumcision or clitoral alteration.
4. psychotic – eye or ear removal, genital self-mutilation and extreme amputation

5. organic brain diseases – which allow repetitive head banging, hand biting, finger fracturing or eye removal.
6. conventional – nail clipping, trimming of hair and shaving beards.

Pao (1969) differentiated between *delicate* (low lethality) and *coarse* (high lethality) self-mutilators who cut. The 'delicate' cutters were young, multiple episodic of superficial cuts and generally had borderline personality disorder diagnosis. The 'coarse' cutters were older and generally psychotic. Ross and McKay (1979) categorized self-mutilators into 9 groups: *cutting, biting, abrading, severing, inserting, burning, ingesting or inhaling* and *hitting and constricting*

After the 1970s the paradigm of self-harm shifted from a focus on Freudian psycho-sexual drives of the patients.

Walsh and Rosen (1988) created four categories numbered by Roman Numerals I-IV, defining *Self-mutilation* as rows II, III and IV

Classification	Examples of Behavior	Degree of Physical Damage	Psychological State	Social Acceptability
I	Ear piercing, nail biting, small tattoos, cosmetic surgery (not considered self-harm by the majority of the population)	Superficial to mild	Benign	Mostly accepted
II	Piercings, saber scars, ritualistic clan scarring, sailor and gang tattoos	Mild to moderate	Benign to agitated	Subculture acceptance
III	Wrist or body cutting, self-inflicted cigarette burns and tattoos, wound excoriation	Mild to moderate	Psychic crisis	Accepted by some subgroups but not by the general population
IV	Autocastration, self-enucleation, amputation	Severe	Psychotic decompensation	Unacceptable

Favazza and Rosenthal (1993) reviewed hundreds of studies and divided self-mutilation into two categories: *culturally sanctioned self-mutilation* and *deviant self-mutilation*. Favazza also created two subcategories of sanctioned self-mutilations; *rituals* and *practices*. The *rituals* are mutilations repeated generationally and "reflect the traditions, symbolism, and beliefs of a society" (p. 226). *Practices* are historically transient and cosmetic such as piercing of earlobes, nose, eyebrows as well as male circumcision (for non-Jews) while *Deviant self-mutilation* is equivalent to self-harm.

Society and culture

Self-harm is known to have been a regular ritual practice by cultures such as the ancient Maya civilization, in which the Maya priesthood performed auto-sacrifice by cutting and piercing their bodies in order to draw blood. A reference to the priests of Baal "cutting themselves with blades until blood flowed" can be found in the Hebrew Bible.. However, in Judaism, such self-harm is forbidden under Mosaic law.

Self-harm is also practiced by the sadhu or Hindu ascetic, in Catholic mortification of the flesh, in ancient Canaanite mourning rituals as described in the Ras Shamra tablets and in the Shi'ite annual ritual of self-flagellation, using chains and swords, that takes place during Ashura where the Shi'ite sect mourne the martyrdom of Imam Hussein.

In other animals

Self-mutilation in non-human mammals is a well-established, although not a widely known phenomenon and its study under zoo or laboratory conditions could lead to a better understanding of self-harm in human patients. Zoo or laboratory rearing and isolation are important factors leading to increased susceptibility to self-harm in higher mammals, e.g. macaque monkeys. Lower mammals are also known to mutilate themselves under laboratory conditions after administration of drugs. For example pemoline, clonidine, amphetamine, and very high (toxic) doses of caffeine or theophylline are known to precipitate self-harm in lab animals. In dogs, canine obsessive-compulsive disorder can lead to self-inflicted injuries, for example canine lick granuloma. Captive birds are sometimes known to engage in feather-plucking, causing damage to feathers that can range from feather shredding to the removal of most or all feathers within the birds reach, or even the mutilation of skin or muscle tissue.

Feather-plucking in a Moluccan Cockatoo

Further reading

- Bogdashina, O. (2003), *Sensory Perceptual Issues in Autism and Asperger Syndrome, Different Sensory Experiences, Different Perceptual Worlds.*, Jessica Kingsley, ISBN 978-1-84310-166-6
- Farber, S. (2002), *When the Body Is the Target: Self-Harm, Pain, and Traumatic Attachments*, Jason Aronson Inc, ISBN 978-0-76570-371-2
- Favazza, A.R (1996), *Bodies Under Siege: Self-Mutilation and Body Modification in Culture and Psychiatry.*, Johns Hopkins University Press, ISBN 978-0-80185-300-5

- Griffin, J. & Tyrrell, I. (2000), *The Shackled Brain: How to release locked in patterns of psychological trauma.*, Organising Idea Monograph: 5, European Therapy Studies Institute, ISBN 1-899398-11-2
- Hawton, K. and Rodham, K. (2006), *By Their Own Young Hand: Deliberate Self-harm and Suicidal Ideas in Adolescents*, Jessica Kingsley, ISBN 978-1-84310-230-4
- Kaminski, M.M. (2004), *Games Prisoners Play.*, Princeton University Press, ISBN 0-691-11721-7
- Kern, J. (2007), *Scars That Wound: Scars That Heal*, Standard Publishing, ISBN 978-0-7847-2104-9
- Levenkron, S. (1998), *Cutting: Understanding and Overcoming Self-Mutilation*, W. W. Norton and Company., ISBN 978-0-39302-741-9
- McVey-Noble, M.; Khemlani-Patel, S.;Neziroglu, F (2006), *When Your Child is Cutting: A Parent's Guide to Helping Children Overcome Self Injury*, California: New Harbinger, ISBN 978-1572244375
- Miller, D. (1994), *Women Who Hurt Themselves.*, Basic Books, ISBN 978-0-46509-219-2
- Plante, L. G. (2007), *Bleeding to Ease the Pain: cutting. self-injury, and the adolescent search for self.*, Praeger Publishers, ISBN 978-0-27599-062-6
- Smith, C. (2006), *Cutting it Out: a journey through psychotherapy and self-harm.*, Jessica Kingsley Publishers, ISBN 978-1-84310-266-3
- Strong, M. (1998), *A Bright Red Scream: Self-Mutilation and the Language of Pain.*, Viking Press, ISBN 978-0-67087-781-2
- Whittenhall, E. (2006), *Cutting: Self-Injury and Emotional Pain.*, InterVarsity Press, ISBN 978-0-83084-990-1

External links

- Information about self-harm [4] from the Royal College of Psychiatrists
- Men Who Self Harm [5] BBC Radio 4 item discussing Self-Harm.
- Understanding self-harm [6] from Mind: A mental health charity in England and Wales
- Youth & Self Injury [7] Information from the Canadian Mental Health Association

Self-inflicted wound

A **self-inflicted wound** (**SIW**), is the act of harming oneself where there are no underlying psychological problems related to the self-injury, but where the injurer wanted to take advantage of being injured.

Reasons to self-wound

Most self-inflicted wounds occur during wartime, for various possible reasons.

Potential draftees may self-injure in order to avoid being drafted for health reasons.

The most common reason enlisted soldiers self-wound is to render themselves unable to continue serving in combat, thus resulting in their removal from the combat line to a hospital. Thus, self-injury can be used to avoid a more serious combat injury or a combat death.

In prison camps, such as gulags and concentration camps, people sometimes self-injure so that they will not be forced to work and could spend some time in the more comfortable conditions of the infirmary barracks.

Types of wounds

Among the most common type of wounds are a rifle shot to the hand, arm, leg, or foot.

Punishments

In most militaries, deliberately self-inflicted wounds are considered to be a serious military offense. Most self-inflicted wounds go unnoticed, though consequences are often severe if caught.

In the British army during World War I, the penalty for self-inflicted wound was capital punishment, which at that time was death by firing squad. In the British Army, some 3,894 men were found guilty, though none were executed but instead were sent to prison for lengthy periods.

In Nazi concentration camps, self-injury was dangerous as the incapacitated were often just executed, but in some lower-stringency camps it has indeed been documented.

History

There have been many reports of SIW during World War I, placing certain soldiers under suspicion for some injuries which could have been genuine accidents.

During World War II, almost all armies (most often mentioned are the Soviet Army and the Wehrmacht) had cases of self-inflicted injury.

Attention seeking

Enjoying the attention of others is quite socially acceptable. In some instances, however, the need for attention can lead to difficulties. The term **attention seeking** (or **attention-seeking**) is generally reserved for such situations, where excessive and "inappropriate attention seeking" is seen.

Styles

The following styles of attention seeking have been identified:

- **Extroverted positive overt style** - associated with narcissism, bragging and boasting. May also include shocking exhibitionist behavior such as streaking.
- **Extroverted positive subdued style** - similar but more subtle such as wearing designer clothes, wearing sexy clothes or dominating the conversation.
- **Extroverted negative overt style** - to gain pity and reassurance.
- **Extroverted negative subdued style** - making a negative statement to the world by, for example, dressing as a goth, freak or punk.

In different pathologies or contexts

- **Attention-deficit hyperactivity disorder**
- **Münchausen by Internet**
- **Münchausen syndrome**
- **Münchausen syndrome by proxy**
- **Personality disorders** - A sustained pattern of attention seeking in adults is often associated with, in particular, histrionic personality disorder - but it may instead be associated with narcissistic personality disorder or borderline personality disorder. The expression drama queen is associated with histrionic behavior.
- **Self-destructive behaviour** - It is a common misconception that self-destructive behaviour is inherently attention seeking, or at least that attention is a primary motive. While this is undoubtedly true in some cases, normally the motivation runs much deeper than that. Many self-injurers are very self-conscious of their wounds and scars and feel guilty about their behavior leading them to go to

great lengths to conceal their behavior from others.
- **Voluntary false confession**

Tactical ignoring

Main article: Tactical ignoring

Tactical ignoring, also known as planned ignoring, is a behavioral management strategy used in response to challenging behavior that seeks to receive attention or to gain a reaction from others. It is a commonly used strategy when the person displaying the attention-seeking behavior still feels rewarded by a negative response.

See also
- Exaggeration
- Victim playing
- Trolling

Further reading
- Gewirtz, Jacob L *Three determinants of attention-seeking in young children* (1956)
- Gewirtz, Jacob L *A factor analysis of some attention-seeking behaviors of young children* Child Development (1956)
- Harvey, Eric & Mellor, Nigel *Helping Parents Deal With Attention Seeking Behaviour* (2009)
- Leit, Lisa & Jacobvitz, Deborah & Hazen-Swann, Nancy *Conversational Narcissism in Marriage: Narcissistic attention seeking behaviors in face-to-face interactions: Implications for marital stability and partner mental health* (2008)
- Mellor, Nigel *Attention Seeking: A Practical Solution for the Classroom* (1997)
- Mellor, Nigel *The Good, the Bad and the Irritating: A Practical Approach for Parents of Children who are Attention Seeking* (2000)
- Mellor, Nigel *Attention Seeking: A Complete Guide for Teachers* (2008)
- Smith-Martenz, Arden *Attention--seeking misbehaviors* (1990)

External links
- Hysteria, Drama Majors and Drama Queens [1]
- Attention-seeking personality disorders [2]

Psychological pain

Psychological pain, also called sometimes psychalgia, is any mental, or mind, or non-physical suffering. Emotional pain is a particular kind of psychological pain, more closely related to emotions. In the fields of social psychology and personality psychology, the term social pain is used to denote emotional pain caused by harm or threat to social connection; bereavement, embarrassment, shame and hurt feelings are subtypes of social pain. Another kind of psychological pain that is commonly found is spiritual or soul pain.

Recent research in neuroscience suggests that physical pain and psychological pain may share some underlying neurological mechanisms.

In recent years there has been some prominence to quite controversial lawsuits in which the plaintiff seeks redress for pain and suffering that are not physical at all but purely psychological.[*citation needed*]

See also

- Psychogenic pain
- Psychological trauma

Self-injury Awareness Day

Self-injury Awareness Day (SIAD) is a grassroots annual global awareness event / campaign on March 1, where on this day, and in the weeks leading up to it, some people choose to be more open about their own self-harm, and awareness organizations make special efforts to raise awareness about self-harm and self-injury. Some people wear an orange awareness ribbon or wristband to encourage awareness of self-harm.

The orange ribbon of self harm awareness.

Enucleation of the eye

Intervention: Enucleation of the eye	
ICD-10 code:	
ICD-9 code:	16.4 [1]
Other codes:	

Enucleation is removal of the eye, leaving the eye muscles and remaining orbital contents intact. This type of ocular surgery is indicated for a number of different ocular tumors, in eyes that have suffered severe trauma, and in eyes that are blind and painful due to other disease.

Auto-enucleation (oedipism) and other forms of serious self inflicted eye injury are an extremely rare form of severe self-harm which usually results from serious mental illnesses such as schizophrenia. The name comes from Oedipus, who gouged out his eyes in penance after having sex with his mother and killing his father. Some patients have apparently been inspired by the Gospel of Matthew, which states: *"...if the right eye offend thee, pluck it out and cast it from thee"* (5:29).

Classification

There are three types of eye removal

- Evisceration - removal of the internal eye contents, but the sclera is left behind with the extraocular muscles still attached.
- Enucleation - removal of the eyeball, but the adjacent structures of the eye socket and eyelids remain. An intraocular tumor excision requires an enucleation, not an evisceration.
- Exenteration - removal of the contents of the eye socket (orbit) including the eyeball, fat, muscles and other adjacent structures of the eye. The eyelids may also be removed in cases of cutaneous cancers and unrelenting infection. Exenteration is sometimes done together with Maxillectomy which is removal of the maxilla or the upper jaw bone/cheekbone

Reasons for eye removal

- Cancer of the eye (retinoblastoma, melanomas, any other cancers of the eye or orbit)
- Severe injury of the eye when the eye cannot be saved or attempts to save the eye have failed
- End stage glaucoma
- Painful, blind eye
- In cases of sympathetic ophthalmia (inflammation of the eye) to prevent travel to other eye, in which, if untreated can cause blindness
- Congenital cystic eye
- In a deceased person, so the cornea can be used for a living person who needs a corneal transplant by a surgical operation called keratoplasty.
- Constant infection in a blind, or otherwise useless eye.

Orbital implants and ocular prostheses

Removal of the eye by enucleation or evisceration can relieve pain and minimize further risk to life and well-being of an individual with the above noted conditions. In addition, procedures to remove the eye should address the resulting appearance of the orbit. Orbital implants and ocular prostheses are used by the surgeon to restore a more natural appearance.

An orbital implant is placed after removal of the eye to restore volume to the eye socket and enhance movement or motility of an ocular prosthesis and eyelids. The eyeball is a slightly elongated sphere with a diameter of approximately 24 millimetres. To avoid a sunken appearance to the eye socket, an implant approximating this volume can be placed into the space of the removed eye, secured, and covered with Tenon's capsule and conjunctiva (the mucous membrane covering the natural sclera). Implants can be made of many materials with the most common being plastic, hydroxylapatite, metal alloy or glass.

Later, once the conjunctiva has healed and post-operative swelling has subsided, an ocular prosthesis can be placed to provide the appearance of a natural eye. The prosthesis is fabricated by an ocularist. Its form is that of a cupped disc so that it can fit comfortably in the pocket behind the eyelids overlying the conjunctiva that covers the orbital implant. The external portion of the ocular prosthesis is painted and finished to mimic a natural eye color, shape and luster. It can be removed and cleaned periodically by the individual or a care giver.

The two part system of orbital implant and ocular prosthesis provides a stable, and well tolerated aesthetic restoration of the eye socket. Although vision is not restored by removal of the eye with placement of an orbital implant and ocular prosthesis, a natural appearance can result. The implant can be moved by intact extraocular muscles that will track or move simultaneously with the other eye. The visible ocular prosthesis can couple with the orbital implant and thus move simultaneously with the other eye. The eyelids can move and blink over the prosthesis as well.

See also

- Phantom eye syndrome

External links

- LostEye.com (Support and Information) [2]
- Leading conditions of Eye Loss [3]
- Stories of Eye Loss [4]

Major depressive disorder

For other depressive disorders, see Mood disorder.

Major Depressive Disorder	
Classification and external resources	
Vincent van Gogh's 1890 painting *At Eternity's Gate*	
ICD-10	F 32. [1], F 33. [2]
ICD-9	296 [3]
OMIM	608516 [4]
DiseasesDB	3589 [5]
MedlinePlus	003213 [6]
eMedicine	med/532 [7]
MeSH	D003865 [8]

Major depressive disorder (also known as **recurrent depressive disorder**, **clinical depression**, **major depression**, **unipolar depression**, or **unipolar disorder**) is a mental disorder characterized by an all-encompassing low mood accompanied by low self-esteem, and by loss of interest or pleasure in normally enjoyable activities. The term "major depressive disorder" was selected by the American Psychiatric Association to designate this symptom cluster as a mood disorder in the 1980 version of the *Diagnostic and Statistical Manual of Mental Disorders* (DSM-III), and has become widely used since. The general term **depression** is often used to denote the disorder; but as it can also be used in reference to other types of psychological depression, it is avoided in favor of more precise terminology for the disorder in clinical and research use. Major depression is a disabling condition which adversely affects a person's family, work or school life, sleeping and eating habits, and general health. In the United States, around 3.4% of people with major depression commit suicide, and up to 60% of people who commit suicide had depression or another mood disorder.

The diagnosis of major depressive disorder is based on the patient's self-reported experiences, behavior reported by relatives or friends, and a mental status exam. There is no laboratory test for major depression, although physicians generally request tests for physical conditions that may cause similar symptoms.Gelder,Mayou and Geddes(2005) state if depressive disorder is not detected in the early stages it may result in a slow recovery and affect or worsen the persons physical health.The most common time of onset is between the ages of 20 and 30 years, with a later peak between 30 and 40 years.

Typically, patients are treated with antidepressant medication and, in many cases, also receive psychotherapy or counseling. Hospitalization may be necessary in cases with associated self-neglect or a significant risk of harm to self or others. A minority are treated with electroconvulsive therapy (ECT), under a short-acting general anaesthetic. The course of the disorder varies widely, from one episode lasting weeks to a lifelong disorder with recurrent major depressive episodes. Depressed individuals have shorter life expectancies than those without depression, in part because of greater susceptibility to medical illnesses and suicide. It is unclear whether or not medications affect the risk of suicide. Current and former patients may be stigmatized.

The understanding of the nature and causes of depression has evolved over the centuries, though this understanding is incomplete and has left many aspects of depression as the subject of discussion and research. Proposed causes include psychological, psycho-social, hereditary, evolutionary and biological factors. Certain types of long-term drug use can both cause and worsen depressive symptoms. Psychological treatments are based on theories of personality, interpersonal communication, and learning. Most biological theories focus on the monoamine chemicals serotonin, norepinephrine and dopamine, which are naturally present in the brain and assist communication between nerve cells.

Symptoms and signs

Major depression significantly affects a person's family and personal relationships, work or school life, sleeping and eating habits, and general health. Its impact on functioning and well-being has been equated to that of chronic medical conditions such as diabetes.

A person having a major depressive episode usually exhibits a very low mood, which pervades all aspects of life, and an inability to experience pleasure in activities that were formerly enjoyed. Depressed people may be preoccupied with, or ruminate over, thoughts and feelings of worthlessness, inappropriate guilt or regret, helplessness, hopelessness, and self-hatred. In severe cases, depressed people may have symptoms of psychosis. These symptoms include delusions or, less commonly, hallucinations, usually unpleasant. Other symptoms of depression include poor concentration and memory (especially in those with melancholic or psychotic features), withdrawal from social situations and activities, reduced sex drive, and thoughts of death or suicide.

Insomnia is common among the depressed. In the typical pattern, a person wakes very early and cannot get back to sleep, but insomnia can also include difficulty falling asleep. Insomnia affects at least 80% of depressed people. Hypersomnia, or oversleeping, can also happen, affecting 15% of the depressed people. Some antidepressants may also cause insomnia due to their stimulating effect.

A depressed person may report multiple physical symptoms such as fatigue, headaches, or digestive problems; physical complaints are the most common presenting problem in developing countries, according to the World Health Organization's criteria for depression. Appetite often decreases, with resulting weight loss, although increased appetite and weight gain occasionally occur. Family and friends may notice that the person's behavior is either agitated or lethargic.

The concept of depression is more controversial in regards to children, and depends on the view that is taken about when self-image develops and becomes fully established. Depressed children may often display an irritable mood rather than a depressed mood, and show varying symptoms depending on age and situation. Most lose interest in school and show a decline in academic performance. They may be described as clingy, demanding, dependent, or insecure. Diagnosis may be delayed or missed when symptoms are interpreted as normal moodiness. Depression may also coincide with attention-deficit hyperactivity disorder (ADHD), complicating the diagnosis and treatment of both.

Older depressed persons may have cognitive symptoms of recent onset, such as forgetfulness, and a more noticeable slowing of movements. Depression often coexists with physical disorders common among the elderly, such as stroke, other cardiovascular diseases, Parkinson's disease, and chronic obstructive pulmonary disease.

Causes

The biopsychosocial model proposes that biological, psychological, and social factors all play a role in causing depression. The diathesis–stress model specifies that depression results when a preexisting vulnerability, or diathesis, is activated by stressful life events. The preexisting vulnerability can be either genetic, implying an interaction between nature and nurture, or schematic, resulting from views of the world learned in childhood.

These interactive models have gained empirical support. For example, researchers in New Zealand took a prospective approach to studying depression, by documenting over time how depression emerged among an initially normal cohort of people. The researchers concluded that variation among the serotonin transporter (5-HTT) gene affects the chances that people who have dealt with very stressful life events will go on to experience depression. Specifically, depression may follow such events, but seems more likely to appear in people with one or two short alleles of the 5-HTT gene. Additionally, a Swedish study estimated the heritability of depression—the degree to which individual differences in occurrence are associated with genetic differences—to be around 40% for women and 30% for men, and evolutionary psychologists have proposed that the genetic basis for depression lies deep in the history of naturally selected adaptations. A substance-induced mood disorder resembling major depression has been causally linked to long-term drug use or drug abuse, or to withdrawal from certain sedative and hypnotic drugs.

Biological

Main article: Biology of depression

Monoamine hypothesis

Most antidepressant medications increase the levels of one or more of the monoamines—the neurotransmitters serotonin, norepinephrine and dopamine—in the synaptic cleft between neurons in the brain. Some medications affect the monoamine receptors directly.

Serotonin is hypothesized to regulate other neurotransmitter systems; decreased serotonin activity may allow these systems to act in unusual and erratic ways. According to this "permissive hypothesis", depression arises when low serotonin levels promote low levels of norepinephrine, another monoamine neurotransmitter. Some antidepressants enhance the levels of norepinephrine directly, whereas others raise the levels of dopamine, a third monoamine neurotransmitter. These observations gave rise to the monoamine hypothesis of depression. In its contemporary formulation, the monoamine hypothesis postulates that a deficiency of certain neurotransmitters is responsible for the corresponding features of depression: "Norepinephrine may be related to alertness and energy as well as anxiety, attention, and interest in life; [lack of] serotonin to anxiety, obsessions, and compulsions; and dopamine to attention, motivation, pleasure, and reward, as well as interest in life." The proponents of this theory recommend the choice of an antidepressant with mechanism of action that impacts the most prominent symptoms. Anxious and irritable patients should be treated with SSRIs or norepinephrine reuptake inhibitors, and those experiencing a loss of energy and enjoyment of life with norepinephrine- and dopamine-enhancing drugs.

In the past two decades, research has revealed multiple limitations of the monoamine hypothesis, and its explanatory inadequacy has been highlighted within the psychiatric community. Intensive investigation has failed to find convincing evidence of a primary dysfunction of a specific monoamine system in patients with major depressive disorders[citation needed]. The medications tianeptine and opipramol have long been known to have antidepressant properties despite the fact that the former is a serotonin reuptake enhancer and the latter has no effect on the monoamine system. Experiments with pharmacological agents that cause depletion of monoamines have shown that this depletion does not cause depression in healthy people nor does it worsen symptoms in depressed patients—although an intact monoamine system is necessary for antidepressants to achieve therapeutic effectiveness. According to an essay published by the Public Library of Science (PLoS), the monoamine hypothesis, already limited, has been further oversimplified when presented to the general public as a mass marketing tool.

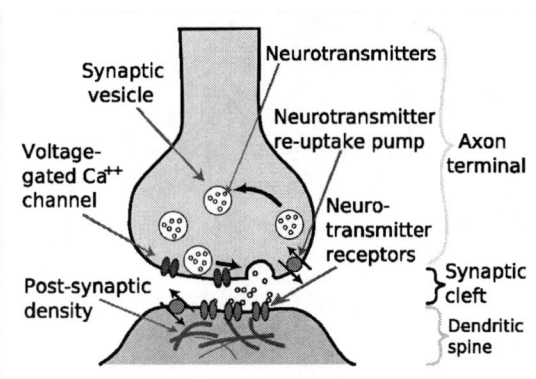

Schematic of a synapse between an axon of one neuron and a dendrite of another. Synapses are specialized gaps between neurons. Electrical impulses arriving at the axon terminal trigger release of packets of chemical messengers (neurotransmitters), which diffuse across the synaptic cleft to receptors on the adjacent dendrite temporarily affecting the likelihood that an electrical impulse will be triggered in the latter neuron. Once released the neurotransmitter is rapidly metabolized or pumped back into a neuron. Antidepressants influence the overall balance of these processes.

Other theories

MRI scans of patients with depression have revealed a number of differences in brain structure compared to those who are not depressed. Although there is some inconsistency in the results, meta-analyses have shown there is evidence for smaller hippocampal volumes and increased numbers of hyperintensive lesions. Hyperintensities have been associated with patients with a late age of onset, and have led to the development of the theory of vascular depression.

There may be a link between depression and neurogenesis of the hippocampus, a center for both mood and memory. Loss of hippocampal neurons is found in some depressed individuals and correlates with impaired memory and dysthymic mood. Drugs may increase serotonin levels in the brain, stimulating neurogenesis and thus increasing the total mass of the hippocampus. This increase may help to restore mood and memory. Similar relationships have been observed between depression and an area of the anterior cingulate cortex implicated in the modulation of emotional behavior. One of the neurotrophins responsible for neurogenesis is brain-derived neurotrophic factor (BDNF). The level of BDNF in the blood plasma of depressed subjects is drastically reduced (more than threefold) as compared to the norm. Antidepressant treatment increases the blood level of BDNF. Although decreased plasma BDNF levels have been found in many other disorders, there is some evidence that BDNF is involved in the cause of depression and the mechanism of action of antidepressants.

There is some evidence that major depression may be caused in part by an overactive hypothalamic-pituitary-adrenal axis (HPA axis) that results in an effect similar to the neuro-endocrine response to stress. Investigations reveal increased levels of the hormone cortisol and enlarged pituitary and adrenal glands, suggesting disturbances of the endocrine system may play a role in some psychiatric disorders, including major depression. Oversecretion of corticotropin-releasing hormone from the hypothalamus is thought to drive this, and is implicated in the cognitive and arousal symptoms.

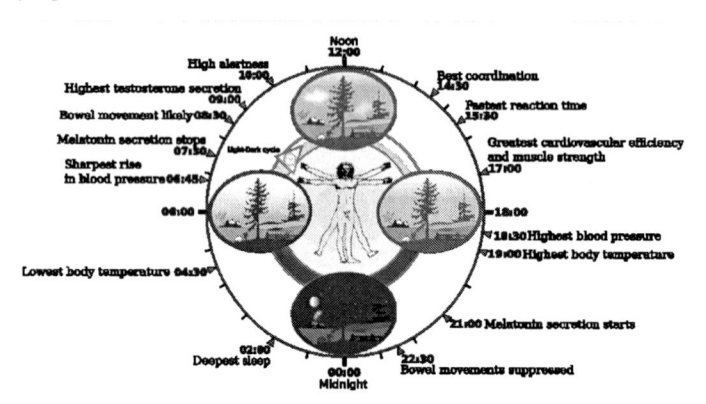

Depression may be related to abnormalities in the circadian rhythm, or biological clock. For example, rapid eye movement (REM) sleep—the stage in which dreaming occurs—may be quick to arrive and intense in depressed people. REM sleep depends on decreased serotonin levels in the brain stem, and is impaired by compounds, such as antidepressants, that increase serotonergic tone in brain stem structures. Overall, the serotonergic system is least active during sleep and most active during wakefulness. Prolonged wakefulness due to sleep deprivation activates serotonergic neurons, leading to processes similar to the therapeutic effect of antidepressants, such as the selective serotonin reuptake inhibitors (SSRIs). Depressed individuals can exhibit a significant lift in mood after a night of sleep deprivation. SSRIs may directly depend on the increase of central serotonergic neurotransmission for their therapeutic effect, the same system that impacts cycles of sleep and wakefulness.

Depression may be related to the same brain mechanisms that control the cycles of sleep and wakefulness.

Research on the effects of light therapy on seasonal affective disorder suggests that light deprivation is related to decreased activity in the serotonergic system and to abnormalities in the sleep cycle, particularly insomnia. Exposure to light also targets the serotonergic system, providing more support for the important role this system may play in depression. Sleep deprivation and light therapy both target the same brain neurotransmitter system and brain areas as antidepressant drugs, and are now used clinically to treat depression. Light therapy, sleep deprivation and sleep time displacement (sleep phase advance therapy) are being used in combination quickly to interrupt a deep depression in hospitalized patients.

The hormone estrogen has been implicated in depressive disorders due to the increase in risk of depressive episodes after puberty, the antenatal period, and reduced rates after menopause. Conversely, the premenstrual and postpartum periods of low estrogen levels are also associated with increased risk. Sudden withdrawal of, fluctuations in or periods of sustained low levels of estrogen have been linked to significant mood lowering. Clinical recovery from depression postpartum, perimenopause, and postmenopause was shown to be effective after levels of estrogen were stabilized or restored. Other research has explored potential roles of molecules necessary for overall cellular functioning: cytokines. The symptoms of major depressive disorder are nearly identical to those of sickness behavior, the response of the body when the immune system is fighting an infection. This raises the possibility that depression can result from a maladaptive manifestation of sickness behavior as a result of abnormalities in circulating cytokines. The involvement of pro-inflammatory cytokines in depression is strongly suggested by a meta-analysis of the clinical literature showing higher blood concentrations of IL-6 and TNF-α in depressed subjects compared to controls.

Psychological

Various aspects of personality and its development appear to be integral to the occurrence and persistence of depression, with negative emotionality as a common precursor. Although depressive episodes are strongly correlated with adverse events, a person's characteristic style of coping may be correlated with their resilience. Additionally, low self-esteem and self-defeating or distorted thinking are related to depression. Depression is less likely to occur, as well as quicker to remit, among those who are religious. It is not always clear which factors are causes or which are effects of depression; however, depressed persons who are able to reflect upon and challenge their thinking patterns often show improved mood and self-esteem.

American psychiatrist Aaron T. Beck, following on from the earlier work of George Kelly and Albert Ellis, developed what is now known as a cognitive model of depression in the early 1960s. He proposed that three concepts underlie depression: a triad of negative thoughts composed of cognitive errors about oneself, one's world, and one's future; recurrent patterns of depressive thinking, or *schemas*; and distorted information processing. From these principles, he developed the structured technique of cognitive behavioral therapy (CBT). According to American psychologist Martin Seligman, depression in humans is similar to learned helplessness in laboratory animals, who remain in unpleasant situations when they are able to escape, but do not because they initially learned they had no control.

Attachment theory, which was developed by English psychiatrist John Bowlby in the 1960s, predicts a relationship between depressive disorder in adulthood and the quality of the earlier bond between the infant and their adult caregiver. In particular, it is thought that "the experiences of early loss, separation and rejection by the parent or caregiver (conveying the message that the child is unlovable) may all lead to insecure internal working models ... Internal cognitive representations of the self as unlovable and of attachment figures as unloving [or] untrustworthy would be consistent with parts of Beck's cognitive triad". While a wide variety of studies has upheld the basic tenets of attachment theory, research has been inconclusive as to whether self-reported early attachment and later depression are demonstrably related.

Depressed individuals often blame themselves for negative events, and, as shown in a 1993 study of hospitalized adolescents with self-reported depression, those who blame themselves for negative occurrences may not take credit for positive outcomes. This tendency is characteristic of a depressive attributional, or pessimistic explanatory style. According to Albert Bandura, a Canadian social psychologist associated with social cognitive theory, depressed individuals have negative beliefs about themselves, based on experiences of failure, observing the failure of social models, a lack of social persuasion that they can succeed, and their own somatic and emotional states including tension and stress. These influences may result in a negative self-concept and a lack of self-efficacy; that is, they do not believe they can influence events or achieve personal goals.

An examination of depression in women indicates that vulnerability factors—such as early maternal loss, lack of a confiding relationship, responsibility for the care of several young children at home, and unemployment—can interact with life stressors to increase the risk of depression. For older adults, the factors are often health problems, changes in relationships with a spouse or adult children due to the transition to a care-giving or care-needing role, the death of a significant other, or a change in the availability or quality of social relationships with older friends because of their own health-related life changes.

The understanding of depression has also received contributions from the psychoanalytic and humanistic branches of psychology. From the classical psychoanalytic perspective of Austrian psychiatrist Sigmund Freud, depression, or *melancholia*, may be related to interpersonal loss and early life experiences. Existential therapists have connected depression to the lack of both meaning in the present and a vision of the future. The founder of humanistic psychology, American psychologist Abraham Maslow, suggested that depression could arise when people are unable to attain their needs or to self-actualize (to realize their full potential).

Social

Poverty and social isolation are associated with increased risk of mental health problems in general. Child abuse (physical, emotional, sexual, or neglect) is also associated with increased risk of developing depressive disorders later in life. Such a link has good face validity given that it is during the years of development that a child is learning how to become a social being. Abuse of the child by the caregiver is bound to distort the developing personality and create a much greater risk for depression and many other debilitating mental and emotional states. Disturbances in family functioning, such as parental (particularly maternal) depression, severe marital conflict or divorce, death of a parent, or other disturbances in parenting are additional risk factors. In adulthood, stressful life events are strongly associated with the onset of major depressive episodes. In this context, life events connected to social rejection appear to be particularly related to depression. Evidence that a first episode of depression is more likely to be immediately preceded by stressful life events than are recurrent ones is consistent with the hypothesis that people may become increasingly sensitized to life stress over successive recurrences of depression.

The relationship between stressful life events and social support has been a matter of some debate; the lack of social support may increase the likelihood that life stress will lead to depression, or the absence of social support may constitute a form of strain that leads to depression directly. There is evidence that neighborhood social disorder, for example, due to crime or illicit drugs, is a risk factor, and that a high neighborhood socioeconomic status, with better amenities, is a protective factor. Adverse conditions at work, particularly demanding jobs with little scope for decision-making, are associated with depression, although diversity and confounding factors make it difficult to confirm that the relationship is causal.

Evolutionary

Main article: Evolutionary approaches to depression

From the standpoint of evolutionary theory, major depression is hypothesized, in some instances, to increase an individual's reproductive fitness. Evolutionary approaches to depression and evolutionary psychology posit specific mechanisms by which depression may have been genetically incorporated into the human gene pool, accounting for the high heritability and prevalence of depression by proposing that certain components of depression are adaptations, such as the behaviors relating to attachment and social rank. Current behaviors can be explained as adaptations to regulate relationships or resources, although the result may be maladaptive in modern environments.

From another viewpoint, a counseling therapist may see depression, not as a biochemical illness or disorder, but as "a species-wide evolved suite of emotional programmes that are mostly activated by a perception, almost always over-negative, of a major decline in personal usefulness, that can sometimes be linked to guilt, shame or perceived rejection". This suite may have manifested in aging hunters in humans' foraging past, who were marginalized by their declining skills, and may continue to appear in alienated members of today's society. The feelings of uselessness generated by such marginalization could hypothetically prompt support from friends and kin. Additionally, in a manner analogous to that in which physical pain has evolved to hinder actions that may cause further injury, "psychic misery" may have evolved to prevent hasty and maladaptive reactions to distressing situations.

Drug and alcohol use

See also: Mood disorder#Substance-induced mood disorders

According to the DSM-IV, a diagnosis of mood disorder cannot be made if the cause is believed to be due to "the direct physiological effects of a substance"; when a syndrome resembling major depression is believed to be caused immediately by substance abuse or by an adverse drug reaction, it is referred to as, "substance-induced mood disturbance". Alcoholism or excessive alcohol consumption significantly increases the risk of developing major depression. Like alcohol, the benzodiazepines are central nervous system depressants; this class of medication is commonly used to treat insomnia, anxiety, and muscular spasms. Similar to alcohol, benzodiazepines increase the risk of developing major depression. This increased risk may be due in part to the effects of drugs on neurochemistry, such as decreased levels of serotonin and norepinephrine. Chronic use of benzodiazepines also can cause or worsen depression, or depression may be part of a protracted withdrawal syndrome.

Diagnosis

Further information: depression (differential diagnoses)

Clinical assessment

Further information: Rating scales for depression

A diagnostic assessment may be conducted by a suitably trained general practitioner, or by a psychiatrist or psychologist, who records the person's current circumstances, biographical history, current symptoms and family history. The broad clinical aim is to formulate the relevant biological, psychological and social factors that may be impacting on the individual's mood. The assessor may also discuss the person's current ways of regulating their mood (healthy or otherwise) such as alcohol and drug use. The assessment also includes a mental state examination, which is an assessment of the person's current mood and thought content, in particular the presence of themes of hopelessness or pessimism, self-harm or suicide, and an absence of positive thoughts or plans. Specialist mental health services are rare in rural areas, and thus diagnosis and management is largely left to primary care clinicians. This issue is even more marked in developing countries. The score on a rating scale alone is insufficientWikipedia:Avoid weasel words to diagnose depression, but it provides an indication of the severity of symptoms for a time period, so a person who scores above a given cut-off point can be more thoroughly evaluated for a depressive disorder diagnosis. Several rating scales are used for this purpose. Screening programs have been advocated to improve detection of depression, but there is evidence that they do not improve detection rates, treatment, or outcome.

Primary care physicians and other non-psychiatrist physicians have difficulty diagnosing depression, in part because they are trained to recognize and treat physical symptoms, and depression can cause a myriad of physical (psychosomatic) symptoms. Non-psychiatrists miss two-thirds of cases and unnecessarily treat other patients.

Before diagnosing a major depressive disorder, a doctor generally performs a medical examination and selected investigations to rule out other causes of symptoms. These include blood tests measuring TSH and thyroxine to exclude hypothyroidism; basic electrolytes and serum calcium to rule out a metabolic disturbance; and a full blood count including ESR to rule out a systemic infection or chronic disease. Adverse affective reactions to medications or alcohol misuse are often ruled out, as well. Testosterone levels may be evaluated to diagnose hypogonadism, a cause of depression in men.

Subjective cognitive complaints appear in older depressed people, but they can also be indicative of the onset of a dementing disorder, such as Alzheimer's disease. Cognitive testing and brain imaging can help distinguish depression from dementia. A CT scan can exclude brain pathology in those with psychotic, rapid-onset or otherwise unusual symptoms. No biological tests confirm major depression. Investigations are not generally repeated for a subsequent episode unless there is a medical indication.

DSM-IV-TR and ICD-10 criteria

The most widely used criteria for diagnosing depressive conditions are found in the American Psychiatric Association's revised fourth edition of the *Diagnostic and Statistical Manual of Mental Disorders* (DSM-IV-TR), and the World Health Organization's *International Statistical Classification of Diseases and Related Health Problems* (ICD-10) which uses the name *recurrent depressive disorder*. The latter system is typically used in European countries, while the former is used in the US and many other non-European nations, and the authors of both have worked towards conforming one with the other.

Major depressive disorder is classified as a mood disorder in DSM-IV-TR. The diagnosis hinges on the presence of single or recurrent major depressive episodes. Further qualifiers are used to classify both the episode itself and the course of the disorder. The category Depressive Disorder Not Otherwise Specified is diagnosed if the depressive episode's manifestation does not meet the criteria for a major depressive episode. The ICD-10 system does not use the term *major depressive disorder*, but lists very similar criteria for the diagnosis of a depressive episode (mild, moderate or severe); the term *recurrent* may be added if there have been multiple episodes without mania.

Major depressive episode

Main article: Major depressive episode

A major depressive episode is characterized by the presence of a severely depressed mood that persists for at least two weeks. Episodes may be isolated or recurrent and are categorized as mild (few symptoms in excess of minimum criteria), moderate, or severe (marked impact on social or occupational functioning). An episode with psychotic features—commonly referred to as *psychotic depression*—is automatically rated as severe. If the patient has had an episode of mania or markedly elevated mood, a diagnosis of bipolar disorder is made instead. Depression without mania is sometimes referred to as *unipolar* because the mood remains at one emotional state or "pole".

DSM-IV-TR excludes cases where the symptoms are a result of bereavement, although it is possible for normal bereavement to evolve into a depressive episode if the mood persists and the characteristic features of a major depressive episode develop. The criteria have been criticized because they do not take into account any other aspects of the personal and social context in which depression can occur. In addition, some studies have found little empirical support for the DSM-IV cut-off criteria, indicating they are a diagnostic convention imposed on a continuum of depressive symptoms of varying severity and duration: Excluded are a range of related diagnoses, including dysthymia, which involves a chronic but milder mood disturbance; recurrent brief depression, consisting of briefer depressive episodes; minor depressive disorder, whereby only some of the symptoms of major depression are present; and adjustment disorder with depressed mood, which denotes low mood resulting from a psychological response to an identifiable event or stressor.

Subtypes

The DSM-IV-TR recognizes five further subtypes of MDD, called *specifiers*, in addition to noting the length, severity and presence of psychotic features:

- **Melancholic depression** is characterized by a loss of pleasure in most or all activities, a failure of reactivity to pleasurable stimuli, a quality of depressed mood more pronounced than that of grief or loss, a worsening of symptoms in the morning hours, early morning waking, psychomotor retardation, excessive weight loss (not to be confused with anorexia nervosa), or excessive guilt.
- **Atypical depression** is characterized by mood reactivity (paradoxical anhedonia) and positivity, significant weight gain or increased appetite (comfort eating), excessive sleep or sleepiness (hypersomnia), a sensation of heaviness in limbs known as leaden paralysis, and significant social impairment as a consequence of hypersensitivity to perceived interpersonal rejection.
- **Catatonic depression** is a rare and severe form of major depression involving disturbances of motor behavior and other symptoms. Here the person is mute and almost stuporose, and either remains immobile or exhibits purposeless or even bizarre movements. Catatonic symptoms also occur in schizophrenia or in manic episodes, or may be caused by neuroleptic malignant syndrome.
- **Postpartum depression**, or **mental and behavioural disorders associated with the puerperium, not elsewhere classified**, refers to the intense, sustained and sometimes disabling depression experienced by women after giving birth. Postpartum depression has an incidence rate of 10–15% among new mothers. The DSM-IV mandates that, in order to qualify as postpartum depression, onset occur within one month of delivery. It has been said that postpartum depression can last as long as three months.
- **Seasonal affective disorder** (SAD) is a form of depression in which depressive episodes come on in the autumn or winter, and resolve in spring. The diagnosis is made if at least two episodes have occurred in colder months with none at other times, over a two-year period or longer.

Differential diagnoses

Main article: Depression (differential diagnoses)

To confer major depressive disorder as the most likely diagnosis, other potential diagnoses must be considered, including dysthymia, adjustment disorder with depressed mood or bipolar disorder. Dysthymia is a chronic, milder mood disturbance in which a person reports a low mood almost daily over a span of at least two years. The symptoms are not as severe as those for major depression, although people with dysthymia are vulnerable to secondary episodes of major depression (sometimes referred to as *double depression*). Adjustment disorder with depressed mood is a mood disturbance appearing as a psychological response to an identifiable event or stressor, in which the resulting emotional or behavioral symptoms are significant but do not meet the criteria for a major depressive episode. Bipolar disorder, also known as *manic–depressive disorder*, is a condition in which depressive phases alternate with periods of mania or hypomania. Although depression is currently categorized as a separate disorder, there is ongoing debate because individuals diagnosed with major depression often experience some hypomanic symptoms, indicating a mood disorder continuum.

Other disorders need to be ruled out before diagnosing major depressive disorder. They include depressions due to physical illness, medications, and substance abuse. Depression due to physical illness is diagnosed as a mood disorder due to a general medical condition. This condition is determined based on history, laboratory findings, or physical examination. When the depression is caused by a substance abused including a drug of abuse, a medication, or exposure to a toxin, it is then diagnosed as a substance-induced mood disorder. In such cases, a substance is judged to be etiologically related to the mood disturbance.

Schizoaffective disorder is different from major depressive disorder with psychotic features because in the schizoaffective disorder at least two weeks of delusions or hallucinations must occur in the absence of prominent mood symptoms.

Depressive symptoms may be identified during schizophrenia, delusional disorder, and psychotic disorder not otherwise specified, and in such cases those symptoms are considered associated features of these disorders, therefore, a separate diagnosis is not deemed necessary unless the depressive symptoms meet full criteria for a major depressive episode. In that case, a diagnosis of depressive disorder not otherwise specified may be made as well as a diagnosis of schizophrenia.

Some cognitive symptoms of dementia such as disorientation, apathy, difficulty concentrating and memory loss may get confused with a major depressive episode in major depressive disorder. They are especially difficult to determine in elderly patients. In such cases, the premorbid state of the patient may be helpful to differentiate both disorders. In the case of dementia, there tends to be a premorbid history of declining cognitive function. In the case of a major depressive disorder patients tend to exhibit a relatively normal premorbid state and abrupt cognitive decline associated with the depression.

Prevention

A 2008 meta-analysis found that behavioral interventions, such as interpersonal therapy, are effective at preventing new onset depression. Because such interventions appear to be most effective when delivered to individuals or small groups, it has been suggested that they may be able to reach their large target audience most efficiently through the Internet. However, an earlier meta-analysis found preventive programs with a competence-enhancing component to be superior to behaviorally oriented programs overall, and found behavioral programs to be particularly unhelpful for older people, for whom social support programs were uniquely beneficial. Additionally, the programs that best prevented depression comprised more than eight sessions, each lasting between 60 and 90 minutes; were provided by a combination of lay and professional workers; had a high-quality research design; reported attrition rates; and had a well-defined intervention. The "Coping with Depression" course (CWD) is claimed to be the most successful of psychoeducational interventions for the treatment and prevention of depression (both for its adaptability to various populations and its results), with a risk reduction of 38% in major depression and an efficacy as a treatment comparing favorably to other psychotherapies.

Management

The three most common treatments for depression are psychotherapy, medication, and electroconvulsive therapy. Psychotherapy is the treatment of choice for people under 18, while electroconvulsive therapy is only used as a last resort. Care is usually given on an outpatient basis, while treatment in an inpatient unit is considered if there is a significant risk to self or others.

Treatment options are much more limited in developing countries, where access to mental health staff, medication, and psychotherapy is often difficult. Development of mental health services is minimal in many countries; depression is viewed as a phenomenon of the developed world despite evidence to the contrary, and not as an inherently life-threatening condition.

Psychotherapy

Psychotherapy can be delivered, to individuals or groups, by mental health professionals, including psychotherapists, psychiatrists, psychologists, clinical social workers, counselors, and suitably trained psychiatric nurses. With more complex and chronic forms of depression, a combination of medication and psychotherapy may be used. In people under 18, according to the National Institute for Health and Clinical Excellence, medication should only be offered in conjunction with a psychological therapy, such as CBT, interpersonal therapy, or family therapy. Psychotherapy has been shown to be effective in older people. Successful psychotherapy appears to reduce the recurrence of depression even after it has been terminated or replaced by occasional booster sessions.

The most-studied form of psychotherapy for depression is CBT, which teaches clients to challenge self-defeating, but enduring ways of thinking (cognitions) and change counter-productive behaviours. Research beginning in the mid-1990s suggested that CBT could perform as well or better than antidepressants in patients with moderate to severe depression. CBT may be effective in depressed adolescents, although its effects on severe episodes are not definitively known. Combining fluoxetine with CBT appeared to bring no additional benefit, or, at the most, only marginal benefit. Several variables predict success for cognitive behavioral therapy in adolescents: higher levels of rational thoughts, less hopelessness, fewer negative thoughts, and fewer cognitive distortions. CBT is particularly beneficial in preventing relapse. Several variants of cognitive behavior therapy have been used in depressed patients, most notably rational emotive behavior therapy, and more recently mindfulness-based cognitive therapy.

Psychoanalysis is a school of thought, founded by Sigmund Freud, which emphasizes the resolution of unconscious mental conflicts. Psychoanalytic techniques are used by some practitioners to treat clients presenting with major depression. A more widely practiced, eclectic technique, called psychodynamic psychotherapy, is loosely based on psychoanalysis and has an additional social and interpersonal focus. In a meta-analysis of three controlled trials of Short Psychodynamic Supportive Psychotherapy, this modification was found to be as effective as medication for mild to moderate depression.

Logotherapy, a form of existential psychotherapy developed by Austrian psychiatrist Viktor Frankl, addresses the filling of an "existential vacuum" associated with feelings of futility and meaninglessness. It is posited that this type of psychotherapy may be useful for depression in older adolescents.

Antidepressants

The effects of prescription antidepressants are somewhat superior to those of psychotherapy, especially in cases of chronic major depression, although in short-term trials more patients—especially those with less serious forms of depression—cease medication than cease psychotherapy, most likely due to adverse effects from the medication and to patients' preferences for psychological therapies over pharmacological treatments.

To find the most effective antidepressant medication with minimal side effects, the dosages can be adjusted, and if necessary, combinations of different classes of antidepressants can be tried. Response rates to the first antidepressant administered range from 50–75%, and it can take at least six to eight weeks from the start of medication to remission, when the patient is back to their normal self. Antidepressant medication treatment is usually continued for 16 to 20 weeks after remission, to minimize the chance of recurrence, and even up to one year of continuation is recommended. People with chronic depression may need to take medication indefinitely to avoid relapse.

Selective serotonin reuptake inhibitors (SSRIs), such as sertraline, escitalopram, fluoxetine, paroxetine, and citalopram are the primary medications prescribed owing to their effectiveness, relatively mild side effects, and because they are less toxic in overdose than other antidepressants. Patients who do not respond to one SSRI can be switched to another antidepressant, and this results in improvement in almost 50% of cases. Another option is to switch to the atypical antidepressant bupropion. Venlafaxine, an antidepressant with a different mechanism of action, may be modestly more effective than SSRIs. However, venlafaxine is not recommended in the UK as a first-line treatment because of evidence suggesting its risks may outweigh benefits, and it is specifically discouraged in children and adolescents. For adolescent depression, fluoxetine and escitalopram are the two recommended choices. Antidepressants have not been found to be beneficial in children. Any antidepressant can cause low serum sodium levels (also called hyponatremia); nevertheless, it has been reported more often with SSRIs. It is not uncommon for SSRIs to cause or worsen insomnia; the sedating antidepressant mirtazapine can be used in such cases.

Monoamine oxidase inhibitors, an older class of antidepressants, have been plagued by potentially life-threatening dietary and drug interactions. They are still used only rarely, although newer and better tolerated agents of this class have been developed.

The terms "refractory depression" and "treatment-resistant depression" are used to describe cases that do not respond to adequate courses of at least two antidepressants. In many major studies, only about 35% of patients respond well to medical treatment. It may be difficult for a doctor to decide when someone has treatment-resistant depression or whether the problem is due to coexisting disorders, which are common among patients with major depression.

A team of psychologists from multiple American universities found that antidepressant drugs hardly have better effects than a placebo in cases of mild or moderate depression. The study focused on paroxetine and imipramine.

Pharmacological augmentation

A medication with a different mode of action may be added to bolster the effect of an antidepressant in cases of treatment resistance. Medication with lithium salts has been used to augment antidepressant therapy in those who have failed to respond to antidepressants alone. Furthermore, lithium dramatically decreases the suicide risk in recurrent depression. Addition of a thyroid hormone, triiodothyronine may work as well as lithium, even in patients with normal thyroid function. Addition of atypical antipsychotics when the patient has not responded to an antidepressant is also known to increase the effectiveness of antidepressant drugs, albeit offset by increased side effects.

Comparative efficacy of medication and psychotherapy

Two recent meta-analyses of clinical trial results submitted to the FDA concluded that antidepressants are statistically superior to placebo but their overall effect is low-to-moderate. In that respect they often did not exceed the National Institute for Health and Clinical Excellence criteria for a "clinically significant" effect. In particular, the effect size was very small for moderate depression but increased with severity, reaching "clinical significance" for very severe depression. These results were consistent with the earlier clinical studies in which only patients with severe depression benefited from either psychotherapy or treatment with an antidepressant, imipramine, more than from the placebo treatment. Despite obtaining similar results, the authors argued about their interpretation. One author concluded that there "seems little evidence to support the prescription of antidepressant medication to any but the most severely depressed patients, unless alternative treatments have failed to provide benefit." The other author agreed that "antidepressant 'glass' is far from full" but disagreed "that it is completely empty". He pointed out that the first-line alternative to medication is psychotherapy, which does not have superior efficacy.

One interpretation of the research is that antidepressants in general are as effective as psychotherapy for major depression, and that this conclusion holds true for both severe and mild forms of MDD. In contrast, medication gives better results for dysthymia. The subgroup of SSRIs may be slightly more efficacious than psychotherapy. On the other hand, significantly more patients drop off from the antidepressant treatment than from psychotherapy, likely because of the side effects of antidepressants. Successful psychotherapy appears to prevent the recurrence of depression even after it has been terminated or replaced by occasional "booster" sessions. The same degree of prevention can be achieved by continuing antidepressant treatment. However, another argument is that medication and psychotherapy are two very different things and comparisons are not scientifically valid. Psychotherapy involves addressing and understanding the meaning behind emotions, whilst medication involves regulating those emotions through biochemical means. In many cases, both approaches may be necessary either in combination or in sequence.

Antidepressants and suicidality

Main article: Selective serotonin reuptake inhibitor#suicidality

For children, adolescents, and in some studies also for young adults between 18–24 years old, there is a higher risk of both suicidal ideations and suicidal behavior in those treated with SSRIs. For adults, it is unclear whether or not SSRIs affect the risk of suicidality. One review found no connection between SSRIs and the risk of suicide; other studies found an increase in suicide attempts by those who use SSRIs as compared to placebo; and yet other studies found that the widespread use of antidepressants in the new "SSRI-era" appeared to have led to a highly significant decline in suicide rates in most countries with traditionally high baseline suicide rates.

A black box warning was introduced in the United States in 2007 on SSRI and other antidepressant medications due to increased risk of suicide in patients younger than 24 years old. Similar precautionary notice revisions were implemented by the Japanese Ministry of Health.

Electroconvulsive therapy

Main article: Electroconvulsive therapy

Electroconvulsive therapy (ECT) is a procedure whereby pulses of electricity are sent through the brain via two electrodes, usually one on each temple, to induce a seizure while the patient is under a brief period of general anaesthesia. Hospital psychiatrists may recommend ECT for cases of severe major depression which have not responded to antidepressant medication or, less often, psychotherapy or supportive interventions. ECT can have a quicker effect than antidepressant therapy and thus may be the treatment of choice in emergencies such as catatonic depression where the patient has stopped eating and drinking, or where a patient is severely suicidal. ECT is probably more effective than pharmacotherapy for depression in the immediate short-term, although a landmark community-based study found much lower remission rates in routine practice. When ECT is used on its own, the relapse rate within the first six months is very high; early studies put the rate at around 50%, while a more recent controlled trial found rates of 84% even with placebos. The early relapse rate may be reduced by the use of psychiatric medications or further ECT (although the latter is not recommended by some authorities) but remains high. Common initial adverse effects from ECT include short and long-term memory loss, disorientation and headache. Although memory disturbance after ECT usually resolves within one month, ECT remains a controversial treatment, and debate on its efficacy and safety continues.

Deep brain stimulation

Deep brain stimulation (DBS) is a neurosurgical treatment that has been used especially to treat movement disorders such as Parkinson's disease. It requires a neurosurgeon to drill a hole in the skull and insert an electrode into the patient's tissue. Then, a device located in the chest transmits a signal to the implanted electrode through wires located underneath the scalp.

Clinical trials are focused on the use of DBS for epilepsy and depression but the FDA has not approved this use. It requires brain surgery and it is therefore the most invasive form of brain stimulation in the treatment of depression.

Physical exercise

Physical exercise is recommended by U.K. health authorities for management of mild depression but it has only a moderate, statistically insignificant effect on symptoms in most cases of major depressive disorder.

Over-the-counter compounds

St John's wort is available over-the-counter as a herbal remedy in some parts of the world; however, the evidence of its effectiveness for the treatment of major depression is varying and confusing. Its safety can be compromised by inconsistency in pharmaceutical quality and in the amounts of active ingredient in different preparations. Further, it interacts with numerous prescribed medicines including antidepressants, and it can reduce the effectiveness of hormonal contraception.

The efficacy of omega-3 fatty acids for major depression is unclear, with controlled studies and meta-analyses supporting both positive and negative conclusions.

Reviews of short-term clinical trials of S-adenosylmethionine (SAMe) indicate that it may be effective in treating major depression in adults. A 2002 review reported that tryptophan and 5-hydroxytryptophan appear to be better than placebo, but found most of the evidence in their favor to be of poor quality and inconclusive.

Other somatic treatments

Repetitive transcranial magnetic stimulation (rTMS) applies powerful magnetic fields to the brain from outside the head. Multiple controlled studies support the use of this method in treatment-resistant depression; it has been approved for this indication in Europe, Canada, Australia, and the US. rTMS appeared similarly effective for both uncomplicated depression and depression resistant to medication; however, it was inferior to ECT in a side-by-side randomized trial.

Vagus nerve stimulation was approved by the FDA in the United States in 2005 for use in treatment-resistant depression, although it failed to show short-term benefit in the only large double-blind trial when used as an adjunct on treatment-resistant patients; a 2008 systematic review concluded that despite the promising results reported mainly in open studies, further clinical trials are needed to confirm its efficacy in major depression.

Prognosis

Major depressive episodes often resolve over time whether or not they are treated. Outpatients on a waiting list show a 10–15% reduction in symptoms within a few months, with approximately 20% no longer meeting the full criteria for a depressive disorder. The median duration of an episode has been estimated to be 23 weeks, with the highest rate of recovery in the first three months.

Studies have shown that 80% of those suffering from their first major depressive episode will suffer from at least 1 more during their life, with a lifetime average of 4 episodes. Other general population studies indicate around half those who have an episode (whether treated or not) recover and remain well, while the other half will have at least one more, and around 15% of those experience chronic recurrence. Studies recruiting from selective inpatient sources suggest lower recovery and higher chronicity, while studies of mostly outpatients show that nearly all recover, with a median episode duration of 11 months. Around 90% of those with severe or psychotic depression, most of whom also meet criteria for other mental disorders, experience recurrence.

Recurrence is more likely if symptoms have not fully resolved with treatment. Current guidelines recommend continuing antidepressants for four to six months after remission to prevent relapse. Evidence from many randomized controlled trials indicates continuing antidepressant medications after recovery can reduce the chance of relapse by 70% (41% on placebo vs. 18% on antidepressant). The preventive effect probably lasts for at least the first 36 months of use.

Those people who experience repeated episodes of depression are required quick and ongoing treatment in order to prevent more severe, long-term depression. In some cases, people need to take medications for long periods of time or for the rest of their lives.

Cases when outcome is poor are associated with inappropriate treatment, severe initial symptoms that may include psychosis, early age of onset, more previous episodes, incomplete recovery after 1 year, pre-existing severe mental or medical disorder, and family dysfunction as well.

Depressed individuals have a shorter life expectancy than those without depression, in part because depressed patients are at risk of dying by suicide. However, they also have a higher rate of dying from other causes, being more susceptible to medical conditions such as heart disease. Up to 60% of people who commit suicide have a mood disorder such as major depression, and the risk is especially high if a person has a marked sense of hopelessness or has both depression and borderline personality disorder. The lifetime risk of suicide associated with a diagnosis of major depression in the US is estimated at 3.4%, which averages two highly disparate figures of almost 7% for men and 1% for women (although suicide attempts are more frequent in women). The estimate is substantially lower than a previously accepted figure of 15% which had been derived from older studies of hospitalized patients.

Epidemiology

Prevalence

Depression is a major cause of morbidity worldwide. Lifetime prevalence varies widely, from 3% in Japan to 17% in the US. In most countries the number of people who would suffer from depression during their lives falls within an 8–12% range. In North America the probability of having a major depressive episode within a year-long period is 3–5% for males and 8–10% for females. Population studies have consistently shown major depression to be about twice as common in women as in men, although it is unclear why this is so, and whether factors unaccounted for are contributing to this. The relative increase in occurrence is related to pubertal development rather than chronological age, reaches adult ratios between the ages of 15 and 18, and appears associated with psychosocial more than hormonal factors.

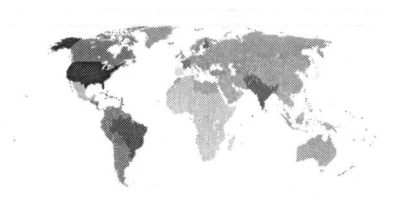

Disability-adjusted life year for unipolar depressive disorders per 100,000 inhabitants in 2002. Mortality and Burden of Disease Estimates for WHO Member States in 2002 [xls]; 2002. no data   ≤ 600   600–700   700–800   800–900   900–1000   1000–1100   1100–1200   1200–1300   1300–1400   1400–1500   1500–1600   ≥ 1600

People are most likely to suffer their first depressive episode between the ages of 30 and 40, and there is a second, smaller peak of incidence between ages 50 and 60. The risk of major depression is increased with neurological conditions such as stroke, Parkinson's disease, or multiple sclerosis and during the first year after childbirth. It is also more common after cardiovascular illnesses, and is related more to a poor outcome than to a better one. Studies conflict on the prevalence of depression in the elderly, but most data suggest there is a reduction in this age group.

Comorbidity

Major depression frequently co-occurs with other psychiatric problems. The 1990–92 *National Comorbidity Survey* (US) reports that 51% of those with major depression also suffer from lifetime anxiety. Anxiety symptoms can have a major impact on the course of a depressive illness, with delayed recovery, increased risk of relapse, greater disability and increased suicide attempts. American neuroendocrinologist Robert Sapolsky similarly argues that the relationship between stress, anxiety, and depression could be measured and demonstrated biologically. There are increased rates of alcohol and drug abuse and particularly dependence, and around a third of individuals diagnosed with ADHD develop comorbid depression. Post-traumatic stress disorder and depression often co-occur.

Depression and pain often co-occur. This may be for the simple reason that is obviously depressing to be in pain, especially if it is chronic or cannot be controlled. This also fits with Seligman's theory of learned helplessness. One or more pain symptoms is present in 65% of depressed patients, and anywhere from five to 85% of patients with pain will be suffering from depression, depending on the setting; there is a lower prevalence in general practice, and higher in specialty clinics. The diagnosis of depression is often delayed or missed, and the outcome worsens. The outcome can also obviously worsen if the depression is noticed but completely misunderstood

Depression is also associated with a 1.5- to 2-fold increased risk of cardiovascular disease, independent of other known risk factors, and is itself linked directly or indirectly to risk factors such as smoking and obesity. People with major depression are less likely to follow medical recommendations for treating cardiovascular disorders, which further increases their risk. In addition, cardiologists may not recognize underlying depression that complicates a cardiovascular problem under their care.

Disease impacts

Depression is often associated with unemployment and poverty. Major depression is currently the leading cause of disease burden in North America and other high-income countries, and the fourth-leading cause worldwide. In the year 2030, it is predicted to be the second-leading cause of disease burden worldwide after HIV, according to the World Health Organization. Delay or failure in seeking treatment after relapse, and the failure of health professionals to provide treatment, are two barriers to reducing disability.

History

Main article: History of depression

The Ancient Greek physician Hippocrates described a syndrome of melancholia as a distinct disease with particular mental and physical symptoms; he characterized all "fears and despondencies, if they last a long time" as being symptomatic of the ailment. It was a similar but far broader concept than today's depression; prominence was given to a clustering of the symptoms of sadness, dejection, and despondency, and often fear, anger, delusions and obsessions were included.

The term *depression* itself was derived from the Latin verb *deprimere*, "to press down". From the 14th century, "to depress" meant to subjugate or to bring down in spirits. It was used in 1665 in English author Richard Baker's *Chronicle* to refer to someone having "a great depression of spirit", and by English author Samuel Johnson in a similar sense in 1753. The term also came in to use in physiology and economics. An early usage referring to a psychiatric symptom was by French psychiatrist Louis Delasiauve in 1856, and by the 1860s it was appearing in medical dictionaries to refer to a physiological and metaphorical lowering of emotional function. Since Aristotle, melancholia had been associated with men of learning and intellectual brilliance, a hazard of contemplation and creativity. The newer concept abandoned these associations and through the 19th century, became more associated with women.

Although *melancholia* remained the dominant diagnostic term, *depression* gained increasing currency in medical treatises and was a synonym by the end of the century; German psychiatrist Emil Kraepelin may have been the first to use it as the overarching term, referring to different kinds of melancholia as *depressive states*.

Sigmund Freud likened the state of melancholia to mourning in his 1917 paper *Mourning and Melancholia*. He theorized that objective loss, such as the loss of a valued relationship through death or a romantic break-up, results in subjective loss as well; the depressed individual has identified with the object of affection through an unconscious, narcissistic process called the *libidinal cathexis* of the ego. Such loss results in severe melancholic symptoms more profound than mourning; not only is the outside world viewed negatively, but the ego itself is compromised. The patient's decline of self-perception is revealed in his belief of his own blame, inferiority, and unworthiness. He also emphasized early life experiences as a predisposing factor. Meyer put forward a mixed social and biological framework emphasizing *reactions* in the context of an individual's life, and argued that the term *depression* should be used instead of *melancholia*. The first version of the DSM (DSM-I, 1952) contained *depressive reaction* and the DSM-II (1968) *depressive neurosis*, defined as an excessive reaction to internal conflict or an identifiable event, and also included a depressive type of manic-depressive psychosis within Major affective disorders.

In the mid-20th century, researchers theorized that depression was caused by a chemical imbalance in neurotransmitters in the brain, a theory based on observations made in the 1950s of the effects of reserpine and isoniazid in altering monoamine neurotransmitter levels and affecting depressive symptoms.

The term *Major depressive disorder* was introduced by a group of US clinicians in the mid-1970s as part of proposals for diagnostic criteria based on patterns of symptoms (called the "Research Diagnostic Criteria", building on earlier Feighner Criteria), and was incorporated in to the DSM-III in 1980. To maintain consistency the ICD-10 used the same criteria, with only minor alterations, but using the DSM diagnostic threshold to mark a *mild depressive episode*, adding higher threshold categories for moderate and severe episodes. The ancient idea of *melancholia* still survives in the notion of a melancholic subtype.

The new definitions of depression were widely accepted, albeit with some conflicting findings and views. There have been some continued empirically based arguments for a return to the diagnosis of melancholia. There has been some criticism of the expansion of coverage of the diagnosis, related to the development and promotion of antidepressants and the biological model since the late 1950s.

Sociocultural aspects

See also: List of people with depression

People's conceptualizations of depression vary widely, both within and among cultures. "Because of the lack of scientific certainty," one commentator has observed, "the debate over depression turns on questions of language. What we call it—'disease,' 'disorder,' 'state of mind'—affects how we view, diagnose, and treat it." There are cultural differences in the extent to which serious depression is considered an illness requiring personal professional treatment, or is an indicator of something else, such as the need to address social or moral problems, the result of biological imbalances, or a reflection of individual differences in the understanding of distress that may reinforce feelings of powerlessness, and emotional struggle.

American president Abraham Lincoln appears to have had at least two major depressive episodes.

The diagnosis is less common in some countries, such as China. It has been argued that the Chinese traditionally deny or somatize emotional depression (although since the early 1980s the Chinese denial of depression may have modified drastically). Alternatively, it may be that Western cultures reframe and elevate some expressions of human distress to disorder status. Australian professor Gordon Parker and others have argued that the Western concept of depression "medicalizes" sadness or misery. Similarly, Hungarian-American psychiatrist Thomas Szasz and others argue that depression is a metaphorical illness that is inappropriately regarded as an actual disease. There has also been concern that the DSM, as well as the field of descriptive psychiatry that employs it, tends to reify abstract phenomena such as depression, which may in fact be social constructs. American archetypal psychologist James Hillman writes that depression can be healthy for the soul, insofar as "it brings refuge, limitation, focus, gravity, weight, and humble powerlessness." Hillman argues that therapeutic attempts to eliminate depression echo the Christian theme of resurrection, but have the unfortunate effect of demonizing a soulful state of being.

Historical figures were often reluctant to discuss or seek treatment for depression due to social stigma about the condition, or due to ignorance of diagnosis or treatments. Nevertheless, analysis or interpretation of letters, journals, artwork, writings or statements of family and friends of some historical personalities has led to the presumption that they may have had some form of depression. People who may have had depression include English author Mary Shelley, American-British writer Henry James, and American president Abraham Lincoln. Some well-known contemporary people with possible depression include Canadian songwriter Leonard Cohen and American playwright and novelist Tennessee Williams. Some pioneering psychologists, such as Americans William James and John B. Watson, dealt with their own depression.

There has been a continuing discussion of whether neurological disorders and mood disorders may be linked to creativity, a discussion that goes back to Aristotelian times. British literature gives many examples of reflections on depression. English philosopher John Stuart Mill experienced a several-months-long period of what he called "a dull state of nerves", when one is "unsusceptible to enjoyment or pleasurable excitement; one of those moods when what is pleasure at other times, becomes insipid or indifferent". He quoted English poet Samuel Taylor Coleridge's "Dejection" as a perfect description of his case: "A grief without a pang, void, dark and drear, / A drowsy, stifled, unimpassioned grief, / Which finds no natural outlet or relief / In word, or sigh, or tear." English writer Samuel Johnson used the term "the black dog" in the 1780s to describe his own depression, and it was subsequently popularized by depression sufferer former British Prime Minister Sir Winston Churchill.

Social stigma of major depression is widespread, and contact with mental health services reduces this only slightly. Public opinions on treatment differ markedly to those of health professionals; alternative treatments are held to be more helpful than pharmacological ones, which are viewed poorly. In the UK, the Royal College of Psychiatrists and the Royal College of General Practitioners conducted a joint Five-year Defeat Depression campaign to educate and reduce stigma from 1992 to 1996; a MORI study conducted afterwards showed a small positive change in public attitudes to depression and treatment.

Notes

Selected cited works

- American Psychiatric Association. *Diagnostic and statistical manual of mental disorders, Fourth Edition, Text Revision: DSM-IV-TR*. Washington, DC: American Psychiatric Publishing, Inc.; 2000a. ISBN 0890420254.
- Barlow DH. *Abnormal psychology: An integrative approach (5th ed.)*. Belmont, CA, USA: Thomson Wadsworth; 2005. ISBN 0534633560.
- Beck AT, Rush J, Shaw BF, Emery G. *Cognitive Therapy of depression*. New York, NY, USA: Guilford Press; 1987. ISBN 0898629195.
- Simon, Karen Michele; Freeman, Arthur M.; Epstein, Norman (1986). *Depression in the family*. New York: Haworth Press. ISBN 0-86656-624-4.
- Hergenhahn BR. *An Introduction to the History of Psychology*. 5th ed. Belmont, CA, USA: Thomson Wadsworth; 2005. ISBN 0534554016.
- May R. *The discovery of being: Writings in existential psychology*. New York, NY, USA: W. W. Norton & Company; 1994. ISBN 0393312402.
- Hadzi-Pavlovic, Dusan; Parker, Gordon. *Melancholia: a disorder of movement and mood: a phenomenological and neurobiological review*. Cambridge, UK: Cambridge University Press; 1996. ISBN 0-521-47275-X.

- Royal Pharmaceutical Society of Great Britain. *[[British National Formulary [9]] (BNF 56)]*. UK: BMJ Group and RPS Publishing; 2008. ISBN 9780853697787.
- Sadock, Virginia A.; Sadock, Benjamin J.; Kaplan, Harold I.. *Kaplan & Sadock's synopsis of psychiatry: behavioral sciences/clinical psychiatry*. Hagerstwon, MD: Lippincott Williams & Wilkins; 2003ref= CITEREFSadock2002.

External links

- BBC Headroom: [10] Understanding Depression
- DSM-IV diagnostic criteria for major depressive disorder [11] – DSM-IV-TR text from behavenet.com
- Depression [12] at the Open Directory Project
- NHS Evidence – search results for Depression [13]
- Depression Alliance [14] – Depression Alliance is a UK charity for people with clinical depression and anxiety

Euthanasia

Euthanasia

Part of a series on
Euthanasia
Types
Animal · Child · Voluntary Non-voluntary · Involuntary
Views
Religious (Buddhist · Catholic)
Groups
Dignitas · Dignity in Dying Exit International
People
Jack Kevorkian · Philip Nitschke
Books
Final Exit *The Peaceful Pill Handbook*
Jurisdictions
Australia · Canada Mexico · Netherlands New Zealand · Switzerland United Kingdom · United States
Laws
Rights of the Terminally Ill Act 1995 Oregon Death with Dignity Act Washington Death with Dignity Act
Court cases

Euthanasia

Washington v. Glucksberg (1997)
Gonzales v. Oregon (2006)
Baxter v. Montana (2009)
Alternatives
Assisted suicide
Palliative care
Principle of double effect
Terminal sedation
Other issues
Suicide tourism
Groningen Protocol
Euthanasia device

Euthanasia (from the Greek εὐθανασία meaning "good death": εὖ, *eu* (well or good) + θάνατος, *thanatos* (death)) refers to the practice of ending a life in a manner which relieves pain and suffering. According to the House of Lords Select Committee on Medical Ethics, the precise definition of euthanasia is "a deliberate intervention undertaken with the express intention of ending a life, to relieve intractable suffering."

Euthanasia is categorized in different ways, which include voluntary, non-voluntary, or involuntary and active or passive. Euthanasia is usually used to refer to active euthanasia, and in this sense, euthanasia is usually considered to be criminal homicide, but voluntary, passive euthanasia is widely non-criminal.

The controversy surrounding euthanasia centers around a two-pronged argument by opponents which characterizes euthanasia as either voluntary "suicides", or as involuntary murders. (Hence, opponents argue that a broad policy of "euthanasia" is tantamount to eugenics). Much hinges on whether a particular death was considered an "easy", "painless", or "happy" one, or whether it was a "wrongful death". Proponents typically consider a death that increased suffering to be "wrongful", while opponents typically consider any deliberate death as "wrongful". "Euthanasia's" original meaning introduced the idea of a "rightful death" beyond that only found in natural deaths.

Euthanasia is the most active area of research in contemporary bioethics.

Etymology

Like other terms borrowed from history, the "euthanasia" has had different meanings depending on usage. The first apparent usage of the term "euthanasia" belongs to the historian Suetonius who described how the Emperor Augustus, "dying quickly and without suffering in the arms of his wife, Livia, experienced the 'euthanasia' he had wished for." The word "euthanasia" was first used in a medical context by Francis Bacon in the 17th century, to refer to an easy, painless, happy death, during which it was a "physician's responsibility to alleviate the 'physical sufferings' of the body." Bacon referred to an "outward euthanasia"—the term "outward" he used to distinguish from a spiritual concept—the euthanasia "which regards the preparation of the soul."

In current parlance it has come to mean different but related things depending on philosophy and political persuasion: Opponents to euthanasia and assisted suicide, refer to an "active causation of a patient's death by a physician".[citation needed] Proponents instead refer to palliative care and easing of suffering.[citation needed]

Classification of euthanasia

Euthanasia may be classified according to whether a person gives informed consent into three types: voluntary, non-voluntary and involuntary.

There is a debate within the medical and bioethics literature about whether or not the non-voluntary (and by extension, involuntary) killing of patients can be regarded as euthanasia, irrespective of intent or the patient's circumstances. In the definitions offered by Beauchamp & Davidson and, later, by Wreen, consent on the part of the patient was not considered to be one of their criteria. However, others see consent as essential. For example, in a discussion of euthanasia presented in 2003 by the European Association of Palliative Care (EPAC) Ethics Task Force, the authors offered the unambiguous statement:

> Medicalized killing of a person without the person's consent, whether nonvoluntary (where the person in unable to consent) or involuntary (against the person's will) is not euthanasia: it is murder. Hence, euthanasia can be voluntary only.

Voluntary euthanasia

Main article: Voluntary euthanasia

Euthanasia conducted with the consent of the patient is termed voluntary euthanasia. Voluntary euthanasia is legal in Belgium, Luxembourg, the Netherlands, Switzerland, and the U.S. states of Oregon and Washington. When the patient brings about his or her own death with the assistance of a physician, the term assisted suicide is often used instead.

Non-voluntary euthanasia

Main article: Non-voluntary euthanasia

Euthanasia conducted where the consent of the patient is unavailable is termed non-voluntary euthanasia. Examples include child euthanasia, which is illegal worldwide but decriminalised under certain specific circumstances in the Netherlands under the Groningen Protocol.

Involuntary euthanasia

Main article: Involuntary euthanasia

Euthanasia conducted against the will of the patient is termed involuntary euthanasia.

Procedural decision

Voluntary, non-voluntary and involuntary euthanasia can all be further divided into passive or active variants. A number of authors consider these terms to be misleading and unhelpful.

Passive euthanasia

Passive euthanasia entails the withholding of common treatments, such as antibiotics, necessary for the continuance of life.

Active euthanasia

Active euthanasia entails the use of lethal substances or forces to kill and is the most controversial means.

Legal status

Main article: Legality of euthanasia

West's Encyclopedia of American Law states that "a 'mercy killing' or euthanasia is generally considered to be a criminal homicide" and is normally used as a synonym of homicide committed at a request made by the patient.

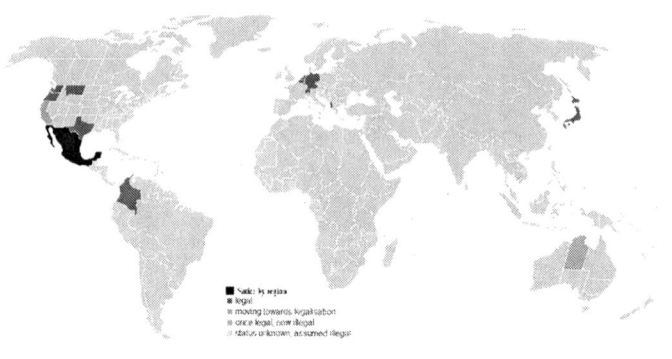

Map of the legality of euthanasia.

The judicial sense of the term "homicide" includes any intervention undertaken with the express intention of ending a life, even to relieve intractable suffering. Not all homicide is unlawful. Two designations of homicide that carry no criminal punishment are justifiable and excusable homicide. In most countries this is not the status of euthanasia. The term "euthanasia" is usually confined to the active variety; the University of Washington website states that "euthanasia generally means that the physician would act directly, for instance by giving a lethal injection, to end the patient's life". Physician-assisted suicide is thus not classified as euthanasia by the US State of Oregon, where it is legal under the Oregon Death with

Dignity Act, and despite its name, it is not legally classified as suicide either. Unlike physician-assisted suicide, withholding or withdrawing life-sustaining treatments with patient consent (voluntary) is almost unanimously considered, at least in the United States, to be legal. The use of pain medication in order to relieve suffering, even if it hastens death, has been held as legal in several court decisions.

Some governments around the world have legalized voluntary euthanasia but generally it remains as a criminal homicide. In the Netherlands and Belgium, where euthanasia has been legalized, it still remains homicide although it is not prosecuted and not punishable if the perpetrator (the doctor) meets certain legal exceptions.

See also

- Medical law
- Principle of double effect

Voluntary euthanasia

Part of a series on
Euthanasia
Types
Animal · Child · Voluntary Non-voluntary · Involuntary
Views
Religious (Buddhist · Catholic)
Groups
Dignitas · Dignity in Dying Exit International
People
Jack Kevorkian · Philip Nitschke
Books
Final Exit *The Peaceful Pill Handbook*
Jurisdictions

Australia · Canada Mexico · Netherlands New Zealand · Switzerland United Kingdom · United States
Laws
Rights of the Terminally Ill Act 1995 Oregon Death with Dignity Act Washington Death with Dignity Act
Court cases
Washington v. Glucksberg (1997) *Gonzales v. Oregon* (2006) *Baxter v. Montana* (2009)
Alternatives
Assisted suicide Palliative care Principle of double effect Terminal sedation
Other issues
Suicide tourism Groningen Protocol Euthanasia device

Voluntary euthanasia (from the Greek ευθανασία meaning "good death": ευ-, eu- (well or good) + θάνατος, thanatos (death)) refers to the practice of ending a life in a painless manner. Voluntary euthanasia (VE) and physician-assisted suicide (PAS) have been the focus of great controversy in recent years.

As of 2009, some forms of voluntary euthanasia are legal in Belgium, Luxembourg, the Netherlands, Switzerland, and the U.S. states of Oregon and Washington.

Assisted suicide

Main article: Assisted suicide

Assisted suicide is where the patient actively takes the last step in their death. The term "assisted suicide" is contrasted with "active euthanasia" when the difference between providing the means and actively administering lethal medicine is considered important, though in practice, the distinction can appear very hard to draw. For example, Swiss law on assisted suicide allows assisted suicide, while all forms of active euthanasia (like lethal injection) remain prohibited.

Some jurisdictions declare that a person dying as a result of physician assisted suicide does not commit suicide. This ensures that terminally ill people choosing assisted suicide options do not have reduced insurance claims compared to people dying in "natural" way. For example, the Oregon Death with Dignity Act defines that "... participation under the Act is not suicide, so should not affect insurance benefits by that definition."

Other terminology

Voluntary refusal of food and fluids (VRFF) or Patient Refusal of Nutrition and Hydration (PRNH) is bordering on euthanasia. Some authors classify it as a form of passive euthanasia, while others treat it separately because it is treated differently from legal point of view and often perceived as a more ethical option. VRFF is sometimes suggested as a legal alternative to euthanasia in jurisdictions disallowing euthanasia.[citation needed]

History

The term euthanasia comes from the Greek words "eu"-meaning good and "thanatos"-meaning death, which combined means "well-death" or "dying well". Hippocrates mentions euthanasia in the Hippocratic Oath, which was written between 400 and 300 BC The original Oath states: "To please no one will I prescribe a deadly drug nor give advice which may cause his death." Despite this, the ancient Greeks and Romans generally did not believe that life needed to be preserved at any cost and were, in consequence, tolerant of suicide in cases where no relief could be offered to the dying or, in the case of the Stoics and Epicureans, where a person no longer cared for his life.

English Common Law from the 14th century until the middle of the last century made suicide a criminal act in England and Wales. Assisting others to kill themselves remains illegal in that jurisdiction. However, in the 16th century, Thomas More, considered a saint by Roman Catholics, described a utopian community and envisaged such a community as one that would facilitate the death of those whose lives had become burdensome as a result of "torturing and lingering pain", see The meaning of the work.

Modern history

Since the 19th Century, euthanasia has sparked intermittent debates and activism in North America and Europe. According to medical historian Ezekiel Emanuel, it was the availability of anesthesia that ushered in the modern era of euthanasia. In 1828, the first known anti-euthanasia law in the United States was passed in the state of New York, with many other localities and states following suit over a period of several years. After the Civil War, voluntary euthanasia was promoted by advocates, including some doctors. Support peaked around the turn of the century in the US and then grew again in the 1930s.

In an article in the *Bulletin of the History of Medicine*, Brown University historian Jacob M. Appel documented extensive political debate over legislation to legalize physician-assisted suicide in both Iowa and Ohio in 1906. Appel indicates social activist Anna S. Hall was the driving force behind this movement. According to historian Ian Dowbiggin, leading public figures, including Clarence Darrow and Jack London, advocated for the legalization of euthanasia.

Euthanasia societiesWikipedia:Avoid weasel words were formed in England in 1935 and in the USA in 1938 to promote euthanasia. Although euthanasia legislation did not pass in the USA or England, in 1937, doctor-assisted euthanasia was declared legal in Switzerland as long as the doctor ending the life had nothing to gain. During this same era, US courts tackled cases involving critically ill people who requested physician assistance in dying as well as "mercy killings", such as by parents of their severely disabled children.[citation needed]

Post-War history

During the post-war period, prominent proponents of euthanasia included Glanville Williams (*The Sanctity of Life and the Criminal Law*) and clergyman Joseph Fletcher ("Morals and medicine"). By the 1960s, advocacy for a right-to-die approach to voluntary euthanasia increased.

Australia

See also: Euthanasia in Australia

In 1996, the world's first euthanasia legislation, the Rights of the Terminally Ill Act 1996, was passed in the Northern Territory of Australia. Four patients died under the Act, using a euthanasia device designed by Dr Philip Nitschke. The legislation was overturned in 1997 by Australia's Federal Parliament in 1997. In response to the overturning of the Act, Dr Nitschke founded EXIT International. In 2009, an Australian quadriplegic was granted the right to refuse sustenance and be allowed to die. The Supreme Court of Western Australia ruled that it was up to Christian Rossiter, aged 49, to decide if he was to continue to receive medical care (tube feeding) and that his carers had to abide by his wishes. Chief Justice Wayne Martin also stipulated that his carers, Brightwater Care, would not be held criminally responsible for following his instructions. Rossiter died on September 21, 2009 following a chest infection.

Europe

See also: Euthanasia in the United Kingdom and Euthanasia in the Netherlands

In 1957 in Britain, Judge Devlin ruled in the trial of Dr John Bodkin Adams that causing death through the administration of lethal drugs to a patient, if the intention is solely to alleviate pain, is not considered murder even if death is a potential or even likely outcome. In 1993, the Netherlands decriminalized doctor-assisted suicide, and in 2002, restrictions were loosened. During that year, physician-assisted suicide was approved in Belgium. Belgium's at the time most famous author Hugo

Claus, suffering from Alzheimer's disease, was among those that asked for euthanasia. He died in March 2008, assisted by an Antwerp doctor.

United States

See also: Euthanasia in the United States

A key turning point in the debate over voluntary euthanasia (and physician assisted dying), at least in the United States, was the public furor over the case of Karen Ann Quinlan. The Quinlan case paved the way for legal protection of voluntary passive euthanasia. In 1977, California legalized living wills and other states soon followed suit.

In 1980 the Hemlock Society USA was founded in Santa Monica by Derek Humphry. It was the first group in America to provide information to the terminally ill in case they wanted a hastened death. Hemlock also campaigned and partially financed drives to reform the law. In 2003 Hemlock was merged with End of Life Choices, which changed its name to Compassion and Choices.

In 1990, Dr. Jack Kevorkian, a Michigan physician, became infamous for encouraging and assisting people in committing suicide which resulted in a Michigan law against the practice in 1992. Kevorkian was tried and convicted in 1999 for a murder displayed on television. Also in 1990, the Supreme Court approved the use of non-active euthanasia.

In 1994, Oregon voters approved the Death with Dignity Act, permitting doctors to assist terminal patients with six months or less to live to end their lives. The U.S. Supreme Court allowed such laws in 1997. The Bush administration failed in its attempt to use drug law to stop Oregon in 2001, in the case *Gonzales v. Oregon*. In 1999, non-active euthanasia was permitted in Texas.[*citation needed*]

Most recently, amid U.S. government roadblocks and controversy in the Terri Schiavo case, where a Floridian who was in a vegetative state since 1990, had her feeding tube removed in 2005. Her husband had won the right to take her off life support, which he claimed she would want but was difficult to confirm as she had no living will and the rest of her family claimed otherwise.Wikipedia:Link rot

In November 2008, Washington Initiative 1000 made Washington the second U.S. state to legalize physician-assisted suicide.

China and Hong Kong

While active euthanasia remains illegal in China, it is gaining increasing acceptance among doctors and the general populace.

In Hong Kong, support for euthanasia among the general public is higher among those who put less importance on religious belief, those who are non-Christian, those who have higher family incomes, those who have more experience in taking care of terminally ill family members, and those who are older.

Arguments for and against voluntary euthanasia

Since World War II, the debate over euthanasia in Western countries has centered on voluntary euthanasia within regulated health care systems. In some cases, judicial decisions, legislation, and regulations have made voluntary euthanasia an explicit option for patients and their guardians. Proponents and critics of such voluntary euthanasia policies offer the following reasons for and against official voluntary euthanasia policies:

Reasons given for voluntary euthanasia

- Choice: Proponents of voluntary euthanasia emphasize that choice is a fundamental principle for liberal democracies and free market systems.
- Quality of Life: The pain and suffering a person feels during a disease, even with pain relievers, can be incomprehensible to a person who has not gone through it. Even without considering the physical pain, it is often difficult for patients to overcome the emotional pain of losing their independence.
- Opinion of Witnesses: Those who witness others die are "particularly convinced" that the law should be changed to allow assisted death.
- Economic costs and human resources: Today in many countries there is a shortage of hospital space. The energy of doctors and hospital beds could be used for people whose lives could be saved instead of continuing the life of those who want to die which increases the general quality of care and shortens hospital waiting lists. It is a burden to keep people alive past the point they can contribute to society, especially if the resources used could be spent on a curable ailment.

Reasons given against voluntary euthanasia

- Professional role: Critics argue that voluntary euthanasia could unduly compromise the professional roles of health care employees, especially doctors. They point out that European physicians of previous centuries traditionally swore some variation of the Hippocratic Oath, which in its ancient form excluded euthanasia: "To please no one will I prescribe a deadly drug nor give advice which may cause his death.." However, since the 1970s, this oath has largely fallen out of use.
- Moral/Theological: Some people, including many Christians, consider euthanasia of some or all types to be morally unacceptable. This view usually treats euthanasia to be a type of murder and voluntary euthanasia as a type of suicide, the morality of which is the subject of active debate.
- Necessity: If there is some reason to believe the cause of a patient's illness or suffering is or will soon be curable, the correct action is sometimes considered to attempt to bring about a cure or engage in palliative care.
- Feasibility of implementation: Euthanasia can only be considered "voluntary" if a patient is mentally competent to make the decision, i.e., has a rational understanding of options and consequences. Competence can be difficult to determine or even define.

- Consent under pressure: Given the economic grounds for voluntary euthanasia, critics of voluntary euthanasia are concerned that patients may experience psychological pressure to consent to voluntary euthanasia rather than be a financial burden on their families. Even where health costs are mostly covered by public money, as in various European countries, voluntary euthanasia critics are concerned that hospital personnel would have an economic incentive to advise or pressure people toward euthanasia consent.

Slippery Slope

It has been claimed that permitting voluntary euthanasia to occur will lead to the support and legalization of non-voluntary and involuntary euthanasia, as a slippery slope. Although studies of the Netherlands after the introduction of voluntary euthanasia found that there was no evidence to support this claim, the introduction of legal non-voluntary euthanasia into the Netherlands in the form of the Groningen Protocol has led to renewed debate. The Groningen Protocol has been identified by some as having the "potential to validate the slippery-slope argument against allowing euthanasia in selected populations", and in examining the Netherlands situation, some researchers have claimed that the protocol is evidence that the slippery slope exists. For example, William Lanier points to the Groningen Protocol as evidence that a slippery slope is "playing out in real time", while Ola Didrik Saugstad warns neonatologists against taking a path down the slope which will end in the Dutch practice. Countering this view, others have argued that there is a lack of evidence upon which to form a determination, and it has been argued that the public nature of the decisions and their evaluation by a prosecutor prevent a "slippery slope" from occurring – although effectiveness of these legal restrictions has been brought into question, as it has been argued that the Netherlands have seen the gradual introduction of more lax legal restrictions since euthanasia was first legalized and there are still a significant percentage of cases of euthanasia practiced illegally ergo violating even the current legal permissions.

The mechanisms under slippery slope are discussed in literature. For example, *The Mechanism of slippery slope* in *Harvard Law Review* shows the judicial logic that could eventually lead to gradually break the legal restrictions for euthanasia.

Euthanasia opponent Ian Dowbiggin linked the Nazi's Euthanasia Program - Action T4 to the resistance in the West to involuntary euthanasia. He believes that the revulsion inspired by the Nazis led to some of the early advocates of euthanasia in all its forms in the U.S. and U.K. removing non-voluntary euthanasia from their proposed platforms.

Medical Ethics on Euthanasia

Euthanasia brings about many ethical issues regarding a patient's death. Some physicians say euthanasia is a rational choice for competent patients to choose to die to escape unbearable suffering. Others feel that aiding in the patient's death goes against a physician's duty to preserve life.

For voluntary euthanasia In America

Physicians who are in favor of euthanasia state that to keep euthanasia or physician-assisted suicide (PAS) illegal is a violation of patient freedoms. They believe that any competent terminally-ill patient should have the right to choose death or refuse life-saving treatment. The U.S. Constitution does not state that the government can keep a person from committing suicide and if PAS was a right, patients could die with dignity and leave others with a positive memory and not what they had become. Suicide and assistance from their physician is seen as the only option those patients have. By allowing PAS and euthanasia, the patient can say their final goodbyes to their loved ones and leave the world by choice. With the suffering and the knowledge from the doctor, this may also suggest that PAS is a humane answer to the excruciating pain.

Not only will PAS and euthanasia help with psychological suffering and give autonomy to the patient, PAS can help reduce health care costs and free up doctors and nurses. By keeping a terminally-ill patient alive, the patient must pay for any medical necessary procedures. These procedures can include x-rays, prescribed drugs, or any lab tests that needs to be performed. All of these procedures can run up a medical costs ranging from $50,000 to $100,000. Since the bills will continue to come for the patient, they will lose more of the money they would want to leave behind for their family. If the patient wants to end the suffering, the reason for racking up the bills and keeping the patient alive are lacking (13). Also, the costly treatment to keep the terminally-ill patient alive from medical funding cannot be used for other types of care, like prenatal, where it would save lives and improve long-term quality of life. Along with reduced health care costs, more doctors and nurses could be freed up. A shortage of medical staff is a critical problem hospitals face and studies have found that understaffed hospitals make many mistakes and provide less quality care. Attending to terminally-ill patients, who would rather die, is not the best use of the medical staff. If PAS and euthanasia were legalized, more staff would have time to care for others and there would be an increase in the quality of care administered.

Physician-assisted suicide and euthanasia can lower health care costs, free up doctors and nurses, and give back the right to the patient to practice autonomy. By keeping PAS and euthanasia illegal, each terminally-ill patient is being discriminated against because they are not able put this option into action. Those patients because of their disability do not have the same right as any other person in the United States.

Against voluntary euthanasia

Many physicians and medical staff have numerous reasons for prohibiting the legalization of PAS and euthanasia. A main reason against PAS is the violation of the Hippocratic oath that some doctors take. The Hippocratic oath states "I will not give a lethal drug to anyone if I am asked, nor will I advise such a plan,". By being a part of PAS and prescribing a lethal dosage of a drug could weaken the doctor-patient relationship because of the oath some doctors take (13).

Another reason for prohibiting PAS and euthanasia is the option of abusing PAS if it were to become legal. Poor or uninsured patients may not have the money or no access to proper care will have limited options, and they could be pressured towards assisted death. For emotionally and physiologically disturbed patients, they could abuse the PAS option and those patients could convince their doctor to help end their life. By keeping PAS and euthanasia illegal, doctors have opportunity to right their wrong diagnoses and prevent leaning towards suicide of a redeemable person (13), there are cases where patients who are not terminally ill are mistakenly admitted into hospices and such patients could become subject to euthanasia. By having more time with the terminally-ill patient, the doctor is giving them constant care and medical attention. Many people believe that the unbearable pain can be controlled to tolerable levels if given proper care from the hospital staff.

Voluntary euthanasia and the Law

Main article: Euthanasia and the law

During the 20th Century, efforts to change government policies on euthanasia have met limited success in Western countries. Country policies are described here in alphabetical order, followed by the exceptional case of the Netherlands. Euthanasia policies have also been developed by a variety of NGOs, most notably medical associations and advocacy organizations.

Voluntary euthanasia and religion

Main article: Religious views on euthanasia

There are many different religious views among on the issue of voluntary euthanasia, although many moral theologians are critical of the procedure.

Euthanasia protocols

See also: Lethal injection#Euthanasia protocol

Euthanasia can be accomplished either through an oral, intravenous, or intramuscular administration of drugs, or by oxygen deprivation (anoxia), as in some euthanasia machines. In individuals who are incapable of swallowing lethal doses of medication, an intravenous route is preferred. The following is a Dutch protocol for parenteral (intravenous) administration to obtain euthanasia:

Intravenous administration is the most reliable and rapid way to accomplish euthanasia. A coma is first induced by intravenous administration of 20 mg/kg sodium thiopental (Nesdonal) in a small volume (10 ml physiological saline). Then a triple intravenous dose of a non-depolarizing neuromuscular muscle relaxant is given, such as 20 mg pancuronium bromide (Pavulon) or 20 mg vecuronium bromide (Norcuron). The muscle relaxant should preferably be given intravenously, in order to ensure optimal availability. Only for pancuronium bromide (Pavulon) are there substantial indications that the agent may also be given intramuscularly in a dosage of 40 mg.

A euthanasia device invented by Dr Philip Nitschke that facilitated euthanasia through heavy doses of drugs. The laptop screen led the user through a series of steps and questions to ensure he or she was fully prepared. The machine in a museum.

With regards to voluntary euthanasia, many people argue that 'equal access' should apply to access to suicide as well, so therefore disabled people who cannot kill themselves should have access to voluntary euthanasia.

Euthanasia in the arts

Literature

Apart from *The Old Law*, a 17th century tragicomedy written by Thomas Middleton, William Rowley, and Philip Massinger, one of the early books to deal with euthanasia in a fictional context is Anthony Trollope's 1882 dystopian novel, *The Fixed Period*. Ricarda Huch's novel *The Deruga Case* (1917) is about a physician who is acquitted after performing euthanasia on his dying ex-wife.

'Quality of Mercy' in *The Prosecution Rests* is a fable exploring the facets of aging, Alzheimer's disease, and euthanasia. The story line makes no judgment but frees the reader to decide.

In the book *The Giver*, euthanasia is used as a form of punishment.

Film

The films *Children of Men* and *Soylent Green* depict instances of government-sponsored euthanasia in order to strengthen their dystopian themes. The protagonist of the film *Johnny Got His Gun* is a brutally mutilated war veteran whose request for euthanasia furthers the work's anti-war message. The recent films *Mar Adentro* and *Million Dollar Baby* argue more directly in favor of euthanasia by illustrating the suffering of their protagonists. These films have provoked debate and controversy in their home countries of Spain and the United States respectively.

Media

In March 2010, the PBS FRONTLINE TV program in the United States showed a documentary called "The Suicide Tourist" which told the story of Professor Craig Ewert, his family, and the Swiss group Dignitas, and their decision to commit assisted suicide in Switzerland after he was diagnosed and suffering with ALS (Lou Gehrig's Disease).

Music

Thrash metal band Megadeth's 1994 album *Youthanasia* (the title is a pun on euthanasia) implies that society is euthanizing its youth.

See also

- Arthur Koestler, author, vice-president of EXIT (now the Voluntary Euthanasia Society).
- Bertrand Dawson, 1st Viscount Dawson of Penn - physician to George V, to whom he gave a lethal injection.
- Chantal Sébire
- George Exoo
- Derek Humphry - Founder of the Hemlock Society, President of ERGO, past-president of the World Federation of Right to Die Societies and author of *Final Exit*.
- Diane Pretty
- Dignitas (euthanasia group in Switzerland)
- Dr. Death (book by Jonathon Kellerman)
- Euthanasia machine, a DIY option for individuals
- Euthanasia: Opposing Viewpoints (2000), listing key sources in an anthology
- Final Exit (book)
- Futile medical care
- International Task Force on Euthanasia and Assisted Suicide
- Jack Kevorkian
- John Bodkin Adams, Eastbourne, England doctor, tried for murder in 1957 but claimed euthanasia. Acquitted.

- Kaishakunin - Assists in the Japanese ritual seppuku (suicide)
- Karen Ann Quinlan and Terri Schiavo case - Cases of persistent vegetative state
- Killick Millard - Founder of the Voluntary Euthanasia Legalisation Society in Great Britain
- Peter Singer - bioethicist, utilitarian
- Philip Nitschke
- Principle of double effect
- Senicide
- Suicide tourism
- Terminal sedation
- Terry Wallis

Bibliography

Neutral

- Battin, Margaret P., Rhodes, Rosamond, and Silvers, Anita, eds. *Physician assisted suicide: expanding the debate*. NY: Routledge, 1998.
- Emanuel, Ezekiel J. 2004. "The history of euthanasia debates in the United States and Britain" in *Death and dying: a reader*, edited by T. A. Shannon. Lanham, MD: Rowman & Littlefield Publishers.
- Dennis J. Horan, David Mall, eds. (1977). *Death, dying, and euthanasia*. Frederick, MD: University Publications of America. ISBN 0-89093-139-9.
- Kopelman, Loretta M., deVille, Kenneth A., eds. *Physician-assisted suicide: What are the issues?* Dordrecht: Kluwer Academic Publishers, 2001. (E.g., Engelhardt on secular bioethics)
- Magnusson, Roger S. "The sanctity of life and the right to die: social and jurisprudential aspects of the euthanasia debate in Australia and the United States" in Pacific Rim Law & Policy Journal (6:1), January 1997.
- Palmer, "Dr. Adams' Trial for Murder" in The Criminal Law Review. (Reporting on R. v. Adams with Devlin J. at 375f.) 365-377, 1957.
- Paterson, Craig, "A History of Ideas Concerning Suicide, Assisted Suicide and Euthanasia" (2005). Available at SSRN: http://ssrn.com/abstract=1029229
- PCSEPMBBR, United States. President's Commission for the Study of Ethical Problems in Medicine and Biomedical and Behavioral Research. 1983. Deciding to forego life-sustaining treatment: a report on the ethical, medical, and legal issues in treatment decisions. Washington, DC: President's Commission for the Study of Ethical Problems in Medicine and Biomedical and Behavioral Research: For sale by the Supt. of Docs. U.S. G.P.O.
- Robertson, John. 1977. Involuntary euthanasia of defective newborns: a legal analysis. In Death, dying, and euthanasia, edited by D. J. Horan and D. Mall. Washington: University Publications of America. Original edition, Stanford Law Review 27 (1975) 213-269.

- Stone, T. Howard, and Winslade, William J. "Physician-assisted suicide and euthanasia in the United States" in *Journal of Legal Medicine* (16:481-507), December 1995.

Viewpoints

- Giorgio Agamben; translated by Daniel Heller-Roazen (1998). *Homo sacer: sovereign power and bare life*. Stanford, Calif: Stanford University Press. ISBN 0-8047-3218-3.
- Raphael Cohen-Almagor (2001). *The right to die with dignity: an argument in ethics, medicine, and law*. New Brunswick, N.J: Rutgers University Press. ISBN 0-8135-2986-7.
- Appel, Jacob. 2007. A Suicide Right for the Mentally Ill? A Swiss Case Opens a New Debate. Hastings Center Report, Vol. 37, No. 3.
- Brock, Dan. *Life and Death* Cambridge University Press, 1993.
- Dworkin, R. M. Life's Dominion: An Argument About Abortion, Euthanasia, and Individual Freedom. New York: Knopf, 1993.
- Fletcher, Joseph F. 1954. Morals and medicine; the moral problems of: the patient's right to know the truth, contraception, artificial insemination, sterilization, euthanasia. Princeton, N.J.K.: Princeton University Press.
- Derek Humphry, Ann Wickett (1986). *The right to die: understanding euthanasia*. San Francisco: Harper & Row. ISBN 0-06-015578-7.
- Kamisar, Yale. 1977. Some non-religious views against proposed 'mercy-killing' legislation. In Death, dying, and euthanasia, edited by D. J. Horan and D. Mall. Washington: University Publications of America. Original edition, Minnesota Law Review 42:6 (May 1958).
- Kelly, Gerald. "The duty of using artificial means of preserving life" in Theological Studies (11:203-220), 1950.
- Panicola, Michael. 2004. Catholic teaching on prolonging life: setting the record straight. In Death and dying: a reader, edited by T. A. Shannon. Lanham, MD: Rowman & Littlefield Publishers.
- Paterson, Craig. Assisted Suicide and Euthanasia: An Natural Law Ethics Approach. Aldershot, Hampshire: Ashgate, 2008.
- Rachels, James. The End of Life: Euthanasia and Morality. New York: Oxford University Press, 1986.
- Sacred congregation for the doctrine of the faith. 1980. The declaration on euthanasia. Vatican City: The Vatican.
- Tassano, Fabian. *The Power of Life or Death: Medical Coercion and the Euthanasia Debate*. Foreword by Thomas Szasz, MD. London: Duckworth, 1995. Oxford: Oxford Forum, 1999.

External links

- Religion and Ethics - Euthanasia [1] - many views of euthanasia, for, against, and religious, from the BBC
- Stanford Encyclopedia of Philosophy entry [2]

Non-voluntary euthanasia

Part of a series on
Euthanasia
Types
Animal · Child · Voluntary Non-voluntary · Involuntary
Views
Religious (Buddhist · Catholic)
Groups
Dignitas · Dignity in Dying Exit International
People
Jack Kevorkian · Philip Nitschke
Books
Final Exit *The Peaceful Pill Handbook*
Jurisdictions
Australia · Canada Mexico · Netherlands New Zealand · Switzerland United Kingdom · United States
Laws
Rights of the Terminally Ill Act 1995 Oregon Death with Dignity Act Washington Death with Dignity Act
Court cases

Washington v. Glucksberg (1997) *Gonzales v. Oregon* (2006) *Baxter v. Montana* (2009)
Alternatives
Assisted suicide Palliative care Principle of double effect Terminal sedation
Other issues
Suicide tourism Groningen Protocol Euthanasia device

Non-voluntary euthanasia (sometimes known as **mercy killing**) is euthanasia conducted where the explicit consent of the individual concerned is unavailable. In the modern world, the term is usually applied to medical situations, such as the termination of newborns born with severe spina bifida (child euthanasia), performed in the Netherlands under the *Groningen Protocol*. The majority of non-voluntary euthanasia today takes place in the form of terminal sedation or continuous deep sedation of terminally ill patients, with up to a third of doctors reporting that they have made decisions that hasten the death of patients.

Len Doyal, a professor of medical ethics and former member of the ethics committee of the British Medical Association, said in 2006 that "[p]roponents of voluntary euthanasia should support non-voluntary euthanasia under appropriate circumstances and with proper regulation".

It may be contrasted with involuntary euthanasia, where euthanasia is performed against the will of the patient.

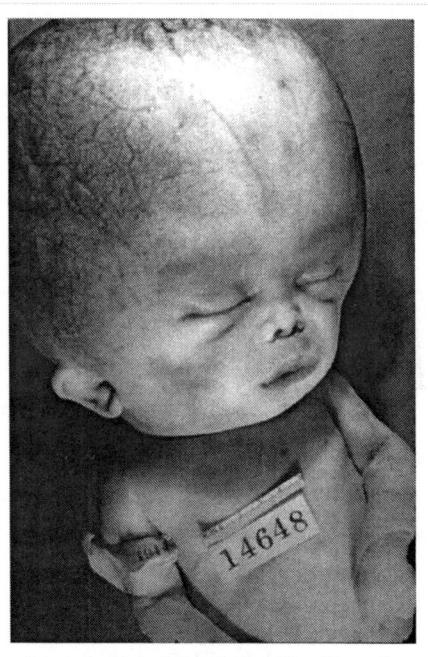

Severe hydrocephalus. Infants like this can be subject to non-voluntary euthanasia in the Netherlands if the parents decide it and the doctor agrees.

Substituted judgement

The decision can be made based on what the incapacitated individual would have wanted, or it could be made on substituted judgment of what the decision maker would want were he or she in the incapacitated person's place, or finally, the decision could be made by the doctor by his own decision

Legal status

Non-voluntary euthanasia is illegal in all countries in the world, and is only practised in the Netherlands (see Groningen Protocol) under an agreement between physicians and district attorneys that was ratified by the Dutch *National Association of Pediatricians*.

Slippery slope debate

Non-voluntary euthanasia has been cited as one of the possible outcomes of the slippery slope argument, in which it is claimed that permitting voluntary euthanasia to occur will lead to the support and legalization of non-voluntary and involuntary euthanasia. Although studies of the Netherlands after the introduction of voluntary euthanasia found that there was no evidence to support this claim, the introduction of legal non-voluntary euthanasia into the Netherlands in the form of the Groningen Protocol has led to renewed debate. The Groningen Protocol has been identified by some as having the "potential to validate the slippery-slope argument against allowing euthanasia in selected populations", and in examining the Netherlands situation, some researchers have claimed that the protocol is evidence that the slippery slope exists. For example, William Lanier points to the Groningen Protocol as evidence that a slippery slope is "playing out in real time", while Ola Didrik Saugstad warns neonatologists against taking a path down the slope which will end in the Dutch practice. Countering this view, others have argued that there is a lack of evidence upon which to form a determination, and it has been argued that the public nature of the decisions and their evaluation by a prosecutor prevent a "slippery slope" from occurring – although effectiveness of these legal restrictions has been brought into question, as it has been argued that the Netherlands have seen the gradual introduction of more lax legal restrictions since euthanasia was first legalized and there are still a significant percentage of cases of euthanasia practiced illegally ergo violating even the current legal permissions.

The mechanisms under slippery slope are discussed in literature. For example, *The Mechanism of slippery slope* in *Harvard Law Review* shows the judicial logic that could eventually lead to gradually break the legal restrictions for euthanasia.

Euthanasia opponent Ian Dowbiggin linked the Nazi's Action T4 to the resistance in the West to involuntary euthanasia. He believes that the revulsion inspired by the Nazis led to some of the early advocates of euthanasia in all its forms in the U.S. and U.K. removing non-voluntary euthanasia from their proposed platforms.

Involuntary euthanasia

Part of a series on
Euthanasia
Types
Animal · Child · Voluntary Non-voluntary · Involuntary
Views
Religious (Buddhist · Catholic)
Groups
Dignitas · Dignity in Dying Exit International
People
Jack Kevorkian · Philip Nitschke
Books
Final Exit *The Peaceful Pill Handbook*
Jurisdictions
Australia · Canada Mexico · Netherlands New Zealand · Switzerland United Kingdom · United States
Laws
Rights of the Terminally Ill Act 1995 Oregon Death with Dignity Act Washington Death with Dignity Act
Court cases
Washington v. Glucksberg (1997) *Gonzales v. Oregon* (2006) *Baxter v. Montana* (2009)
Alternatives

Involuntary euthanasia

Assisted suicide
Palliative care
Principle of double effect
Terminal sedation
Other issues
Suicide tourism
Groningen Protocol
Euthanasia device

Involuntary euthanasia is euthanasia performed on a patient against their will. It is contrasted with voluntary euthanasia (euthanasia performed with the patient's consent) and non-voluntary euthanasia (where the patient is unable to give their informed consent, for example child euthanasia). Involuntary euthanasia is widely opposed and is regarded as a crime in legal jurisdictions, and is sometimes used as a reason for not changing laws relating to other forms of euthanasia.

Historically, involuntary euthanasia has received some support from parts of the pro-euthanasia movement. For example, in 1937 a bill that included provisions for involuntary euthanasia was proposed in Nebraska, although it never went before the state legislature; and in 1943 a committee was formed by the Euthanasia Society of America that was to draft a bill that incorporated involuntary euthanasia for "idiots, imbeciles, and congenital monstrosities".

Legality of euthanasia

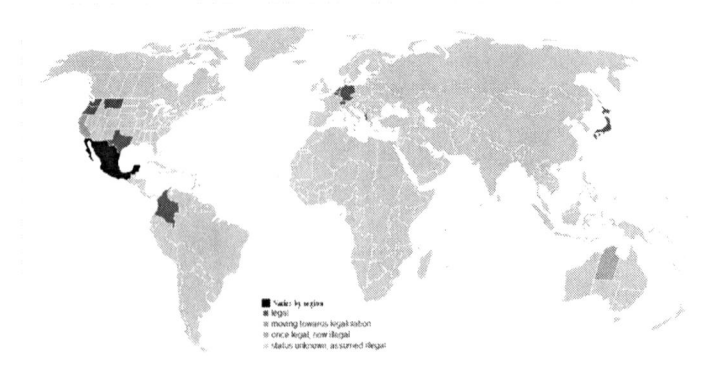

Map of the legality of euthanasia.

Part of a series on
Euthanasia
Types
Animal · Child · Voluntary Non-voluntary · Involuntary
Views
Religious (Buddhist · Catholic)
Groups
Dignitas · Dignity in Dying Exit International
People
Jack Kevorkian · Philip Nitschke
Books
Final Exit *The Peaceful Pill Handbook*
Jurisdictions
Australia · Canada Mexico · Netherlands New Zealand · Switzerland United Kingdom · United States
Laws
Rights of the Terminally Ill Act 1995 Oregon Death with Dignity Act Washington Death with Dignity Act
Court cases
Washington v. Glucksberg (1997) *Gonzales v. Oregon* (2006) *Baxter v. Montana* (2009)
Alternatives
Assisted suicide Palliative care Principle of double effect Terminal sedation

Other issues
Suicide tourism
Groningen Protocol
Euthanasia device

Efforts to change **government policies** on **euthanasia** in the 20th century have met limited success in Western countries. Euthanasia policies have also been developed by a variety of NGOs, most notably medical associations and advocacy organizations.

Euthanasia law by country

Albania

Euthanasia was legalized in Albania in 1999, it was stated that any form of voluntary euthanasia was legal under the rights of the terminally ill act of 1995. Passive euthanasia is considered legal should three or more family members consent to the decision. Albania's euthanasia policy has been controversial among life groups and the Catholic Church.

Resources: Bardhyl Çipi, Department of Forensic Medicine, Faculty of Medicine, Tirana University. Some philosophical, juridical and bioethical problems of end of life: death criterion and euthanasia. A paper analyzing the situation in Albania. From The third international symposium on bioethics [1], Ukraine, Kiev, April 2004.

Australia

Main article: Euthanasia in Australia

Euthanasia was legalized in Australia's Northern Territory, by the Rights of the Terminally Ill Act 1995. Soon after, the law was voided by an amendment by the Commonwealth to the Northern Territory (Self-Government) Act 1978. The powers of the Northern Territory legislature, unlike those of the State legislatures, are not guaranteed by the Australian constitution. However, before the Commonwealth government made this amendment, three people had already practiced legal voluntary euthanasia (PAS), aided by Dr Philip Nitschke. The first person was a carpenter, Bob Dent, who died on 22 September 1996. In August 2009, the Supreme Court of Western Australia ruled that it was up to Christian Rossiter, a 49 year old quadriplegic, to decide if he was to continue to receive medical care (tube feeding) and that his carers had to abide by his wishes. Chief Justice Wayne Martin also stipulated that his carers, Brightwater Care, would not be held criminally responsible for following his instructions. Rossiter died on 21 September, 2009 following a chest infection.

Legality of euthanasia

Belgium

The Belgian parliament legalized euthanasia in late September 2002. Proponents of euthanasia state that prior to the law, several thousand illegal acts of euthanasia were carried out in Belgium each year. According to proponents, the legislation incorporated a complicated process, which has been criticized as an attempt to establish a "bureaucracy of death".

Canada

Main article: Euthanasia in Canada

Canadian laws on living wills and passive euthanasia are a legal dilemma. Documents which set out guidelines for dealing with life-sustaining medical procedures are under the Provinces control, in Ontario under the Health Care Consent Act, 1996.

Germany

On 25 June 2010, the Federal Court of Justice of Germany legalised passive euthanasia with patient consent.

India

In a first step towards legalising euthanasia, The Law Commission of India, Ministry of Law and Justice has decided to recommend to the Indian Government to allow terminally ill to end their lives.

Ireland

In Ireland, it is illegal for a doctor (or anyone) to *actively* contribute to someone's death. It is not, however, illegal to remove life support and other treatment (the "right to die") should a person (or their next of kin) request it - in other words, passive euthanasia is legal. A September 2010 Irish Times poll showed that a majority, 57% of adults, believed that doctor-assisted suicide should be legal for terminally ill patients who request it.

Japan

The Japanese government has no official laws on the status of euthanasia and the Supreme Court of Japan has never ruled on the matter. Rather, to date, Japan's euthanasia policy has been decided by two local court cases, one in Nagoya in 1962, and another after an incident at Tokai University in 1995. The first case involved "passive euthanasia" (消極的安死 *shōkyokuteki anrakushi*) (i.e., allowing a patient to die by turning off life support) and the latter case involved "active euthanasia" (積極的安死 *sekkyokuteki anrakushi*) (e.g., through injection). The judgments in these cases set forth a legal framework and a set of conditions within which both passive and active euthanasia could be legal. Nevertheless, in both of these particular cases the doctors were found guilty of violating these

Legality of euthanasia

conditions when taking the lives of their patients. Further, because the findings of these courts have yet to be upheld at the national level, these precedents are not necessarily binding. Nevertheless, at present, there is a tentative legal framework for implementing euthanasia in Japan.

In the case of passive euthanasia, three conditions must be met:

1. the patient must be suffering from an incurable disease, and in the final stages of the disease from which he/she/ is unlikely to make a recovery;
2. the patient must give express consent to stopping treatment, and this consent must be obtained and preserved prior to death. If the patient is not able to give clear consent, their consent may be determined from a pre-written document such as a living will or the testimony of the family;
3. the patient may be passively euthanized by stopping medical treatment, chemotherapy, dialysis, artificial respiration, blood transfusion, IV drip, etc.

For active euthanasia, four conditions must be met:

1. the patient must be suffering from unbearable physical pain;
2. death must be inevitable and drawing near;
3. the patient must give consent. (Unlike passive euthanasia, living wills and family consent will not suffice.)
4. the physician must have (ineffectively) exhausted all other measures of pain relief.

they are still dicussing this though

Luxembourg

The country's parliament passed a bill legalizing euthanasia on 20 February 2008 in the first reading with 30 of 59 votes in favour. On 19 March 2009, the bill passed the second reading, making Luxembourg the third European Union country, after the Netherlands and Belgium, to decriminalise euthanasia. Terminally ill people will be able to have their lives ended after receiving the approval of two doctors and a panel of experts (Err/Huss law in french)

Mexico

Main article: Euthanasia in Mexico

In Mexico, active euthanasia is illegal but since 7 January 2008 the law allows the terminally ill —or closest relatives, if unconscious— to refuse medication or further medical treatment to extend life (also known as passive euthanasia) in Mexico City, in the central state of Aguascalientes (since 6 April 2009) and, since 1 September 2009, in the Western state of Michoacán. A similar law extending the same provisions at the national level has been approved by the senate and an initiative decriminalizing active euthanasia has entered the same legislative chamber on 13 April 2007.

The Netherlands

Main article: Euthanasia in the Netherlands

In 2002, The Netherlands legalized euthanasia including physician assisted suicide. The law codified a twenty year old convention of not prosecuting doctors who have committed euthanasia in very specific cases, under very specific circumstances. The Ministry of Public Health, Wellbeing and Sports claims that this practice "allows a person to end their life in dignity after having received every available type of palliative care."

The United Nations has reviewed and commented on the Netherlands euthanasia law.

New Zealand

Main article: Euthanasia in New Zealand

Two attempts have been made in the Parliament passing Bills to legalize it, but euthanasia remains illegal in New Zealand

Norway

Euthanasia remains illegal, though a caregiver may receive a reduced punishment for taking the life of someone who consents to it, or for, out of compassion, taking the life of a person that is "hopelessly sick".

The second largest political party, the Progress Party, have several times tried to legalize euthanasia.

Switzerland

Main article: Euthanasia in Switzerland

In Switzerland, deadly drugs may be prescribed to a Swiss person or to a foreigner, where the recipient takes an active role in the drug administration. More generally, article 115 of the Swiss penal code, which came into effect in 1942 (having been written in 1918), considers assisting suicide a crime if and only if the motive is selfish.

The United Kingdom

Main article: Euthanasia in the United Kingdom

Euthanasia is illegal in the United Kingdom. Any person found to be assisting suicide is breaking the law and can be convicted of assisting suicide or attempting to do so (e.g. if a doctor gives a patient in great pain a bottle of morphine to take (to commit suicide) when the pain gets too great). Although two-thirds of Britons think it should be legal,[citation needed] in 2004 the 'Assisted Dying for the Terminally-Ill Bill' was rejected in the lower political chamber, the House of Commons, by a 4-1 margin. Currently, Dr Nigel Cox is the only British doctor to have been convicted of attempted euthanasia. He was given a 12 month suspended sentence in 1992. The principle of double effect is however firmly established. In 1957 Judge Devlin in the trial of Dr John Bodkin Adams ruled that causing death through the administration of lethal drugs to a patient, if the intention is solely to alleviate pain, is not considered murder even if death is a potential or even likely outcome.

United States

Main article: Euthanasia in the United States

Active euthanasia is illegal in most of the United States. Patients retain the rights to refuse medical treatment and to receive appropriate management of pain at their request (passive euthanasia), even if the patients' choices hasten their deaths. Additionally, futile or disproportionately burdensome treatments, such as life-support machines, may be withdrawn under specified circumstances.

Council of Europe

In 2005 the Parliamentary Assembly of the Council of Europe rejected a draft Resolution which would have called upon Member States to legalise euthanasia.

Non-governmental organizations

There are a number of historical studies about the thorough euthanasia-related policies of professional associations. In the Academy of Neurology (AAN). In their analysis, Brody et al. found it necessary to distinguish such topics as euthanasia, physician-assisted suicide, informed consent and refusal, advance directives, pregnant patients, surrogate decision-making (including neonates), DNR orders, irreversible loss of consciousness, quality of life (as a criterion for limiting end-of-life care), withholding and withdrawing intervention, and futility. Similar distinctions presumably are found outside the U.S., as with the highly contested statements of the British Medical Association.

On euthanasia (narrowly-defined here as directly causing death), Brody sums up the U.S. medical NGO arena:

> The debate in the ethics literature on euthanasia is just as divided as the debate on physician-assisted suicide, perhaps more so. Slippery-slope arguments are often made, supported by claims about abuse of voluntary euthanasia in the Netherlands.... Arguments against it are based on the integrity of medicine as a profession. In response, autonomy and quality-of-life-base arguments are made in support of euthanasia, underscored by claims that when the only way to relieve a dying patient's pain or suffering is terminal sedation with loss of consciousness, death is a preferable alternative -- an argument also made in support of physician-assisted suicide.

Other NGOs that advocate for and against various euthanasia-related policies are found throughout the world. Among proponents, perhaps the leading NGO is the UK's Dignity in Dying, the successor to the

(Voluntary) Euthanasia Society. In addition to professional and religious groups, there are NGOs opposed to euthanasia found in various countries.

Murder–Suicide

Murder–suicide

Suicide
Social aspects
Legislation · Philosophy Religious views · Euthanasia Assisted suicide · Right to die Benevolent suicide
Suicide crisis
Assessment of risk · Crisis hotline · Intervention · Prevention · Suicide watch
Suicide types
Copycat · Cult · Euthanasia · Familicide · Forced · Honor · Internet · Mass · Murder–suicide · Parasuicide · Suicide attack · By cop · Pact
Epidemiology
Gender · Suicide rate
History
List of suicides · Suicide methods
Related phenomena
Ideation · Self-harm · Suicide note · Locations · Failed suicide attempt
By country
China · Japan · South Korea · United States

Homicide

Murder

Note: Varies by jurisdiction

Assassination · Child murder
Consensual homicide
Contract killing · Felony murder rule
Honor killing · Human sacrifice
Lust murder · Lynching
Mass murder · Murder–suicide
Proxy murder · Lonely hearts killer
Serial killer · Spree killer
Torture murder · Feticide
Double murder · Misdemeanor murder
Crime of passion · Internet homicide
Depraved-heart murder

Manslaughter

in English law
Negligent homicide
Vehicular homicide

Non-criminal homicide

Note: Varies by jurisdiction

Justifiable homicide
Capital punishment
Human sacrifice
Feticide
Medicide

By victim or victims

Suicide

Family

Familicide · Avunculicide
Prolicide (Filicide • Infanticide • Neonaticide)
Fratricide / Sororicide
Mariticide / Uxoricide
Parricide (Matricide • Patricide)
Other
Amicicide
Genocide / Democide
Gendercide
Omnicide
Regicide / Tyrannicide
Pseudocide
Deicide

A **murder–suicide** is an act in which an individual kills one or more other persons before killing him or herself. The combination of murder and suicide can take various forms, including:

- Suicide to facilitate murder, as in suicide bombing
- Murder to facilitate suicide, such as driving a car of four off a bridge.
- Suicide after murder to escape punishment
- Suicide after murder as a form of self-punishment due to guilt
- Joint suicide in the form of killing the other with consent, and then killing oneself

Many spree killings have ended in suicide, such as in many school shootings. Some cases of cult suicide may also involve murder.

Homicide and Suicide

Ajax, son of Telamon, preparing suicide. Reproduction from a black-figure amphora depiction by Exekias (550–525 BC).

According to the psychiatrist Karl A. Menninger, murder and suicide are interchangeable acts – suicide sometimes forestalling murder, and vice versa. Following Freudian logic, severe repression of natural instincts due to early childhood abuse, may lead the death instinct to emerge in a twisted form. The cultural anthropologist Ernest Becker, whose theories on the human notion of death is strongly influenced by Freud, views the fear of death as a universal phenomenon, a fear repressed in the unconscious and of which people are largely unaware. This fear can move individuals toward heroism, but also to scapegoating. Failed attempts to achieve heroism, according to this view, can lead to mental illness and/or antisocial behavior.

In a research specifically related to murder–suicide, Milton Rosenbaum (1990) discovered the murder–suicide perpetrators to be vastly different from perpetrators of homicide alone. Whereas murderer–suicides were found to be highly depressed and overwhelmingly men, other murderers were not generally depressed and more likely to include women in their ranks. In the U.S. the overwhelming number of cases are male-on-female and involve guns. Around one-third of partner homicides end in the suicide of the perpetrator. From national and international data and interviews with family members of murder–suicide perpetrators, the following are the key predictors of murder–suicide:access to a gun, a history of substance abuse, the male partner some years older than the female partner, a break-up or pending break-up, a history of battering, suicidal ideation by the perpetrator.

Though there's no national tracking system for murder–suicides in the United States, medical studies into the phenomenon estimate between 1,000 to 1,500 deaths per year in the US , with the majority occurring between spouses or intimate partners, males were the vast majority of the perpetrators, and over 90% of murder suicides involved a firearm. Depression, financial problems, and other problems are generally motivators.

See also

- Crime of passion
- Mass murder
- Phil Hartman
- School shooting
- Serial killer
- Spree killer
- Shinjū
- Suicide attack
- Terrorism

Further reading

- van Wormer, K. & Roberts, A.R.(2009) Death by Domestic Violence:Preventing the Murders and Murder–Suicides. Westport, CT:Praeger

External links

- QPR Institute [1] statistics from a suicide prevention program

Suicide pact

Suicide
Social aspects
Legislation · Philosophy Religious views · Euthanasia Assisted suicide · Right to die Benevolent suicide
Suicide crisis
Assessment of risk · Crisis hotline · Intervention · Prevention · Suicide watch
Suicide types
Copycat · Cult · Euthanasia · Familicide · Forced · Honor · Internet · Mass · Murder–suicide · Parasuicide · Suicide attack · By cop · Pact

Epidemiology
Gender · Suicide rate
History
List of suicides · Suicide methods
Related phenomena
Ideation · Self-harm · Suicide note · Locations · Failed suicide attempt
By country
China · Japan · South Korea · United States

A **suicide pact** describes the suicides of two or more individuals in an agreed-upon plan. The plan may be to die together, or separately and closely timed. Suicide pacts are important concepts in the study of suicide, and have occurred throughout history, as well as in fiction.

Suicide pacts are generally distinct from mass suicide. The latter refers to incidents in which a larger number of people kill themselves together for the same ideological reason, often within a religious, political, military or paramilitary context. Suicide pacts, on the other hand, usually involve small groups of people (such as married or romantic partners, family members, or friends) whose motivations are intensely personal and individual.

A suicide pact negotiated over the internet, often between complete strangers, is an **Internet suicide**.

See also

- "The Constitution is not a suicide pact," a recurring concept in American jurisprudence
- "Bridgend suicide incidents," where 24 teenagers committed suicide in early 2007 in Bridgend County
- Suicide prevention contract, the opposite of a suicide pact.
- A suicide pact is mentioned in the skit "Normal Guy" on The Lonely Island comedy album Incredibad.

References

- "UK records first online suicide pact" [1], *The Age*, September 30, 2005
- "Brad Delp: Details Emerge About His Tragic Suicide" [2], *Guitar World*, April 27, 2007

School shooting

Terrorism
Definitions History of terrorism International conventions Anti-terrorism legislation Counter-terrorism
By ideology
Anarchist · Communist · Eco-terrorism · Ethnic Narcoterrorism · Nationalist Religious (Islamic · Christian · Jewish)
Types and tactics
Agro-terrorism · Aircraft hijacking (list) Anti-abortion violence · Bioterrorism · Car bombing (list) Environmental · Hostage-taking · Improvised explosive device Insurgency · Kidnapping · Letter bomb · Nuclear Paper terrorism · Piracy · Propaganda of the deed Proxy bomb · Redemption movement · School shooting Suicide attack (list) · Weapon of mass destruction
State involvement
State terrorism State sponsorship Iran · Pakistan · Russia Sri Lanka · United States
Organization
Terrorist financing Terrorist front organization Terrorist training camp Lone-wolf fighter Clandestine cell system
Historical
Reign of Terror Red Terror · White Terror
Lists

> Designated organizations
> Charities accused of ties to terrorism
> Terrorist incidents

A **school shooting** is an incident in which gun violence occurs at an educational institution.

Definition

The term *school shooting* most commonly describes acts committed by either a student or intruders from outside the school campus. They are to be distinguished from crowd-containment shootings by law-enforcement personnel, such as the shootings at Kent State and Jackson State in the United States, or the October 6, 1976 Massacre in Thailand. They are also differentiated from other kinds of school violence, such as the mass killings of the Bath School disaster (which involved a homemade bomb rather than shooting), the Cologne school massacre (which involved a flamethrower); or terror attacks involving multiple kinds of weapons, such as the Ma'alot massacre, or the Beslan school hostage crisis in which at least 334 hostages were killed, including 186 children.

One of the most prominent school shootings was that at Columbine High School, near Littleton, Colorado. On Tuesday, April 20, 1999, students Eric Harris and Dylan Klebold murdered thirteen people on the school campus before they committed suicide, bringing the total to fifteen.

In the United States, one-on-one public-school violence, such as beatings and stabbings or gang related violence, is more common in some densely-populated areas. Inner-city or urban schools were much more likely than other schools to report serious violent crimes, with 17 percent of city principals reporting at least one serious crime compared to 11 percent of urban schools, 10 percent of rural schools, and five percent of suburban schools in the 1997 school year. However school shootings in other countries may take on more national origious overtones, such as the Mercaz HaRav massacre.

Profiling

School shooting is a topic of intense interest in the United States. Though companies like MOSAIC Threat Assessment Systems sell products and services designed to identify potential threats, a thorough study of all United States school shootings by the U.S. Secret Service warned against the belief that a certain "type" of student would be a perpetrator. Any profile would fit too many students to be useful and may not apply to a potential perpetrator. Some lived with both parents in "an ideal, All-American family." Some were children of divorce, or lived in foster homes. A few were loners, but most had close friends. Some experts such as Alan Lipman have warned against the dearth of empirical validity of profiling methods.

While it may be simplistic to assume a straightforward "profile", the study did find certain similarities among the perpetrators. "The researchers found that killers do not 'snap'. They plan. They acquire weapons. These children take a long, considered, public path toward violence." Princeton's Katherine

Newman points out that, far from being "loners", the perpetrators are "joiners" whose attempts at social integration fail, that they let their thinking and even their plans be known, sometimes frequently over long periods of times.

Many of the shooters told Secret Service investigators that alienation or persecution drove them to violence. According to the United States Secret Service, instead of looking for traits, the Secret Service urges adults to ask about behavior:

> 1. What has this child said?
> 2. Do they have grievances?
> 3. What do their friends know?
> 4. Do they have access to weapons?
> 5. Are they depressed or despondent?

One "trait" that has not yet attracted as much attention is the gender difference: nearly all school shootings are perpetrated by young males, and in some instances the violence has clearly been gender-specific. Bob Herbert addressed this in an October 2006 New York Times editorial. Only two female school shooting incidents have been documented.

School shootings receive extensive media coverage and are infrequent. They have sometimes resulted in nationwide changes of schools' policies concerning discipline and security. Some experts have described fears about school shootings as a type of moral panic.

Such incidents may also lead to nationwide discussion on gun laws.

Notable school shootings

Main article: List of school-related attacks

North America

United States

Name	Location	Date	Year	Death toll
University of Texas Massacre	Austin, Texas, United States	August 1	1966	16
SC State killings[1]	Orangeburg, South Carolina, United States	February 8	1968	3
Kent State shootings[1]	Kent, Ohio, United States	May 4	1970	4
Jackson State shootings[1]	Jackson, Mississippi, United States	May 14–15	1970	2

Olean High School shooting[1]	Olean, New York, United States	December 30	1974	3
California State University, Fullerton massacre	Fullerton, California, United States	July 12	1976	7
Cleveland Elementary School shooting	San Diego, California, United States	January 29	1979	2
Deer Creek Middle School shooting	Littleton, Colorado, United States	April 7	1982	1
Parkway South Middle School shooting	Manchester, Missouri, United States	January 20	1983	2
Goddard Middle School shooting	Goddard, Kansas, United States	January 21	1985	1
Portland Junior High School shooting	Portland, Connecticut, United States	December 10	1985	1
Pine Forest Senior High School	Fayetteville, North Carolina, United States	May 6	1986	0
Pinellas Park High School shooting	Largo, Florida, United States	February 11	1988	1
Hubbard Woods School shooting	Winnetka, Illinois, United States	May 20	1988	1
Atlantic Shores Christian School shooting	Chesapeake, Virginia, United States	December 16	1988	1
Cleveland School massacre	Stockton, California, United States	January 17	1989	6
University of Iowa shooting	Iowa City, Iowa, United States	November 1	1991	6
Lindhurst High School shooting	Olivehurst, California, United States	May 1	1992	4
Palo Duro High School shooting	Amarillo, Texas, United States	September 11	1992	0
Berkner High School shooting	Richardson, TX, United States	November 6	1992	1
Edward Tilden High School shooting	Chicago, Illinois, United States	November 20	1992	1
Simon's Rock College of Bard shooting	Great Barrington, Massachusetts, United States	December 14	1992	2
East Carter High School shooting	Grayson, Kentucky, United States	January 18	1993	2
Amityville High School shooting	Amityville, New York, United States	February 1	1993	1
Reseda High School shooting	Reseda, California, United States	February 22	1993	1
Wauwatosa West High School shooting	Wauwatosa, Wisconsin, United States	December 1	1993	1
Central Middle School shooting	Sheridan, Wyoming, United States	September 17	1993	1
Margaret Leary Elementary School shooting	Butte, Montana, United States	April 12	1994	1
Grimsley High School shooting	Greensboro, North Carolina, United States	October 12	1994	1
Wickliffe Middle School shooting	Wickliffe, Ohio, United States	November 7	1994	1

School shooting

Blackville-Hilda High School shooting	Blackville, South Carolina, United States	October 12	1995	2
Richland High School shooting	Lynnville, Tennessee, United States	November 15	1995	2
Frontier Middle School shooting	Moses Lake, Washington, United States	February 2	1996	3
Hamilton High School shooting	Scottdale, Georgia, United States	February 2	1996	1
San Diego State University shooting	San Diego, California, United States	August 15	1996	3
Hetzel Union Building shooting	State College, Pennsylvania, United States	September 17	1996	1
Bethel Regional High School shooting	Bethel, Alaska, United States	February 19	1997	2
Pearl High School shooting	Pearl, Mississippi, United States	October 1	1997	2
Heath High School shooting	Paducah, Kentucky, United States	December 4	1997	3
Westside Middle School shooting	Jonesboro, Arkansas, United States	March 24	1998	5
Parker Middle School dance shooting[1]	Edinboro, Pennsylvania, United States	April 24	1998	1
Thurston High School shooting	Springfield, Oregon, United States	May 20	1998	2
Columbine High School massacre	Littleton, Colorado, United States	April 20	1999	13
Heritage High School shooting	Conyers, Georgia, United States	May 20	1999	0
Fort Gibson Middle School shooting	Fort Gibson, Oklahoma, United States	December 6	1999	0
Buell Elementary School shooting	Mount Morris Township, Michigan, United States	February 29	2000	1
Lake Worth Middle School shooting	Lake Worth, Florida, United States	May 26	2000	1
University of Arkansas shooting	Fayetteville, Arkansas, United States	August 28	2000	2
Santana High School shooting	Santee, California, United States	March 5	2001	2
Granite Hills High School shooting	El Cajon, California, United States	March 22	2001	0
Martin Luther King, Jr. High School shooting	Manhattan, New York, United States	January 15	2002	0
Appalachian School of Law shooting	Grundy, Virginia, United States	January 16	2002	3
John McDonogh High School shooting	New Orleans, Louisiana, United States	April 14	2003	1
Red Lion Area Junior High School shootings	Red Lion, Pennsylvania, United States	April 24	2003	2
Case Western Reserve University shooting	Cleveland, Ohio, United States	May 9	2003	1
Rocori High School shooting	Cold Spring, Minnesota, United States	September 24	2003	2
Columbia High School shooting	East Greenbush, New York, United States	February 9	2004	0

Fairleigh Dickinson University shooting	Florham Park, New Jersey, United States	April 4	2004	2
Randallstown High School shooting	Randallstown, Maryland, United States	May 7	2004	0
Red Lake Senior High School massacre	Red Lake, Minnesota, United States	March 21	2005	8
Campbell County High School shooting	Jacksboro, Tennessee, United States	November 8	2005	1
Pine Middle School shooting	Reno, Nevada, United States	March 14	2006	0
Essex Elementary School shooting	Essex, Vermont, United States	August 24	2006	2
Orange High School shooting	Hillsborough, North Carolina, United States	August 30	2006	1
Platte Canyon High School shooting	Bailey, Colorado, United States	September 27	2006	2
Weston High School shooting	Cazenovia, Wisconsin, United States	September 29	2006	1
Amish school shooting	Nickel Mines, Lancaster County, Pennsylvania, United States	October 2	2006	6
Henry Foss High School shooting	Tacoma, Washington, United States	January 3	2007	1
Midland Dow High School shooting	Midland, Michigan, United States	March 8	2007	1
University of North Carolina at Greensboro	Greensboro, North Carolina, United States	March 24	2007	0
University of Washington shooting	Seattle, Washington, United States	April 2	2007	2
Virginia Tech massacre	Blacksburg, Virginia, United States	April 16	2007	33
Delaware State University shooting	Dover, Delaware, United States	September 21	2007	1
SuccessTech Academy shooting	Cleveland, Ohio, United States	October 10	2007	1
Louisiana Technical College shooting	Baton Rouge, Louisiana, United States	February 8	2008	3
Mitchell High School shooting	Memphis, Tennessee, United States	February 11	2008	0
E.O. Green School shooting	Oxnard, California, United States	February 12	2008	1
Northern Illinois University massacre	DeKalb, Illinois, United States	February 14	2008	6
Davidson High School Shooting	Mobile, Alabama, United States	March 9	2008	1
Central High School shooting	Knoxville, Tennessee, United States	August 21	2008	1
Henry Ford High School shooting	Detroit, Michigan, United States	October 16	2008	1
2008 University of Central Arkansas shootings	Conway, Arkansas, United States	October 27	2008	2
Dillard High School shooting	Fort Lauderdale, Florida, United States	November 12	2008	1

Henry Ford Community College shooting	Dearborn, Michigan, United States	April 10	2009	2
Wesleyan University[1]	Middletown, Connecticut, United States	May 1	2009	1
Canandaigua Academy shooting	Canandaigua, New York, United States	May 5	2009	1
Harvard University	Cambridge, Massachusetts, United States	May 18	2009	1
Larose-Cut Off Middle School shooting	Larose, Louisiana, United States	May 18	2009	1
Skyline College shooting	San Bruno, California, United States	September 2	2009	0
Atlanta University Center	Atlanta, Georgia, United States	September 3	2009	1
Deer Valley High School shooting	Antioch, California, United States	September 16	2009	0
Northern Virginia Community College	Woodbridge, Virginia, United States	December 8	2009	0
Discovery Middle School	Madison, Alabama, United States	February 6	2010	1
University of Alabama in Huntsville	Huntsville, Alabama, United States	February 12	2010	3
Deer Creek Middle School	Jefferson County, Colorado, United States	February 23	2010	0
Birney Elementary School	Tacoma, Washington, United States	February 26	2010	1
Ohio State University	Columbus, Ohio, United States	March 9	2010	2
Belleville Township HS East	Belleville, Illinois, United States	August 17	2010	1
University of Texas at Austin	Austin, Texas, United States	September 28	2010	1
Alisal High School	Salinas, California, United States	October 1	2010	1
Mid-Atlantic Christian University	Elizabeth City, North Carolina,, United States	October 3	2010	1
Kelly Elementary School	Carlsbad, California, United States	October 8	2010	0

[1] not a "school shooting" in the contemporary sense

Canada

Name	Location	Date	Year	Death toll	Notes
Altona schoolhouse shooting	Altona, Manitoba, Canada	October 10	1902	2	
Centennial Secondary School shooting	Brampton, Ontario Canada	May 28	1975	2	
St Pius X High School School	Ottawa, Ontario, Canada	October 27	1975	1	
École Polytechnique Massacre	Montreal, Quebec, Canada	December 6	1989	14	
Concordia University massacre	Montreal, Quebec, Canada	August 24	1992	4	
W. R. Myers High School shooting	Taber, Alberta, Canada	April 28	1999	1	
Dawson College shooting	Montreal, Quebec, Canada	September 13	2006	1	
C. W. Jefferys Collegiate Institute shooting	Toronto, Ontario, Canada	May 23	2007	1	
Bendale Business and Technical Institute shooting	Toronto, Ontario, Canada	September 16	2008	0	
Central Techincal School shooting	Toronto, Ontario Canada,	September 30	2010	0	

Europe

Name	Location	Date	Year	Death toll	Notes
Bremen school shooting	Bremen, Germany	June 20	1913	5	
Eppstein school shooting	Eppstein, Germany	June 3	1983	6	
Raumanmeri school shooting	Rauma, Finland	January 24	1989	2	
Colston's School	Bristol, United Kingdom	March 5	1991	0	
Aarhus University Shooting	Aarhus, Denmark	April 4	1994	3	
Dunblane massacre	Dunblane, United Kingdom	March 13	1996	18	
Erfurt massacre	Erfurt, Germany	April 26	2002	17	
Coburg shooting	Coburg, Germany	July 3	2003	1	
Terra College	The Hague, Netherlands	January	2004	1	
Grund- und Hauptschule von Rötz shooting	Rötz (Oberpfalz), Germany	March 7	2005	0	
Geschwister Scholl School attack	Emsdetten, Germany	November 20	2006	1	
Jokela school massacre	Tuusula, Finland	November 7	2007	9	
Kauhajoki school shooting	Kauhajoki, Finland	September 23	2008	11	
Winnenden school shooting	Winnenden, Germany	March 11	2009	16	

OAED Vocational College shooting	Athens, Greece	April 10	2009	1
Kanebogen elementary school shooting	Harstad, Norway	April 28	2009	0
Azerbaijan State Oil Academy shooting	Baku, Azerbaijan	April 30	2009	13
Albert-Einstein-Gymnasium	Sankt Augustin, Germany	May 11	2009	0
University of Pécs shooting	Pécs, Hungary	November 26	2009	1

South America, Asia and Australia

Name	Location	Date/Year	Death toll	Notes
Sanaa massacre	Sanaa, Yemen	March 30, 1997	6	
University of the Philippines shooting	Quezon City, Philippines	February 19, 1999	1	
La Trobe University shooting	Melbourne, Australia	August 3, 1999	1	
Monash University shooting	Melbourne, Australia	October 21, 2002	2	
Pak Phanang school shooting	Nakhon Si Thammarat, Thailand	June 6, 2003	2	
Islas Malvinas School shooting	Carmen de Patagones, Argentina	September 28, 2004	4	
Beirut Arab University shooting	Beirut, Lebanon	January 25, 2007	4	
Euro International school shooting	Gurgaon, India	December 12, 2007	1	
Mercaz HaRav shooting	Jerusalem, Israel	March 6, 2008	9	

Impact

Political impact

School shootings have had a political impact, spurring some to press for more stringent gun control laws. The National Rifle Association is opposed to such laws, and some groups have called for fewer gun control laws, citing cases of armed students ending shootings and halting further loss of life, and claiming that the prohibitions against carrying a gun in schools does not deter the gunmen. One such example is the Mercaz HaRav Massacre, where the attacker was not stopped by police but rather a student, Yitzhak Dadon, who stopped the attacker by shooting him with his personal firearm which he lawfully carried concealed. At a Virginia law school, there is a disputed claim that two students retrieved pistols from their cars and stopped the attacker without firing a shot. Also, at a Mississippi high school, the Vice Principal retrieved a firearm from his vehicle and then eventually stopped the attacker as he was driving away from the school. In other cases, such as shootings at Columbine and

Red Lake High Schools, the presence of an armed police officer did nothing to prevent or shorten the shootings.

A ban on the ownership of handguns was introduced in the United Kingdom (with the exception of Northern Ireland) following the Dunblane massacre.

Armed classrooms

Some areas in the US are experimenting with the idea of armed classrooms to deter (or truncate) future attacks, presumably by changing helpless victims into armed defenders. Students at the University of Utah have been allowed to carry concealed pistols (so long as they possess the appropriate state license) since a State Supreme Court decision in 2006. In 2008, Harrold Independent School District in Texas became the first public school district in the U.S. to allow teachers with state-issued firearm-carry permits to carry their arms in the classroom; special additional training and ricochet-resistant ammunition were required for participating teachers.

A commentary in the conservative National Review Online argues that the armed school approach for preventing school attacks, while new in the US, has been used successfully for many years in Israel and Thailand. Teachers and school officials in Israel are allowed and encouraged to carry firearms if they have former military experience in the IDF, which almost all do. Statistics on what percentage of teachers are actually armed is unavailable however.

See also

- List of school-related attacks
- School violence
- Bullying
- School bullying
- Bureau of Alcohol, Tobacco, Firearms and Explosives
- Chencholai bombing, Sri Lanka
- Counter-terrorism
- Federal Bureau of Investigation
- Incendiary device
- Mass murder
- Nagerkovil school bombing, Sri Lanka
- Social rejection
- Suicide bombing
- SWAT
- Terrorism
- Youth subculture

External links

- "Are U.S. Schools Safe?[1]" - CNN In-Depth Special
- "School Killers[2]." - Crime Library
- SchoolShooting.org[3] - Map of school shootings in the US and related info.
- The Depressive and the Psychopath: The FBI's analysis of the Columbine killers' motives[4]
- Schoolboy killing stuns Canada[5] (The Guardian)
- BBC timeline of US school shootings[6]
- Identity annihilation as explanation for school shootings[7]
- *Indianapolis Star*: School violence around the world (November 2004)[8]
- The Scene of the Crime Was the Cause of the Crime[9] - Excerpt from *Going Postal: Rage, Murder, and Rebellion—From Reagan's Workplaces to Clinton's Columbine and Beyond* by Mark Ames.
- Dreading Columbine[10] - Sociological exploration of suburban school shootings.
- Deadly Lessons: Understanding Lethal School Violence[11]
- Teaching Kids to Kill[12]
- Chronology of School Shootings[13]
- Held Hostage at Case Western[14]
- Student Threat Assessment and Management System Guide[15]
- Causes of school shootings. Reviewing the social interaction of pupils.[16]
- SchoolShooters.Info[17]

Reports

- Mass Shootings at Virginia Tech Report of the Review Panel[18]
- U.S. study of school shootings, "The Final Report and Findings of the Safe School Initiative"[19]
- Advice for safe schools, Threat assessment in schools: A Guide to managing threatening situations and to creating safe school climates[20]
- School Violence[21]

Cult suicide

Suicide
Social aspects
Legislation · Philosophy Religious views · Euthanasia Assisted suicide · Right to die Benevolent suicide
Suicide crisis
Assessment of risk · Crisis hotline · Intervention · Prevention · Suicide watch
Suicide types
Copycat · Cult · Euthanasia · Familicide · Forced · Honor · Internet · Mass · Murder–suicide · Parasuicide · Suicide attack · By cop · Pact
Epidemiology
Gender · Suicide rate
History
List of suicides · Suicide methods
Related phenomena
Ideation · Self-harm · Suicide note · Locations · Failed suicide attempt
By country
China · Japan · South Korea · United States

A **cult suicide** is a term used to describe the mass suicide by the members of groups that have been considered cults. In some cases all, or nearly all members have committed suicide at the same time and place. Groups that have committed such mass suicides and that have been called cults include Heaven's Gate, Order of the Solar Temple, and Peoples Temple (in the Jonestown incident). In other cases, such as the Filippians, a group has apparently supported mass suicide without necessarily encouraging all members to participate.

Known cult suicides

Peoples Temple

Main article: Jonestown

On November 18, 1978, 918 Americans died in Peoples Temple-related incidents, including 909 members of the Temple, led by Jim Jones, in Jonestown, Guyana. The dead included 274 children. A tape of the Temple's final meeting in a Jonestown pavilion contains repeated discussions of the group committing "revolutionary suicide," including reference to people taking the poison and the vats to be used. On that tape, Jones tells Temple members that Russia, with whom the Temple had been negotiating a potential exodus for months, would not take them after the Temple had murdered Congressman Leo Ryan, NBC reporter Don Harris and three others at a nearby airstrip. When members apparently cried, Jones counseled "Stop this hysterics. This is not the way for people who are Socialists or Communists to die. No way for us to die. We must die with some dignity." At the end of the tape, Jones concludes: "We didn't commit suicide, we committed an act of revolutionary suicide protesting the conditions of an inhumane world." The people in Jonestown died of an apparent cyanide poisoning, except for Jones (injury consistent with self-inflicted gunshot wound) and his personal nurse. The Temple had spoken of committing "revolutionary suicide" in prior instances, and members had previously drunk what Jones told them was poison at least once before, but the "Flavor Aid" drink they ingested contained no poison. Concurrently, four other members died in the Temple's headquarters in Georgetown.

Solar Temple

From 1994 to 1997, the Order of the Solar Temple's members began a series of mass suicides, which led to roughly 74 deaths. Farewell letters were left by members, stating that they believed their deaths would be an escape from the "hypocrisies and oppression of this world." Added to this they felt they were "moving on to Sirius." Records seized by the Quebec police showed that some members had personally donated over $1 million to the cult's leader, Joseph Di Mambro.

There was also another attempted mass suicide of the remaining members, which was thwarted in the late 1990s. All the suicide/murders and attempts occurred around the dates of the equinoxes and solstices, which likely held some relation to the beliefs of the group.

Heaven's Gate

On March 26, 1997, 39 followers of Heaven's Gate died in a mass suicide in Rancho Santa Fe, California, which borders San Diego to the north. These people believed, according to the teachings of their cult, that through their suicides they were "exiting their human vessels" so that their souls could go on a journey aboard a spaceship they believed to be following comet Hale-Bopp. Some male members of the cult underwent voluntary castration in preparation for the genderless life they believed awaited them after the suicide. On March 30, 1997, Robert Leon Nichols, a former roadie for the Grateful Dead, was discovered dead in his California trailer, with a note nearby that read in part "I'm going to the spaceship with Hale-Bopp to be with those who have gone before me." Using propane gas rather than vodka and phenobarbital to end his life, Nichols, like the members of Heaven's Gate, had his head covered by a plastic bag and his upper torso covered with a purple shroud. Nichols' connection with the cult is unknown.

In May 1997, two Heaven's Gate members who had not been present for the mass suicide attempted suicide, one completing in the attempt, the other going into coma for two days and then recovering. In February 1998 the survivor, Chuck Humphrey, committed suicide.

Disputed cult suicides

Branch Davidians

Main article: Waco Siege

On April 19, 1993, the Bureau of Alcohol, Tobacco and Firearms siege of the Branch Davidians near Waco, Texas ended with an assault and subsequent firestorm that destroyed the compound and killed most of the inhabitants. During the siege, highly concentrated C.S. gas and pyrotechnic "flash-bang" grenades were fired. Some believe these devices ignited the gasoline stockpiled inside the building.

Richard L. Sherrow, a fire and explosion investigator hired by plaintiffs in a civil lawsuit to investigate the cause of the fire stated in his conclusion that "the fire originated in the southeast corner tower from the tipping of a lit Coleman-type lantern which fell onto combustible materials, most likely bedding materials, as the room was utilized as sleeping quarters, and was most likely caused by violent contact or mechanical shock associated with the CEV removing the corner of the southeast tower directly under the point of origin."

The mainstream media reported immediately after the fire that the Branch Davidians, when being overrun, started fires, and therefore this incident was a "cult suicide" or even a murder-suicide perpetrated by the leaders. However, some independent journalists, academics, and other experts contend that the fires could have been an accident or result of a panic.

The Family International

At the beginning of 2005, The Family International gained renewed media attention due to the premeditated murder-suicide of former member Ricky Rodriguez, biological son of current leader Karen Zerby and informally adopted son of the group's founder, David Berg. It revived allegations that the group is abusive and inciting of suicidal ideation. Thus his death was widely called a "suicide of a cult member", or "cult suicide", though this view was far from universal. The event made it to popular culture in oblique references in NBC shows Third Watch and Law & Order

Defenders of the group contend that Rodriguez's behavior was not typical of the group, and that there is no evidence their members are more suicidal than those in mainstream society.

Las Cañadas suicide sect scare

Heidi Fittkau-Garthe, a German psychologist, and a previously high-profile Brahma Kumaris, was charged in the Canary Islands with a plot of murder-suicide in which 31 group members, including five children, were to ingest poison. After the suicides, they were told they would be picked up by a spaceship and taken to an unspecified destination. However a more recent article in Tenerife News casts doubt that there was any intention on the part of the group to commit suicide.

Movement for the Restoration of the Ten Commandments of God

On March 17, 2000, 778 members of the Movement for the Restoration of the Ten Commandments of God died in Uganda. The theory that all of the members died in a mass suicide was changed to mass murder when decomposing bodies were discovered in pits with signs of strangulation while others had stab wounds. The group had diverged from the Roman Catholic Church in order to emphasize apocalypticism and alleged Marian apparitions. The group had been called inward-looking movement that wore matching uniforms and restricted their speech to avoid saying anything dishonest or sinful. On the suicide itself locals said they held a party at which 70 crates of soft drinks and three bulls were consumed.

This version of events has been criticized, most notably Irving Hexham, and a Ugandan source states that even today "no one can really explain the whys, hows, whats, where, when, etc. they're all dead now!"

See also

- Destructive cult
- Doomsday cult
- Mass suicide
- Victims of poisoning

External links

- "Global charts" [1] World Health Organisation
- "The Creativity Movement" [2] ReligiousTolerance.org
- "From Silver Lake to Suicide: One Family's Secret History of the Jonestown Massacre" [3] by Barry Isaacson

Crime of passion

Homicide
Murder
Note: Varies by jurisdiction
Assassination · Child murder Consensual homicide Contract killing · Felony murder rule Honor killing · Human sacrifice Lust murder · Lynching Mass murder · Murder–suicide Proxy murder · Lonely hearts killer Serial killer · Spree killer Torture murder · Feticide Double murder · Misdemeanor murder Crime of passion · Internet homicide Depraved-heart murder
Manslaughter
in English law Negligent homicide Vehicular homicide
Non-criminal homicide
Note: Varies by jurisdiction
Justifiable homicide Capital punishment Human sacrifice Feticide Medicide
By victim or victims
Suicide
Family

Familicide · Avunculicide
Prolicide
(Filicide • Infanticide • Neonaticide)
Fratricide / Sororicide
Mariticide / Uxoricide
Parricide
(Matricide • Patricide)
Other
Amicicide
Genocide / Democide
Gendercide
Omnicide
Regicide / Tyrannicide
Pseudocide
Deicide

A **crime of passion**, in popular usage, refers to a crime in which the perpetrator commits a crime, especially assault or murder, against someone because of sudden strong impulse such as sudden rage or heartbreak rather than as a premeditated crime. A typical crime of passion might involve an aggressive pub-goer who assaults another guest following an argument or a husband who discovers his wife has made him a cuckold and proceeds to brutally batter or even kill his wife or the man with whom she was involved.

Crime of passion

A triangular love scene of Paolo and Francesca da Rimini in The Divine Comedy (Dante Alighieri), depicted by Ingres.

In the United States civil courts, a crime of passion is referred to as "temporary insanity". This defense was first used by U.S. Congressman Daniel Sickles of New York in 1859 after he had killed his wife's lover, Philip Barton Key, but was most used during the 1940s and 1950s.

In some countries, notably France, *crime passionnel* (or *crime of passion*) was a valid defense during murder cases; during the 19th century, some cases could be a custodial sentence for two years for the murderer, while the spouse was dead; this ended in France as the Napoleonic code was updated in the 1970s so that a specific father's authority upon his whole family was over.

See also

- Murder-suicide
- Honor killing

Suicide Attack

Suicide attack

Kamikaze attack on the USS Bunker Hill, May 1945

Terrorism
Definitions History of terrorism International conventions Anti-terrorism legislation Counter-terrorism
By ideology
Anarchist · Communist · Eco-terrorism · Ethnic Narcoterrorism · Nationalist Religious (Islamic · Christian · Jewish)
Types and tactics
Agro-terrorism · Aircraft hijacking (list) Anti-abortion violence · Bioterrorism · Car bombing (list) Environmental · Hostage-taking · Improvised explosive device Insurgency · Kidnapping · Letter bomb · Nuclear Paper terrorism · Piracy · Propaganda of the deed Proxy bomb · Redemption movement · School shooting Suicide attack (list) · Weapon of mass destruction

State involvement
State terrorism State sponsorship Iran · Pakistan · Russia Sri Lanka · United States
Organization
Terrorist financing Terrorist front organization Terrorist training camp Lone-wolf fighter Clandestine cell system
Historical
Reign of Terror Red Terror · White Terror
Lists
Designated organizations Charities accused of ties to terrorism Terrorist incidents

A **suicide attack** (also known as **suicide bombing**, **homicide bombing**, or "kamikaze") is an attack intended to kill others and inflict widespread damage, in which the attacker expects or intends to die in the process.

Tactics

Historical

In the late 17th century, Qing official Yu Yonghe recorded that injured Dutch soldiers fighting against Koxinga's forces for control of Taiwan in 1661 would use gunpowder to blow up both themselves and their opponents rather than be taken prisoner. However, the Chinese observer may have well confused such suicidal tactics with the standard Dutch military practice of undermining and blowing up positions recently overrun by the enemy which almost cost Koxinga his life during the siege.

During the Belgian Revolution, Dutch Lieutenant Jan van Speijk detonated his own ship in the harbour of Antwerp to prevent being captured by the Belgians.

Another example was the Prussian soldier Karl Klinke on 18 April 1864 at the Battle of Dybbøl, who died blowing a hole in a Danish fortification.

In the 18th century John Paul Jones wrote about Ottoman sailors setting their own ships on fire and ramming the ships of their enemies, although they knew this meant certain death for them.

Modern suicide bombing as a political tool can be traced back to the assassination of Tsar Alexander II of Russia in 1881. Alexander fell victim to a Nihilist plot. While driving on one of the central streets of Saint Petersburg, near the Winter Palace, he was mortally wounded by the explosion of hand-made grenades and died a few hours afterwards. The Tsar was killed by a member of Narodnaya Volya, Ignacy Hryniewiecki, who died while intentionally exploding the bomb during the attack.

Rudolf Christoph Freiherr von Gersdorff intended to assassinate Adolf Hitler by suicide bomb in 1943, but was unable to complete the attack.

During the Battle for Berlin the Luftwaffe flew Selbstopfereinsatz against Soviet bridges over the Oder river. These missions were flown by pilots of the Leonidas Squadron under the command of Lieutenant Colonel Heiner Lange. From 17 April until 20 April 1945, using any aircraft that were available, the Luftwaffe claimed that the squadron destroyed 17 bridges, however the military historian Antony Beevor when writing about the incident thinks that this was exaggerated and that only the railway bridge at Küstrin was definitely destroyed. He comments that "thirty-five pilots and aircraft was a high price to pay for such a limited and temporary success". The missions were called off when the Soviet ground forces reached the vicinity of the squadron's airbase at Jüterbog.

Following World War II, Viet Minh "death volunteers" fought against the French Colonial Forces by using a long stick-like explosive to destroy French tanks.

Modern

The number of attacks using suicide tactics has grown from an average of fewer than five per year during the 1980s to 180 per year between 2000 and 2005, and from 81 suicide attacks in 2001 to 460 in 2005. These attacks have been aimed at diverse military and civilian targets, including in Sri Lanka, Israeli targets in Israel since July 6, 1989, Iraqis since the US-led invasion of that country in 2003, and Pakistanis and Afghans since 2005.

There can be issues in identifying if a bombing was in fact a suicide bombing, but this varies in different regions. For example, in some reports in Bangladesh, troops or police of the targeted state are the sole source for the allegation of a suicide bomber attack, and such eyewitness accounts can be unreliable.

Not all modern suicide attacks are by Islamists, a notable example being the separatist Liberation Tigers of Tamil Eelam in Sri Lanka.

This issue with identifying attacks as suicide bombings is not such a problem in places like Israel, Gaza and the West Bank, where suicide bombing is an overt Islamist strategy against the Israelis that has won the backing of both Hamas and Fatah.

For example, between October 2000 and October 2006 there were 167 clearly identified suicide bomber attacks, with 51 other types of suicide attack. It has been suggested that there were so many volunteers for the "Istishhadia" in the Second Intifada in Israel and the occupied territories, such was the tactics growing popular acceptance, that recruiters and dispatchers had a 'larger pool of candidates' than ever before, with one Fatah interviewee stating that they were' flooded' with applicants.

Suicide attacks are also a common feature of the situation in Iraq and Afghanistan.

Suicide bombings have also become a tactic in Chechnya, first being used in the conflict in 2000 when a man and a woman drove a bomb-laden truck into a Russian army base in Alkhan Kala. A number of suicide attacks have occurred in Russia as a result of the Chechen conflict, ranging from the Moscow theater hostage crisis in 2002 to the Beslan school hostage crisis in 2004. The 2010 Moscow Metro bombings are also believed to result from the Chechen conflict.

There have also been suicide attacks in Western Europe and the United States. The September 11 World Trade Center and Pentagon attacks killed nearly 3000 people in New York, Washington D.C and Shanksville, Pennsylvania in 2001. A further attack in London on 7 July 2005 killed 52 people.

In short, suicide tactics have become commonplace in the modern world, with attacks on a global scale as part of diverse regional conflicts.

Japanese kamikaze

Main articles: Kamikaze, Kaiten, Banzai charge, Fukuryu, and Shinyo (suicide boat)

October 25, 1944: Kamikaze pilot in a Mitsubishi Zero's Model 52 crash dives on escort carrier USS White Plains (CVE-66). The aircraft missed the flight deck and impacted the water just off the port quarter of the ship a few seconds later.

The tactics of the Kamikaze, a ritual act of self-sacrifice by state military forces, occurred during combat in a large scale at the end of World War II. These suicide attacks, carried out by Japanese kamikaze bombers, were used as a military tactic aimed at causing material damage in the war. In the Pacific Allied ships were attacked by kamikaze pilots who caused significant damage by flying their explosive-laden aircraft into military targets.

In these attacks, airplanes were used as flying bombs. Later in the war, as Japan became more desperate, this act became formalized and ritualized, as planes were outfitted with explosives specific to the task of a suicide mission. Kamikaze strikes were a weapon of asymmetric war used by the Empire of Japan against United States Navy and Royal Navy aircraft carriers, although the armoured flight deck of the Royal Navy carriers diminished Kamikaze effectiveness.

The Japanese Navy also used both one and two man piloted torpedoes called *kaiten* on suicide missions. Although sometimes called midget submarines, these were modified versions of the unmanned torpedoes of the time and are distinct from the torpedo-firing midget submarines used earlier in the war, which were designed to infiltrate shore defenses and return to a mother ship after firing their torpedoes. Though extremely hazardous, these midget submarine attacks were not technically suicide missions, as the earlier kaitens had escape hatches. Later kaitens, by contrast, provided no means of escape.

After aiming a two-person kaiten at their target, the two crew members traditionally embraced and shot each other in the head. Social support for such choices was strong, due in part to Japanese cultural history, in which seppuku, honourable suicide, was part of samurai duty. It was also fostered and indoctrinated by the Imperial program to persuade the Japanese soldiers to commit these acts.

Definition

Suicide terrorism is a problematic term to define. There is an ongoing debate on definitions of terrorism itself. Kofi Annan, as Secretary General of the UN, defined terrorism in March 2005 in the General Assembly as any action "intended to cause death or serious bodily harm to civilians or non-combatants" for the purpose of intimidation. This definition would distinguish suicide terrorism from suicide bombing in that suicide bombing does not necessarily target non-combatants, and is not widely accepted.

For example, Jason Burke, a journalist who has lived among Islamic militants himself, whilst preferring the term 'militancy' to 'terrorism', suggests that most define terrorism as 'the use or threat of serious violence' to advance some kind of 'cause', and stresses that terrorism is a tactic, and Burke leaves the target of such actions out of the definition, although he is also clear in calling suicide bombings 'abhorrent'. F. Halliday meanwhile draws attention to the fact that assigning the descriptor of 'terrorist' or 'terrorism' to the actions of a group is a tactic used by states to deny 'legitimacy' and 'rights to protest and rebel', although similar to Burke does not define terrorism in terms of the militance of the victim as did Kofi Annan. His preferred approach is to focus on the specific aspects within terrorism that we can study without using the concept itself, laden as it is with 'such distortion and myth'. This means focusing on the specific components of 'terror' and 'political violence' within terrorism.

With awareness of that debate in mind, suicide terrorism itself has been defined by A. Pedahzur as "A diversity of violent actions perpetrated by people who are aware that the odds they will return alive are close to zero." This captures suicide bombing, and the range of suicide tactics below.

Types

See also: Suicide weapon

After the 1983 Beirut barracks bombing that killed 300 and helped drive US and French Multinational Force troops from Lebanon, the tactic spread to non-Islamist groups like the Tamil Tigers of Sri Lanka, and Islamist groups such as Hamas.

- Suicide attack on foot: explosive belt, satchel charge
- Attempted suicide attack with a plane as target: Richard Reid on American Airlines Flight 63
- Explosives hidden inside the body: 2009 attack on Saudi Prince Muhammad bin Nayef
- Suicide car bomb: 1983 Beirut barracks bombing, Sri Lankan Central Bank bombing, numerous incidents in Iraq since 2003
- Suicide attack by a boat with explosives: USS *Cole* bombing, attacks in Aden, Yemen by Al-Qaeda.
- Suicide attack by a submarine with explosives (human-steered torpedo): Kaiten, used by Japan in World War II
- Suicide attack by wearing an explosive belt or a bra bomb : Assassination of Indian Prime Minister Rajiv Gandhi by Thenmuli Rajaratnam of the Liberation Tigers of Tamil Eelam (LTTE).
- Suicide attack by a bicycle with explosives: Assassination of Sri Lankan President Ranasinghe Premadasa by the Liberation Tigers of Tamil Eelam (LTTE)
- Suicide attack by a hijacked commercial jet airliner with fuel: September 11 attacks, possibly Air France Flight 8969 and attempted by Samuel Byck
- Suicide attack by private plane: 2010 Austin plane crash
- Suicide attack by diverting a bus to an abyss: Tel Aviv Jerusalem bus 405 attack
- Suicide attack with guns: Insurgent attack on the Indian Parliament in December 2001, killing 15 people.
- Suicide attack by a car by using a fast driving car to drive intentionally into a crowd of people or breaching a security barrier: 2009 attack on the Dutch royal family

Profile of attackers

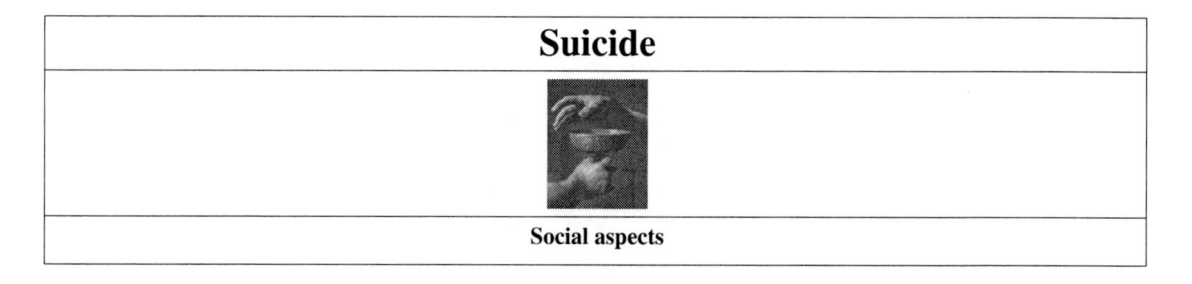

Suicide
Social aspects

Legislation · Philosophy Religious views · Euthanasia Assisted suicide · Right to die Benevolent suicide
Suicide crisis
Assessment of risk · Crisis hotline · Intervention · Prevention · Suicide watch
Suicide types
Copycat · Cult · Euthanasia · Familicide · Forced · Honor · Internet · Mass · Murder–suicide · Parasuicide · Suicide attack · By cop · Pact
Epidemiology
Gender · Suicide rate
History
List of suicides · Suicide methods
Related phenomena
Ideation · Self-harm · Suicide note · Locations · Failed suicide attempt
By country
China · Japan · South Korea · United States

Studies have resulted in conflicting results. Robert Pape, director of the Chicago Project on Suicide Terrorism and expert on suicide bombers, found the majority of suicide bombers came from the educated middle classes, while a 2007 study in Afghanistan[citation needed], a country with a growing number of suicide bombings, found 80% of the suicide attackers had some kind of physical or mental disability[citation needed]. A study of the remains of 110 suicide bombers for the first part of 2007 by Afghan pathologist Dr. Yusef Yadgari, found 80% were missing limbs before the blasts, other suffered from cancer, leprosy, or some other ailments. Also in contrast to earlier findings of suicide bombers, the Afghan bombers were "not celebrated like their counterparts in other Arab nations. Afghan bombers are not featured on posters or in videos as martyrs."

Many subsequent studies of suicide attackers' backgrounds have not shown such a correlation. Forensic psychiatrist Marc Sageman found a lack of antisocial behavior, mental illness, early social trauma or behavioral disorders such as rage, paranoia, narcissism among the 400 members of the Al Qaeda terror network he studied.

Anthropologist Scott Atran found in a 2003 study that this is not a justifiable conclusion. A recently published paper by Harvard University Professor of Public Policy Alberto Abadie "cast[s] doubt on the widely held belief that terrorism stems from poverty, finding instead that terrorist violence is related to a nation's level of political freedom." More specifically this is due to the transition of countries towards democratic freedoms. "Intermediate levels of political freedom are often experienced during times of political transitions, when governments are weak, political instability is elevated, so conditions are favorable for the appearance of terrorism".

Some suicide bombers are educated, with college or university experience, and come from middle class homes. Most suicide bombers do not show signs of psychopathology. Indeed, leaders of the groups who perpetrate these attacks search for individuals who can be trusted to carry out the mission, and those with mental illnesses are not considered ideal candidates.

Use of suicide terror against civilian targets has differing effects on the attackers' goals (see reaction below). Some economists suggest that this tactic goes beyond symbolism and is actually a response to commodified, controlled, or devalued lives, as the suicide attackers apparently consider family prestige and financial compensation from the community as compensation for their own lives.[*citation needed*] Whether such motivation is significant as compared to political or religious feeling remains unclear.

Idealism

The doctrine of asymmetric warfare views suicide attacks as a result of an imbalance of power, in which groups with little significant power resort to suicide bombing as a convenient tactic (see advantages noted above) to demoralize the targeted civilians or government leadership of their enemies. Suicide bombing may also take place as a perceived response to actions or policies of a group with greater power. [*citation needed*] Groups which have significant power have no need to resort to suicide bombing to achieve their aims; consequently, suicide bombing is overwhelmingly used by guerrillas, and other irregular fighting forces. Among many such groups, there are religious overtones to martyrdom: attackers and their supporters may believe that their sacrifice will be rewarded in an afterlife. Suicide attackers often believe that their actions are in accordance with moral or social standards because they are aimed at fighting forces and conditions that they perceive as unjust.

According to Robert Pape, director of the Chicago Project on Suicide Terrorism and expert on suicide bombers, 95% of suicide attacks in recent times have the same specific strategic goal: to cause an occupying state to withdraw forces from a disputed territory. Pape found the targeted countries were ones where the government was democratic and public opinion played a role in determining policy. Other characteristics Pape found were a difference in religion between the attackers and the occupiers and grassroots support for the attacks. Attackers were disproportionately from the educated middle classes. Characteristics which Pape thought to be correlated to suicide bombing and bombers included: Islam, especially the influence of Salafi Islam; brutality and cruelty of the occupiers; competition among militant groups; and poverty, immaturity, poor education, past history of suicide attempts, or social maladjustment of the attackers.

Other researchers have argued that Pape's analysis is fundamentally flawed, particularly his contention that democracies are the main targets of such attacks. Scott Atran found that non-Islamic groups have carried out very few bombings since 2003, while bombing by Muslim or Islamist groups associated with a "global ideology" of "martyrdom" has skyrocketed. In one year, in one Muslim country alone -

2004 in Iraq - there were 400 suicide attacks and 2,000 casualties. Still others argue that perceived religious rewards in the hereafter are instrumental in encouraging Muslims to commit suicide attacks.

Suicide operatives are overwhelmingly male in most groups, but among the Chechen rebels and the Kurdistan Workers Party (PKK) women form a majority of the attackers. So too some groups use teams all or most of the time (Al-Qaeda and Chechen), and others infrequently or never (Palestinians, Lebanese, and PKK). The ritualistic communion of the extremist groups to which they belong ("lone wolf" suicide bombers are rare), in addition to their strongly-held beliefs, helps motivate their decision to commit suicide.[citation needed]

In his book *Dead for Good*, Hugh Barlow describes recent suicide attack campaigns as a new development in the long history of martyrdom that he dubs *predatory martyrdom*. Some individuals who now act alone are inspired by emails, radical books, the internet, various new electronic media, and a general public tolerance of extreme teachers and leaders with terrorist agendas.

Muslim religious motivation

Islamist militant organisations (including Al-Qaeda, Hamas and Islamic Jihad) continue to argue that suicide operations are justified according to Islamic law, despite claims that Islam strictly prohibits suicide and murder.

Irshad Manji, in a conversation with one leader of Islamic Jihad, noted their ideology:

> "What's the difference between suicide, which the Koran condemns, and martyrdom?" I asked. "Suicide," he replied, "is done out of despair. But remember: most of our martyrs today were very successful in their earthly lives." In short, there was a future to live for - and they detonated it anyway.

According to a report compiled by the Chicago Project on Suicide Terrorism, 224 of 300 suicide terror attacks from 1980 to 2003 involved Islamist groups or took place in Muslim-majority lands. Another tabulation found a massiveWikipedia:Manual of Style (dates and numbers) increase in suicide bombings in the two years following Papes study and that the majority of these bombers were motivated by the ideology of Islamist martyrdom. According to another estimate, as of early 2008, 1,121 Muslim suicide bombers have blown themselves up in Iraq.

Recent research on the rationale of suicide bombing as an effective technique to kill enemies has highlighted the importance of the religion of Islam as a driving force. While some scholars cite political and socio-economic factors, others agree that religion provides the framework for suicide bombing because acting in the name of Islam is regarded as martyrdom. Since martyrdom is widely seen as a step towards paradise, those who commit suicide while discarding their community from a common enemy believe that they will reach an ultimate salvation after they die.

A briefing produced by the little-known Pentagon intelligence unit called the Counterintelligence Field Activity (CIFA) cites a number of passages from the Quran dealing with jihad (holy warfare), martyrdom and paradise, where "beautiful mansions" and "maidens" await martyr heroes. In preparation for attacks, suicide terrorists typically recited passages from the Quran to prepare themselves.[citation needed]

The most common citation from the Quran made by Islamic suicide bombers is Sura 9 Ultimatum, Verse 111:

> Allah has bought from the believers their lives and their money in exchange for Paradise. Thus, they fight in the cause of Allah, willing to kill and get killed. Such is His truthful pledge in the Torah, the Gospel, and the Quran - and who fulfills His pledge better than Allah? You shall rejoice in making such an exchange. This is the greatest triumph.

Historically, as long as a Muslim died while attempting to advance the cause of Islam, including by warfare and killing, it was not considered suicide, but a glorious act worthy of paradise.[citation needed] The tantalizing prize of paradise for being killed supply sufficient Quranic justification for modern Muslim suicide attackers, especially those who are dissatisfied with their current lives. As recently as 2010 Muhammad Badi, head of the Muslim Brotherhood, world's largest Muslim group called for a global Muslim jihad against the West, openly calling for all forms of violence including suicide attacks, saying "The improvement and change that the [Muslim] nation seeks can only be attained through jihad and sacrifice and by raising a jihadi generation that pursues death just as the enemies pursue life."

Despite this, some still cling to notions that Islam doesn't permit suicide attacks because they involve suicide, ignoring the extra requirement that the attack advance Islam. According to Charles Kimball, chair of the Department of Religion at Wake Forest University in Winston-Salem, "There is only one verse in the Qur'an that contains a phrase related to suicide", Verse 4:29 of the Quran. It reads:

> O you who believe! Do not consume your wealth in the wrong way-rather through trade mutually agreed to, and do not kill yourselves. Surely God is Merciful toward you.

Some commentators believe that the phrase "do not kill yourselves" is better translated "do not kill each other", and some translations (e.g. by Shakir) reflect that view.[citation needed]

Mainstream Islamic groups such as the European Council for Fatwa and Research rely on the Quranic verse Al-Anam 6:151 as prohibiting suicide: "And take not life, which Allah has made sacred, except by way of justice and law", which sidesteps the question of when Allah considers it just and lawful to do so, such as in jihad. Whether the Quran prohibits it or not, the *hadith* allegedly unambiguously forbid simple selfish suicide for terminal illness, grief, etc.

Nationalism

The Liberation Tigers of Tamil Eelam are considered to have mastered the use of suicide terrorism as "the contemporary terrorist groups engaged in suicide attacks, the LTTE has conducted the largest number of attacks." The LTTE also has a unit, The Black Tigers, which are "constituted exclusively of cadres who have volunteered to conduct suicide operations."

Pape suggests that resentment of foreign occupation and nationalism is the principal motivation for suicide attacks:

> Beneath the religious rhetoric with which [such terror] is perpetrated, it occurs largely in the service of secular aims. Suicide terrorism is mainly a response to foreign occupation rather than a product of Islamic fundamentalism... Though it speaks of Americans as infidels, al-Qaida is less concerned with converting us to Islam than removing us from Arab and Muslim lands.

Muslim views

In January 2006, one of Shia Islam's highest ranking Marja clerics, Ayatollah al-Udhma Yousof al-Sanei also decreed a fatwa against suicide bombing, declaring it as a "terrorist act".

Other views

According to anthropologist Scott Atran and former CIA case officer Marc Sageman, support for suicide actions is triggered by moral outrage at perceived attacks against Islam and sacred values, but this is converted to action as a result of small world factors. There are millions who express sympathy with global jihad (according to a 2006 Gallup study in involving more than 50,000 interviews in dozens of countries, 7 percent of the world's 1.3 billion Muslims - 90 million people - consider the 9/11 attacks "completely justified.") Nevertheless, only some thousands show willingness to commit violence (e.g., 60 arrested in the USA, 2400 in Western Europe, 3200 in Saudi Arabia). They tend to go to violence in small groups consisting mostly of friends, and some kin (although friends tend to become kin as they marry one another's sisters and cousins - there are dozens of such marriages among militant members of Southeast Asia's Jemaah Islamiyah). These groups arise within specific "scenes": neighborhoods, schools (classes, dorms), workplaces and common leisure activities (soccer, paintball, mosque discussion groups, barbershop, café, online chat-rooms).

Case studies

1. In Al Qaeda, about 70 percent join with friends, 20 percent with kin. Interviews with friends of the 9/11 suicide pilots reveal they weren't "recruited" into Qaeda. They were Middle Eastern Arabs isolated even among the Moroccan and Turkish Muslims who predominate in Germany. Seeking friendship, they began hanging out after services at the Masjad al-Quds and other nearby mosques in Hamburg, in local restaurants and in the dormitory of the Technical University in the suburb of Harburg. Three (Mohamed Atta, Ramzi Binalshibh, Marwan al-Shehhi) wound up living together as they self-radicalized. They wanted to go to Chechnya, then Kosovo, only landing in a Qaeda camp in Afghanistan as a distant third choice.

2. Five of the seven plotters in the 11 March 2004 Madrid train bombings who blew themselves up when cornered by police grew up in the tumble-down neighborhood of Jemaa Mezuak in Tetuan, Morocco: Jamal Ahmidan, brothers Mohammed and Rashid Oulad Akcha, Abdennabi Kounjaa, Asri Rifaat. In 2006, at least five more young Mezuaq men went to Iraq on "martyrdom missions": Abdelmonim Al-Amrani, Younes Achebak, Hamza Aklifa, and the brothers Bilal and Munsef Ben Aboud (DNA analysis has confirmed the suicide bombing death of Amrani in Baqubah, Iraq). All 5 attended a local elementary school (Abdelkrim Khattabi), the same one that Madrid's Moroccan bombers attended. And 4 of the 5 were in the same high school class (Kadi Ayadi, just outside Mezuak). They played soccer as friends, went to the same mosque (Masjad al-Rohban of the Dawa Tabligh), mingled in the same restaurants, barbershops and cafes.

3. Hamas's most sustained suicide bombing campaign in 2003-4 involved several buddies from Hebron's Masjad (mosque) al-Jihad soccer team. Most lived in the Wad Abu Katila neighborhood and belonged to the al-Qawasmeh hamula (clan); several were classmates in the neighborhood's local branch of the Palestinian Polytechnic College. Their ages ranged from 18 to 22. At least eight team members were dispatched to suicide shooting and bombing operations by the Hamas military leader in Hebron, Abdullah al-Qawasmeh (killed by Israeli forces in June 2003 and succeeded by his relatives Basel al-Qawasmeh, killed in September 2003, and Imad al-Qawasmeh, captured on 13 October 2004). In retaliation for the assassinations of Hamas leaders Sheikh Ahmed Yassin (22 March 2004) and Abdel Aziz al-Rantissi (17 April 2004), Imad al-Qawasmeh dispatched Ahmed al-Qawasmeh and Nasim al-Ja'abri for a suicide attack on two buses in Beer Sheva (31 August 2004). In December 2004, Hamas declared a halt to suicide attacks.

On 15 January 2008, the son of Mahmoud al-Zahar, the leader of Hamas in the Gaza Strip, was killed (another son was killed in a 2003 assassination attempt on Zahar). Three days later, Israel Defense Minister Ehud Barak ordered Israel Defense Forces to seal all border crossings with Gaza, cutting off the flow of vital supplies to the besieged territory in an attempt to stop rocket barrages on Israeli border towns. Nevertheless, violence from both sides only increased. On 4 February 2008, two friends (Mohammed Herbawi, Shadi Zghayer), who were members of the Masjad al-Jihad soccer team, staged a suicide bombing at commercial center in Dimona, Israel. Herbawi had previously been arrested as a 17-year-old on 15 March 2003 shortly after a suicide bombing on Haifa bus (by Mamoud al-Qawasmeh on 5 March 2003) and coordinated suicide shooting attacks on Israeli settlements by others on the team (7 March 2003, Muhsein, Hazem al-Qawasmeh, Fadi Fahuri, Sufian Hariz) and before another set of suicide bombings by team members in Hebron and Jerusalem on May 17–18, 2003 (Fuad al-Qawasmeh, Basem Takruri, Mujahed al-Ja'abri). Although Hamas claimed responsibility for the Dimona attack, the politburo leadership in Damascus and Beirut was clearly initially unaware of who initiated and carried out the attack. It appears that Ahmad al-Ja'abri, military commander of Hamas's Izz ad-Din al-Qassam Brigades in Gaza (and who is also originally from a Hebron clan) requested the suicide attack through Ayoub Qawasmeh, Hamas's military liaison in Hebron, who knew where to look for eager young men who had self-radicalized together and had already mentally prepared themselves for martyrdom.

Background

The concept of self-sacrifice has long been a part of war. However, many instances of suicide bombing today has intended civilian targets, not military targets alone. "Suicide bombing as a tool of stateless terrorists was dreamed up a hundred years ago by the European anarchists immortalized in Joseph Conrad's 'Secret Agent.'"

The ritual act of self-sacrifice during combat appeared in a large scale at the end of World War II with the Japanese kamikaze bombers. In these attacks, airplanes were used as flying bombs. Later in the war, as Japan became more desperate, this act became formalized and ritualized, as planes were outfitted with explosives specific to the task of a suicide mission. Kamikaze strikes were a weapon of asymmetric war used by the Empire of Japan against United States Navy and Royal Navy aircraft carriers, although the armoured flight deck of the Royal Navy carriers diminished Kamikaze effectiveness.

A Japanese Mitsubishi Zero's suicide attack on the USS Missouri (BB-63), April 11, 1945

The Japanese Navy also used both one and two man piloted torpedoes called *kaiten* on suicide missions. Although sometimes called midget submarines, these were modified versions of the unmanned torpedoes of the time and are distinct from the torpedo-firing midget submarines used earlier in the war, which were designed to infiltrate shore defences and return to a mother ship after firing their torpedoes. Though extremely hazardous, these midget submarine attacks were not technically suicide missions, as the earlier kaitens had escape hatches. Later kaitens, by contrast, provided no means of escape.

After aiming a two-person kaiten at their target, the two crew members traditionally embraced and shot each other in the head. Social support for such choices was strong, due in part to Japanese cultural history, in which seppuku, honourable suicide, was part of samurai duty. It was also fostered and indoctrinated by the Imperial program to persuade the Japanese soldiers to commit these acts.

Suicide attacks were used as a military tactic aimed at causing material damage in war, during the Second World War in the Pacific as Allied ships were attacked by Japanese kamikaze pilots who caused maximum damage by flying their explosive-laden aircraft into military targets, not focused on civilian targets.

During the Battle for Berlin the Luftwaffe flew "Self-sacrifice missions" (*Selbstopfereinsatz*) against Soviet bridges over the River Oder. These 'total missions' were flown by pilots of the *Leonidas* Squadron under the command of Lieutenant Colonel Heiner Lange. From 17 April until 20 April 1945, using any aircraft that were available, the Luftwaffe claimed that the squadron destroyed 17 bridges, however the military historian Antony Beevor when writing about the incident thinks that this was exaggerated and that only the railway bridge at Küstrin was definitely destroyed. He comments that "thirty-five pilots and aircraft was a high price to pay for such a limited and temporary success". The missions were called off when the Soviet ground forces reached the vicinity of the squadron's airbase at Jüterbog.

Following World War II, Viet Minh "death volunteers" fought against the French colonial army by using a long stick-like explosive to detonate French tanks, as part of their urban warfare tactics.

In 1972, in the hall of the Lod airport in Tel Aviv, Israel, three Japanese used grenades and automatic rifles to kill 26 people and wound many more. The group belonged to the Japanese Red Army (JRA) a terrorist organization created in 1969 and allied to the Popular Front for the Liberation of Palestine (PFLP). Until then, no group involved in terrorism had conducted such a suicide operation in Israel. Members of the JRA became instructors in martial art and kamikaze operations at several training camps bringing the suicide techniques to the Middle East [citation needed].

1980 to present

The first modern suicide bombing—involving explosives deliberately carried to the target either on the person or in a civilian vehicle and delivered by surprise—was in 1981; perfected by the factions of the Lebanese Civil War and especially by the Tamil Tigers of Sri Lanka, the tactic had spread to dozens of countries by 2005. Those hardest-hit are Sri Lanka during its prolonged ethnic conflict, Lebanon during its civil war, Israel and the Palestinian Territories since 1994, and Iraq since the US-led invasion in 2003.

The Islamic Dawa Party's car bombing of the Iraqi embassy in Beirut in December 1981 and Hezbollah's bombing of the U.S. embassy in April 1983 and attack on United States Marine and French barracks in October 1983 brought suicide bombings international attention. Other parties to the civil war were quick to adopt the tactic, and by 1999 factions such as Hezbollah, the Amal Movement, the Ba'ath Party, and the Syrian Social Nationalist Party had carried out around 50 suicide bombings between them. (The latter of these groups sent the first recorded female suicide bomber in 1985. Female combatants have existed throughout human history and in many different societies, so it is possible that females who engage in suicidal attacks are not new.) Hezbollah was the only one to attack overseas, bombing the Israeli embassy (and possibly the Argentine-Israeli Mutual Association building) in Buenos Aires; as its military and political power have grown, it has since abandoned the tactic.

Lebanon saw the first bombing, but it was the LTTE Tamil Tigers in Sri Lanka who perfected the tactic and inspired its use elsewhere. Their Black Tiger unit has committed between 76 and 168 (estimates vary) suicide bombings since 1987, the higher estimates putting them behind more than half of the world's suicide bombings between 1980 and 2000. The list of victims include former Indian Prime Minister, Rajiv Gandhi, and the president of Sri Lanka, Ranasinghe Premadasa.

Suicide bombing is a popular tactic among Palestinian terrorist organizations like Hamas, Islamic Jihad, and the Al-Aqsa Martyrs Brigade. Bombers affiliated with these groups often use so-called "suicide belts", explosive devices (often including shrapnel) designed to be strapped to the body under clothing. In order to maximize the loss of life, the bombers seek out cafés or city buses crowded with people at rush hour, or less commonly a military target (for example, soldiers waiting for transport at roadside). By seeking enclosed locations, a successful bomber usually kills a large number of people. In Israel, Palestinian suicide bombers have targeted civilian buses, restaurants, shopping malls, hotels and marketplaces.

Palestinian television has aired a number of music videos and announcements that promote eternal reward for children who seek "*shahada*", which *Palestinian Media Watch* has claimed is "Islamic motivation of suicide terrorists". *The Chicago Tribune* has documented the concern of Palestinian parents that their children are encouraged to take part in suicide operations. Israeli sources have also alleged that Hamas, Islamic Jihad and Fatah operate "Paradise Camps", training children as young as 11 to become suicide bombers.

The Kurdistan Workers' Party has also employed suicide bombings in the scope of its guerrilla attacks on Turkish security forces since the beginning of their insurgency against the Turkish state in 1984. Although the majority of PKK activity is focused on village guards, gendarme, and military posts, they have employed suicide bombing tactics on tourist sites and commercial centers in Western Turkish cities, especially during the peak of tourism season.

The 11 September attacks involved the hijacking of large passenger jets which were deliberately flown into the towers of the World Trade Center in New York City and the Pentagon, killing everyone aboard the planes and thousands more in and around the targeted buildings. The passenger jets selected were required to be fully fueled to fly cross-country, turning the planes themselves into the largest suicide bombs in history. The 'September 11' attacks also had a vast economic and political impact: for the cost of the lives of the 19 hijackers and financial expenditure of around US$100,000, al-Qaeda, the militant Islamist group responsible for the attacks, effected a trillion-dollar drop in global markets within one week, and triggered massive increases in military and security expenditure in response.

On 22 December 2001, Richard Reid attempted to destroy the American Airlines Flight 63 by the means of a bomb hidden in a shoe. He was arrested after his attempt was foiled when he was unable to light the bomb's fuse.

After the U.S.-led invasion of Iraq in 2003, Iraqi and foreign insurgents carried out waves of suicide bombings. They attacked United States military targets, although many civilian targets (e.g. Shiite mosques, international offices of the UN and the Red Cross, Iraqi men waiting to apply for jobs with the new army and police force) were also attacked. In the lead up to the Iraqi parliamentary election, on 30 January 2005, suicide attacks upon civilian and security personnel involved with the elections increased, and there were reports of the insurgents co-opting disabled people as involuntary suicide bombers.

In the first eight months of 2008, Pakistan overtook Iraq and Afghanistan in suicide-bomb with 28 bombings killing 471 people.

> First the targets were American soldiers, then mostly Israelis, including women and children. From Lebanon and Israel, the technique of suicide bombing moved to Iraq, where the targets have included mosques and shrines, and the intended victims have mostly been Shiite Iraqis. The newest testing ground is Afghanistan, where both the perpetrators and the targets are orthodox Sunni Muslims. Not long ago, a bombing in Lashkar Gah, the capital of Helmand Province, killed Muslims, including women, who were applying to go on pilgrimage to Mecca. Overall, the trend is definitively in the direction of Muslim-on-Muslim violence. By a conservative accounting, more than three times as many Iraqis have been killed by suicide bombings in the last 3 years as have Israelis in the last 10. Suicide bombing has become the archetype of Muslim violence — not just to frightened Westerners but also to Muslims themselves.

Public Surveys

The Pew Global Attitudes Project surveys Muslim publics to measure support for suicide bombing and other forms of violence that target civilians in order to defend Islam. In the annual poll, the highest support for such acts has been reported by Palestinians (at approximately 70 percent), except for years in which Palestinians were not surveyed. The lowest support has generally been observed in Turkey (between 3 and 17 percent, depending on the year). The 2009 report concluded that support for suicide bombing has declined in recent years, especially in Pakistan, where support dropped from 33 percent in 2002 (the first year of the survey) to 5 percent in 2009.

Response

World leaders, especially those of countries that experience suicide bombings, usually express resolve to continue on their previous course of affairs after such attacks. They denounce suicide bombings and sometimes vow not to let such bombings deter ordinary people from going about their everyday economic business.

Suicide bombings are sometimes followed by reprisals. As a successful suicide bomber cannot be targeted, the response is often a targeting of those believed to have sent the bomber. In targeting such organizations, Israel often uses military strikes against organizations, individuals, and possibly infrastructure. In the West Bank the IDF formerly demolished homes that belong to families whose children (or renters whose tenants) had volunteered for such missions (whether successfully or not), though an internal review starting in October 2004 brought an end to the policy. The effectiveness of suicide bombings—notably those of the Japanese kamikazes, the Palestinian bombers, and even the September 11, 2001 attacks—is debatable. Although kamikaze attacks could not stop the Allied advance the Pacific, they inflicted more casualties and delayed the fall of Japan for longer than might have been the case using only the conventional methods available to the Japanese Empire. The attacks reinforced the resolution of the World War II Allies to destroy the Imperial force, and may have had a significant effect in the decision to use atomic bombs against Japan.[citation needed]

In the case of the September 11 attacks, the long-term effects remain to be seen, but in the short term, the results were negative for Al-Qaeda, as well as the Taliban Movement. Furthermore, since the September 11 attacks, Western nations have diverted massive resources towards stopping similar actions, as well as tightening up borders, and military actions against various countries that the U.S. and its allies believe to have been involved with terrorism. However, critics of the War on Terrorism suggest that in fact the results were profoundly negative, as the proceeding actions of the United States and other countries has increased the number of recruits, and their willingness to carry out suicide bombings.

It is more difficult to determine whether Palestinian suicide bombings have proved to be a successful tactic. In the Israeli-Palestinian conflict, the suicide bombers were repeatedly deployed since the Oslo Accords. In 1996 , the Israelis elected the conservative candidate Benjamin Netanyahu who promised to restore safety by conditioning every step in the peace process on Israel's assessment of the Palestinian Authority's fulfillment of its obligations in curbing violence as outlined in the Oslo agreements.

In the course of al-Aqsa Intifada which followed the collapse of the Camp David II summit between the PLO and Israel, the number of suicide attacks drastically increased. In response, Israel mobilized its army in order to seal off the Gaza Strip and reinstate military control of the West Bank, patrolling the area with tanks. The Israelis also began a campaign of targeted killings to kill militant Palestinian leaders, using jets and helicopters to deploy high-precision bombs and missiles.

The suicide missions, having killed hundreds and maimed thousands of Israelis, are believed by some to have brought on a move to the political right, increasing public support for hard-line policies towards the Palestinians, and a government headed by the former general, prime minister Ariel Sharon. In response to the suicide bombings, Sharon's government has imposed restrictions on the Palestinian community, making commerce, travel, school, and other aspects of life difficult for the Palestinians, with the average Palestinian suffering due to the choices of the suicide bombers. The Separation barrier under construction seem to be part of the Israeli government's efforts to stop suicide bombers from entering Israel proper.

Social support by some for this activity remained, however, as of the calling of a truce at the end of June 2003. This may be due to the economic or social purpose of the suicide bombing and the bombers' refusal to accept external judgements on those who sanction them.

If the objective is to kill as many people as possible, suicide bombing by terrorists may thus "work" as a tactic in that it costs fewer lives than any conventional military tactic and targeting unarmed civilians is much easier than targeting soldiers. As an objective designed to achieve some form of favorable outcome, especially a political outcome, most believe it to be a failure. Terrorist campaigns involving the targeting of civilians have never won a war. Analysts believe that in order to win or succeed, any guerrilla or terrorist campaign must first transform into something more than a guerrilla or terrorist movement. Such analysts believe that a terrorist cause has little political attraction and success may be achieved only by renouncing terrorism and transforming the passions into politics.[citation needed]

Israeli ultra-right politician and author Obadiah Shoher declared terrorism proper and efficient military tactics, and called for the Jews to answer in kind. Shoher praised Baruch Goldstein who massacred Palestinian worshippers inside a mosque.

Often extremists assert that, because they are outclassed militarily, suicide bombings are necessary. For example, the former leader of Hamas Sheikh Ahmad Yassin stated: "Once we have warplanes and missiles, then we can think of changing our means of legitimate self-defense. But right now, we can only tackle the fire with our bare hands and sacrifice ourselves."

Such views are challenged both from the outside and from within Islam. According to Islamic jurist and scholar Khaled Abou Al-Fadl,

> The classical jurists, nearly without exception, argued that those who attack by stealth, while targeting noncombatants in order to terrorize the resident and wayfarer, are corrupters of the earth. "Resident and wayfarer" was a legal expression that meant that whether the attackers terrorize people in their urban centers or terrorize travelers, the result was the same: all such attacks constitute a corruption of the earth. The legal term given to people who act this way was *muharibun* (those who wage war against society), and the crime is called the crime of *hiraba* (waging war against society). The crime of *hiraba* was so serious and repugnant that, according to Islamic law, those guilty of this crime were considered enemies of humankind and were not to be given quarter or sanctuary anywhere. ... Those who are familiar with the classical tradition will find the parallels between what were described as crimes of *hiraba* and what is often called terrorism today nothing short of remarkable. The classical jurists considered crimes such as assassinations, setting fires, or poisoning water wells – that could indiscriminately kill the innocent – as offenses of *hiraba*. Furthermore, hijacking methods of transportation or crucifying people in order to spread fear and terror are also crimes of *hiraba*. Importantly, Islamic law strictly prohibited the taking of hostages, the mutilation of corpses, and torture.

Usage of term

The usage of the term "suicide bombing" dates back to at least 1940. A 10 August 1940 New York Times article of mentions the term in relation to German tactics. A 4 March 1942 article refers to a Japanese attempt as a "suicide bombing" on an American carrier. The Times (London) of 15 April 1947, page 2, refers to a new pilotless, radio-controlled rocket missile thus: "Designed originally as a counter-measure to the Japanese 'suicide-bomber,' it is now a potent weapon for defence or offence". The quotes are in the original and suggest that the phrase was an existing one. An earlier article (21 Aug 1945, page 6) refers to a kamikaze plane as a "suicide-bomb". Even earlier, though not using the exact phrase, the magazine Modern Mechanix (February 1936) reports the Italians reacted to a possible oil embargo by stating that they would carry out attacks with "a squadron of aviators pledged to crash their death-laden planes in suicidal dives directly onto the decks of British ships".

The term with the meaning "an attacker blowing up himself or a vehicle to kill others" appeared in 1981, when it was used by Thomas Baldwin in an Associated Press article to describe the bombing of the Iraqi Embassy in Beirut.

In order to assign either a more positive or negative connotation to the act, suicide bombing is sometimes referred to by different terms. Islamists often call the act a *isshtahad* (meaning *martyrdom operation*), and the suicide bomber a *shahid* (pl. *shuhada*, literally 'witness' and usually translated as 'martyr'). The term denotes one who died in order to testify his faith in God (Allah), for example those who die while waging *jihad bis saif*; it is applied to suicide bombers, by the Palestinian Authority among others, in part to overcome Islamic strictures against suicide. This term has been embraced by Hamas, Al-Aqsa Martyrs' Brigades, Fatah and other Palestinian factions engaging in suicide bombings. (The title is by no means restricted to suicide bombers and can be used for a wide range of people, including innocent victims; Muhammad al-Durra, for example, is among the most famous *shuhada* of the Intifada, and even a few non-Palestinians such as Tom Hurndall and Rachel Corrie have been called *shahid*).

Homicide bombing

Some effort has been made to replace the term *suicide bombing* with the term **homicide bombing** by commentators and news outlets. The first such use was by White House Press Secretary Ari Fleischer in April 2002. However, it has failed to catch on; the only major media outlets to use it were *Fox News Channel* and the *New York Post* (both owned by News Corporation).

Supporters of the term *homicide bombing* argue that since the primary purpose of such a bombing is to kill other people rather than merely to end one's own life, the term *homicide* is a more accurate description than *suicide*. Others argue that *homicide bombing* is a less useful term, since it fails to capture the distinctive feature of suicide bombings, namely the bombers' use of means which they are aware will inevitably bring about their own deaths.

Another attempted replacement is ***genocide bombing***. The term was coined in 2002 by Canadian member of parliament Irwin Cotler, in an effort to replace the term *homicide bomber* as a substitute for "suicide bomber." The intention was to focus attention on the alleged intention of genocide by militant Palestinians in their calls to "Wipe Israel off the map."

See also

- Pierre Rehov
- Suicide killers
- Child suicide bombers in the Israeli–Palestinian conflict
- List of Hamas suicide attacks
- List of Al-Aqsa Martyrs' Brigades suicide attacks
- List of Palestinian Islamic Jihad suicide attacks
- List of Palestinian militant groups suicide attacks
- 2010 Austin plane crash

Further reading

Book

- Barlow, Hugh (2007). *Dead for Good*. City: Paradigm Publishers. ISBN 1594513244.
- Bloom, Mia (2005). *Dying to Kill*. New York: Columbia University Press. ISBN 0231133200.
- Davis, Joyce M. (2004). *Martyrs: Innocence, Vengeance, and Despair in the Middle East*. Palgrave Macmillan. ISBN 1403966818.
- Falk, Ophir, Morgenstern, Henry (2009). *Suicide Terror: Understanding and Confronting the Threat*. Hoboken: Wiley. ISBN 9780470087299.
- Fall, Bernard (1985). *Hell in a Very Small Place*. New York: Da Capo Press. ISBN 9780306802317.
- Gambetta, Diego (2005). *Making Sense of Suicide Missions*. Oxford Oxfordshire: Oxford University Press. ISBN 0199276994.
- Hafez, Mohammed (2007). *Suicide Bombers in Iraq*. Washington: U.S. Institute of Peace Press. ISBN 9781601270047.
- Hudson, Rex (2002). *Who Becomes a Terrorist and Why*. City: The Lyons Press. ISBN 1585747548.
- Jayawardena, Hemamal (2007). *Forensic Medical Aspects of Terrorist Explosive Attacks*. City: Zeilan Press. ISBN 9780979362422.
- Khosrokhavar, Farhad (2005). *Suicide Bombers*. Sydney: Pluto Press. ISBN 0745322832.
- Oliver, Anne Marie, Steinberg, Paul (2004). *The Road to Martyrs' Square*. New York: Oxford University Press. ISBN 9780195305593.
- Pape, Robert (2005). *Dying to Win*. New York: Random House. ISBN 1400063175.
- Pedahzur, Ami (2005). *Suicide Terrorism*. Cambridge: Polity. ISBN 9780745633831.

- Reuter, Christoph (2004). *My Life Is a Weapon*. Princeton: Princeton University Press. ISBN 9780691126159.
- Scheit, Gerhard (2004) (in German). *Suicide Attack*. City: Ca Ira Verlag. ISBN 3924627878.
- Sheftall, Mordecai (2005). *Blossoms in the Wind*. New York: NAL Caliber. ISBN 9780451214874.
- Skaine, Rosemarie (2006). *Female Suicide Bombers*. Jefferson: McFarland. ISBN 0786426152.
- Swamy, M.R. (1994). *Tigers of Lanka*. City: Vijitha Yapa Publications, Sri Lanka. ISBN 9558095141.
- Matovic, Violeta (2007). *Suicide Bombers Who's Next*. Belgrade: The National Counter Terrorism Committee. ISBN 978-86-908309-2-3.

Web

- Kassim, Sadik H. "The Role of Religion in the Generation of Suicide Bombers" [1]
- Kramer, Martin. (1996). "Sacrifice and "Self-Martyrdom" in Shi'ite Lebanon" [2].
- Sarraj, Dr. Eyad. "Why we have become Suicide Bombers" [3]
- Feffer, John. August 6, 2009. "Our Suicide Bombers: Thoughts on Western Jihad" [4]

External links

- Suicide Terrorism Works [5] Riaz Hassan
- The Economic Logic of Suicide Terrorism by Mark Harrison [6]PDF
- Suicide Bombers - Why do they do it, and what does Islam say about their actions? [7]
- Defending the Transgressed [8] Fatwa against suicide bombing by Shaykh Muhammad Afifi al-Akiti
- Erased In A Moment [9] Suicide Bombing Attacks Against Israeli Civilians [Human Rights Watch]
- Suicide Terrorism: Rationalizing the Irrational [10]
- Athena Intelligence [11] Advanced Research Network on Insurgency and Terrorism: articles on Suicide Terrorism in the Virtual Library
- Suicide Terrorism: Origins and Response [12]
- Video of suicide attack [13] in Colombo, Attempted assassination of Sri Lankan Minister Douglas Devananda by LTTE
- Understanding Suicide Terrorism And How To Stop It [14] - audio interview by *NPR*

Kamikaze

The ***Kamikaze*** (神風, common translation: "divine wind") ([kamikaɯze] Wikipedia:Media helpFile:Kamikaze.ogg) ***Tokubetsu Kougekitai*** (特別攻撃隊) ***Tokkō Tai*** (特攻隊) ***Tokkō*** (特攻) were suicide attacks by military aviators from the Empire of Japan against Allied naval vessels in the closing stages of the Pacific campaign of World War II, designed to destroy as many warships as possible.

Kamikaze pilots would intentionally attempt to crash their aircraft into enemy ships—planes often laden with

USS *Bunker Hill* was hit by *kamikazes* piloted by Ensign Kiyoshi Ogawa (photo below) and another airman on May 11, 1945. 389 personnel were killed or missing from a crew of 2,600.

explosives, bombs, torpedoes and full fuel tanks. The aircraft's normal functions (to deliver torpedoes or bombs or shoot down other aircraft) were put aside, and the planes were converted to what were essentially manned missiles in an attempt to reap the benefits of greatly increased accuracy and payload over that of normal bombs. The goal of crippling as many Allied ships as possible, particularly aircraft carriers, was considered critical enough to warrant the combined sacrifice of pilots and aircraft.

These attacks, which began in October 1944, followed several critical military defeats for the Japanese. They had long lost aerial dominance due to outdated aircraft and the loss of experienced pilots. On a macroeconomic scale, Japan experienced a decreasing capacity to wage war, and a rapidly declining industrial capacity relative to the United States. The Japanese government expressed its reluctance to surrender. In combination, these factors led to the use of *kamikaze* tactics as Allied forces advanced towards the Japanese home islands.

While the term "kamikaze" usually refers to the aerial strikes, the term has sometimes been applied to various other intentional suicide attacks. The Japanese military also used or made plans for Japanese Special Attack Units, including those involving submarines, human torpedoes, speedboats and divers.

Although *kamikaze* was the most common and best-known form of Japanese suicide attack during World War II, they were similar to the "banzai charge" used by Japanese soldiers. The main difference between *kamikaze* and *banzai* is that suicide is essential to the success of a *kamikaze* attack, whereas a *banzai* charge is only *potentially* suicidal — that is, the attackers hope to survive but do not expect to. Western sources often incorrectly consider Operation Ten-Go as a *kamikaze* operation, since it occurred at the Battle of Okinawa along with the mass waves of *kamikaze* planes; however, *banzai* is the more accurate term, since the aim of the mission was for battleship *Yamato* to beach herself and provide support to the island defenders, as opposed to ramming and detonating among enemy naval forces. The tradition of suicide instead of defeat, capture, and perceived shame was deeply entrenched in the Japanese military culture. It was one of the main traditions in the samurai life and the *Bushido* code: loyalty and honor until death.

Ensign Kiyoshi Ogawa, who killed himself in a *kamikaze* attack on USS *Bunker Hill* on May 11, 1945.

Definition and etymology

The Japanese word *Kamikaze* is usually translated as "divine wind" (*kami* is the word for "god", "spirit", or "divinity", and *kaze* for "wind"). The word *kamikaze* originated as the name of major typhoons in 1274 and 1281, which dispersed Mongolian invasion fleets.

In Japanese, the formal term used for units carrying out suicide attacks during 1944–45 is *tokubetsu kōgeki tai* (特別攻□隊), which literally means "special attack unit". This is usually abbreviated to *tokkōtai* (特攻隊). More specifically, air suicide attack units from the Imperial Japanese Navy were officially called *shinpū tokubetsu kōgeki tai* (神風特別攻□隊, "divine wind special attack units"). *Shinpū* is the on-reading (*on'yomi* or Chinese-derived pronunciation) of the same characters that form the word *kamikaze* in Japanese. During World War II, the pronunciation *kamikaze* was used in Japan only informally in relation to suicide attacks, but after the war this usage gained acceptance worldwide and was re-imported into Japan. As a result, the special attack units are sometimes known in Japan as *kamikaze tokubetsu kōgeki tai*.

The Mongol fleet destroyed in a typhoon, ink and water on paper, by Kikuchi Yōsai, 1847

Since the end of the war, the term *kamikaze* has sometimes been used as a *pars pro toto* for other kinds of attack in which an attacker is deliberately sacrificed. These include a variety of suicide attacks, in other historical contexts, such as the proposed use of *Selbstopfer* aircraft by Nazi Germany and various suicide bombings by terrorist organizations around the world (such as the September 11, 2001 attacks), although kamikaze pilots attacked only military targets, while terrorists attack mostly civilian facilities. In English, the word *kamikaze* may also be used in a hyperbolic or metaphorical fashion to refer to non-fatal actions which result in significant loss for the attacker, such as injury or the end of a career.

History

Background

Prior to the formation of *kamikaze* units, deliberate crashes had been used as a last effort when a pilot's plane was severely damaged and he did not want to risk being captured; this was the case in both the Japanese and Allied air forces. According to Axell & Kase, these suicides "were individual, impromptu decisions by men who were mentally prepared to die." In most cases, there is little evidence that these hits were more than accidental collisions, of the kind that sometimes happen in intense sea-air battles. One example of this occurred on December 7, 1941 during the attack on Pearl Harbor. First Lieutenant Fusata Iida's plane had been hit and was leaking fuel, when he apparently used it to make a suicide attack on Kaneohe Naval Air Station. Before taking off, he had told his men that if his plane was badly damaged he would crash it into a "worthy enemy target".

Lt Yoshinori Yamaguchi's Yokosuka D4Y3 (Type 33 *Suisei*) "Judy" in a suicide dive against USS *Essex*. The dive brakes are extended and the non-self-sealing port wing tank is trailing fuel vapor and/or smoke November 25, 1944.

The carrier battles in 1942, particularly Midway, had inflicted irreparable damage on the Imperial Japanese Navy Air Service (IJNAS), such that they could no longer put together a large number of fleet carriers with well-trained aircrews. Japanese planners had assumed a quick war and were ill-prepared to replace the losses of ships, pilots, and sailors; at Midway, the Japanese lost as many aircrewmen in a single day as their pre-war training program had produced in a year. The following Solomons and New Guinea campaigns, notably the Battles of Eastern Solomons and Santa Cruz, would further decimate their veteran aircrews and replacing their combat experience would be impossible. During 1943-44, U.S. forces were steadily advancing towards Japan. Japan's fighter planes were becoming outnumbered and outclassed by newer U.S.-made planes, especially the F6F Hellcat and F4U Corsair. Tropical diseases, as well as shortages of spare parts and fuel, made operations more and more difficult for the

A Japanese *kamikaze* aircraft explodes after crashing into *Essex*' flight deck amidships November 25, 1944

Model 52c Zeroes ready to take part in a *kamikaze* attack (early 1945).

IJNAS. By the Battle of the Philippine Sea in 1944, the Japanese now had to make do with obsolete aircraft and inexperienced aviators, against the better-trained and more experienced US Navy airmen, and its radar-directed combat air patrols. The Japanese lost over 400 carrier-based planes and pilots, effectively putting an end to their carriers' potency, an action referred to by the Allies as the "Great Marianas Turkey Shoot".

On June 19, 1944, planes from the carrier *Chiyoda* approached a US task group. According to some accounts, two made suicide attacks, one of which hit USS *Indiana*.

The important Japanese base of Saipan fell to the Allied forces on July 15, 1944. Its capture provided adequate forward bases which enabled U.S. air forces using the B-29 Superfortress to strike the Japanese home islands. After the fall of Saipan, the Japanese high command predicted that the Allies would try to capture the Philippines, which were strategically important because of their location between the oilfields of Southeast Asia and Japan.

In August 1944, it was announced by the *Domei* news agency that a flight instructor named Takeo Tagata was training pilots in Taiwan for suicide missions.

Another source claims that the first *kamikaze* mission occurred on September 13, 1944. A group of pilots from the army's 31st Fighter Squadron on Negros Island decided to launch a suicide attack the following morning. First Lieutenant Takeshi Kosai and a sergeant were selected. Two 100 kg (220 lb) bombs were attached to two fighters, and the pilots took off before dawn, planning to crash into carriers. They never returned, and there is no record of an enemy plane hitting an Allied ship that day.

According to some sources, on October 14, 1944, USS *Reno* was hit by a deliberately-crashed Japanese plane. However, there is no evidence that the attacker planned to crash.

Rear Admiral Masafumi Arima, the commander of the 26th Air Flotilla (part of the 11th Air Fleet), is also sometimes credited with inventing the *kamikaze* tactic. Arima personally led an attack by about 100 Yokosuka D4Y *Suisei* ("Judy") dive bombers against a large *Essex*-class aircraft carrier, USS *Franklin* near Leyte Gulf, on (or about, accounts vary) October 15, 1944. Arima was killed and part of a plane hit *Franklin*. The Japanese high command and propagandists seized on Arima's example: he was promoted posthumously to Admiral and was given official credit for making the first *kamikaze* attack. However, it is not clear that this was a planned suicide attack, and official Japanese accounts of Arima's attack bore little resemblance to the actual events.

Masafumi Arima

On October 17, 1944, Allied forces assaulted Suluan Island, beginning the Battle of Leyte Gulf. The Imperial Japanese Navy's 1st Air Fleet, based at Manila, was assigned the task of assisting the Japanese ships which would attempt to destroy Allied forces in Leyte Gulf. However, the 1st Air Fleet at that time only had 40 aircraft: 34 A6M Zero carrier-based fighters, three Nakajima B6N *Tenzan* ("Jill") torpedo bombers, one Mitsubishi G4M ("Betty") and two Yokosuka P1Y *Ginga* ("Frances") land-based bombers, and one additional reconnaissance plane. The task facing the Japanese air forces seemed impossible. The 1st Air Fleet commandant, Vice Admiral Takijirō Ōnishi decided to form a suicide attack force, the Special Attack Unit. In a meeting at Mabalacat Airfield (known to the U.S. military as Clark Air Base) near Manila, on October 19, Onishi told officers of the 201st Flying Group headquarters: "I don't think there would be any other certain way to carry out the operation [to hold the Philippines], than to put a 250 kg bomb on a Zero and let it crash into a U.S. carrier, in order to disable her for a week."

First kamikaze unit

Commander Asaiki Tamai asked a group of 23 talented student pilots, all of whom he had trained, to volunteer for the special attack force. All of the pilots raised both of their hands, volunteering to join the operation. Later, Tamai asked Lieutenant Yukio Seki to command the special attack force. Seki is said to have closed his eyes, lowered his head and thought for 10 seconds, before saying: "Please do appoint me to the post." Seki became the 24th *kamikaze* pilot to be chosen. However, Seki later said: "Japan's future is bleak if it is forced to kill one of its best pilots." and "I am not going on this mission for the Emperor or for the Empire... I am going because I was ordered to."

The names of four sub-units within the *Kamikaze* Special Attack Force were *Unit Shikishima*, *Unit Yamato*, *Unit Asahi*, and *Unit Yamazakura*. These names were taken from a patriotic poem (waka or tanka), *Shikishima no Yamato-gokoro wo hito towaba, asahi ni niou yamazakura bana* by the Japanese classical scholar, Motoori Norinaga. The poem reads:

> If someone asks about the *Yamato spirit* [Spirit of Old/True Japan] of *Shikishima* [a poetic name for Japan]—it is the flowers of *yamazakura* [mountain cherry blossom] that are fragrant in the *Asahi* [rising sun].

A less literal translation is:

> Asked about the soul of Japan,
>
> I would say
>
> That it is
>
> Like wild cherry blossoms
>
> Glowing in the morning sun.

Leyte Gulf: the first attacks

On October 25, 1944, during the Battle of Leyte Gulf, the *Kamikaze* Special Attack Force carried out its first mission. Five Zeros, led by Seki, and escorted to the target by leading Japanese ace Hiroyoshi Nishizawa, attacked several escort carriers. One Zero attempted to hit the bridge of USS *Kitkun Bay* but instead exploded on the port catwalk and cartwheeled into the sea. Two others dove at USS *Fanshaw Bay* but were destroyed by anti-aircraft fire. The last two ran at USS *White Plains*. One, under heavy fire and trailing smoke, aborted the attempt on *White Plains* and instead banked toward USS *St. Lo*, plowing into the flight deck. Its bomb caused fires that resulted in the bomb magazine exploding, sinking the carrier. By day's end on October 26, 55 *kamikazes* from the special attack force had also damaged the large escort carriers USS *Sangamon*, *Suwannee*, *Santee*, and the smaller escorts USS *White Plains*, *Kalinin Bay*, and *Kitkun Bay*. In total, seven carriers had been hit, as well as 40 other ships (five sunk, 23 heavily damaged, and 12 moderately damaged).

Starboard horizontal stabilizer from the tail of a "Judy" on the deck of USS *Kitkun Bay*. The "Judy" made a run on the ship approaching from dead astern, it was met by effective fire and the plane passed over the island and exploded. Parts of the plane and the pilot were scattered over the flight deck and the forecastle.

Several suicide attacks during the early days of the Leyte Gulf operation have incorrectly been claimed as the first *kamikaze* attack. Early on October 21, while covering the invasion of Leyte, a Japanese aircraft (variously described as an Aichi D3A dive-bomber or a Mitsubishi Ki-51 of the 6th Flying Brigade, Imperial Japanese Army Air Force) deliberately crashed into the foremast of the heavy cruiser HMAS *Australia*. The attack killed 30 (including the cruiser's Captain, Emile Dechaineux) and wounded 64, including Australian force commander Commodore John Collins. The crash is claimed to be the first *kamikaze* attack on an Allied ship in the official war history of the RAN, and repeated in other sources, although the Special Attack Group did not begin operations until four days later: the crash was the decision of the pilot, not an action he was ordered to commit. The sinking of the ocean tug USS *Sonoma* on October 24 is listed in some sources as the first ship lost to a *kamikaze* strike, but the attack occurred before October 25, and the aircraft used, a Mitsubishi G4M, was not flown by the original four Special Attack Squadrons.

The bridge and forward turrets of the *County*-class heavy cruiser HMAS *Australia*, in September 1944. The officer facing right is Captain Emile Dechaineux, killed on October 21, 1944 in what is incorrectly reported as the first *kamikaze* attack.

Main wave of attacks

Early successes – such as the sinking of *St. Lo* – were followed by an immediate expansion of the program, and over the next few months over 2,000 planes made such attacks.

When Japan began to be subject to intense strategic bombing by B-29s, the Japanese military attempted to use suicide attacks against this threat. During the northern hemisphere winter of 1944-45, the IJAAF formed the 47th Air Regiment, also known as the *Shinten* Special Unit (*Shinten Seiku Ta*) at Narimasu Airfield, Nerima, Tokyo, to defend the Tokyo Metropolitan Area. The unit was equipped with Nakajima Ki-44 *Shoki* ("Tojo") fighters, with which they were to ram United States Army Air Forces (USAAF) B-29s in their attacks on Japan. However, this proved much less successful and practical since an airplane is a much faster, more maneuverable, and smaller target than a warship. The B-29 also had formidable defensive weaponry, so suicide attacks against the plane demanded considerable piloting skill to be successful. That worked against the very purpose of using expendable pilots and even encouraging capable pilots to bail out before impact was ineffective because vital personnel were often lost when they mistimed their exits and were killed as a result.

Kamikaze attacks were being planned at far-flung Japanese bases. On January 8, Onishi formed a second official naval *kamikaze* unit, in Formosa.[citation needed] The unit, *Niitaka* used Zeroes and "Judys", and was based at Takao Airfield. On January 29, 1945, seven Kawasaki Ki-48 "Lilys" from the Japanese Army *Shichisi Mitate* Special group, took off from Palembang, Sumatra to strike the British Pacific Fleet. Vice Admiral Kimpei Teraoka and Captain Riishi Sugiyama of the 601st Air Group organized another second special unit, *Mitate* at Iwo Jima on February 16, as a U.S. invasion force approached.[citation needed] On March 11, the U.S. carrier USS *Randolph* was hit and moderately damaged at Ulithi Atoll, in the Caroline Islands, by a *kamikaze* that had flown almost 4000 km (2500 mi) from Japan, in a mission called Operation Tan No. 2. On March 20, the submarine USS *Devilfish* survived a hit from an aircraft, just off Japan.

USS *Columbia* is attacked by a *kamikaze* off Lingayen Gulf, January 6, 1945.

Purpose-built *kamikaze* planes, as opposed to converted fighters and dive-bombers, were also being constructed. Ensign Mitsuo Ohta had suggested that piloted glider bombs, carried within range of targets by a mother plane, should be developed. The First Naval Air Technical Bureau (*Kugisho*), in Yokosuka, refined Ohta's idea. Yokosuka MXY7 *Ohka* rocket planes, launched from bombers, were first deployed in

The *kamikaze* hits *Columbia* at 17:29. The plane and its bomb penetrated two decks before exploding, killing 13 and wounding 44.

kamikaze attacks from March 1945. U.S. personnel gave them the derisive nickname "Baka Bombs" (*baka* is Japanese for "idiot" or "stupid"). A specially-designed propeller plane, the Nakajima Ki-115 *Tsurugi*, was a simple, easily-built aircraft, intended to use up existing stocks of engines, in a wooden airframe. The landing gear was non-retractable: it was jettisoned shortly after take-off for a suicide mission and then re-used on other planes. During 1945, the Japanese military began stockpiling hundreds of *Tsurugi*, other propeller planes, *Ohkas*, and suicide boats, for use against Allied forces expected to invade Japan. Few were ever used.

Allied defensive tactics

In early 1945, Commander John Thach, a U.S. Navy aviator, who was already famous for developing effective aerial tactics against the Japanese such as the Thach Weave, developed a defensive strategy against *kamikazes* called the "big blue blanket". This recommended larger combat air patrols (CAP), further from the carriers than had previously been the case, a line of picket destroyers and destroyer escorts at least 80 km (50 mi) from the main body of the fleet to provide earlier radar interception, and improved coordination between fighter direction officers on carriers. This plan also called for round-the-clock fighter patrols over Allied fleets, though the U.S. Navy had cut back training of fighter pilots, so there were not enough Navy pilots available to counter the *kamikaze* threat. A final element included intensive fighter sweeps over Japanese airfields, and bombing of Japanese runways with delayed action fuses to make repairs more difficult.

An A6M Zero (A6M5 Model 52) towards the end of its run at the escort carrier USS *White Plains* on October 25, 1944. The aircraft exploded in mid-air, moments after the picture was taken, scattering debris across the deck.

Late in 1944, the British Pacific Fleet (BPF) used the good high altitude performance of their Supermarine Seafires on combat air patrol duties. Seafires were heavily involved in countering the *kamikaze* attacks during the Iwo Jima landings and beyond. The Seafires' best day was August 15, 1945, shooting down eight attacking aircraft for a single loss.

Poor training tended to make *kamikaze* pilots easy targets for experienced Allied pilots, who also flew superior aircraft. The U.S. Fast Carrier Task Force alone could bring over 1,000 fighter aircraft into play. Allied pilots became adept at destroying enemy aircraft before they struck ships.

Allied gunners had begun to develop techniques to negate *kamikaze* attacks. They fired their high-caliber guns into the sea in front of attacking planes flying near sea level, in order to create walls of water which would swamp the attacking planes. Light rapid fire anti-aircraft weapons such as the 40 mm Bofors and Oerlikon 20 mm cannons were ineffective, however heavy anti-aircraft guns such as the 5"/38 caliber gun (127 mm) had the punch to blow *kamikazes* out of the air. Although such tactics could not be used against *Okhas* and other fast, high-angle attacks, these were in turn more vulnerable to anti-aircraft fire. In 1945, large amounts of anti-aircraft shells with radio frequency proximity fuzes became available, these were on average seven times more effective than regular shells.

Final phase

Puffs of smoke left by anti-aircraft shells and the splashes left by cannon and machine gun rounds detail the desperate few seconds of a vain struggle, as the USS Louisville is struck by a kamikaze at the Battle of Lingayen Gulf, January 1945.

The Royal Navy carrier HMS Victorious after three successive kamikaze hits, her armoured deck meant that damage was superficial and she was launching planes within one hour of the attack.

The peak in *kamikaze* attacks came during the period of April–June 1945, at the Battle of Okinawa. On April 6, 1945, waves of planes made hundreds of attacks in Operation *Kikusui* ("floating chrysanthemums"). At Okinawa, *kamikaze* attacks focused at first on Allied destroyers on picket duty, and then on the carriers in the middle of the fleet. Suicide attacks by planes or boats at Okinawa sank or put out of action at least 30 U.S. warships, and at least three U.S. merchant ships, along with some from other Allied forces. The attacks expended 1,465 planes. Many warships of all classes were damaged, some severely, but no aircraft carriers, battleships or cruisers were sunk by *kamikaze* at Okinawa. Most of the ships lost were destroyers or smaller vessels, especially those on picket duty.

U.S. carriers, with their wooden flight decks, appeared to suffer more damage from *kamikaze* hits than the reinforced steel-decked carriers from the British Pacific Fleet. US carriers also suffered considerably heavier casualties from *kamikaze* strikes, for instance 389 men were killed in one attack on USS *Bunker Hill* and this is greater than the combined number of fatal casualties suffered on all six RN armoured carriers from all forms of attack for the entire war; eight *kamikaze* hits on five RN carriers resulted in only twenty fatal casualties while a combined total of 15 bomb hits, most of 500 kg weight or greater, and one torpedo hit on 4 carriers caused 193 fatal casualties earlier in the war - striking proof of the protective value of the armoured flight deck. The resilience of well-armoured vessels was shown on May 4, just after 11:30, when there was a wave of suicide attacks against the BPF. One Japanese plane made a steep dive from "a great height" at the carrier HMS *Formidable* and was engaged by AA guns. Although it was hit by gunfire, the *kamikaze* crashed into the flight deck, making a crater 3 m (9.8 ft) long, 0.6 m (2 ft) wide and 0.6 m (2 ft) deep. A long steel splinter speared down, through the hangar deck and the main boiler room (where it ruptured a steam line), before coming to rest in a fuel tank near the aircraft park, where it started a major fire. Eight personnel were killed and 47 were wounded. One Corsair and 10 Avengers were destroyed. However, the fires were gradually brought under control, and the crater in the deck was repaired with concrete and steel plate. By 17:00, Corsairs were able to land. On May 9, *Formidable* was again damaged by a *kamikaze*, as were the carrier HMS *Victorious* and the battleship HMS *Howe*. The British were able to clear the flight deck and resume flight operations in just hours, while their American counterparts took a few days or even months, as observed by a USN liaison officer on HMS *Indefatigable* who commented: "When a kamikaze hits a U.S. carrier it means 6 months of repair at Pearl [Harbor]. When a kamikaze hits a Limey carrier it's just a case of "Sweepers, man your brooms.""

Sometimes twin-engined aircraft were used in planned *kamikaze* attacks. For example, Mitsubishi Ki-67 *Hiryū* ("Peggy") medium bombers, based on Formosa, undertook *kamikaze* attacks on Allied forces off Okinawa.

Rear Admiral Matome Ugaki, the second in command of the Combined Pacific Fleet, directed the last official *kamikaze* attack, sending "Judies" from the 701st Air Group against the Allied fleet at Okinawa on August 15, 1945.

Effects

As the end of the war approached, the Allies did not suffer significantly more serious losses, despite having far more ships and facing a greater intensity of *kamikaze* attacks. Although causing some of the heaviest casualties on US carriers in 1945, the IJN had sacrificed 2,525 *kamikaze* pilots and the IJAAF 1,387; far more than they had lost in 1942 where they sunk or crippled three carriers (albeit without inflicting significant casualties). In 1942 when US Navy vessels were scarce, the temporary absence of key warships from the combat zone would tie up operational initiatives. However, by 1945, the US Navy was large enough that damaged ships could be detached back home for repair without significantly hampering the fleet's operational capability. The only surface losses were destroyers and smaller ships that lacked the capability to sustain heavy damage. Overall, the *kamikazes* were unable to turn the tide of the war and stop the Allied invasion. The destructive potential of the *kamikaze* sustained postwar funding of Operation Bumblebee until the RIM-8 Talos guided missile became operational in 1959.

A crewman in an AA gun aboard the battleship *New Jersey* watches a *kamikaze* plane descend upon *Intrepid* November 25, 1944

In the immediate aftermath of kamikaze strikes, British carriers with their armoured flight decks appeared to recover more quickly compared to their US counterparts. However, post-war analysis showed that some British carriers such as HMS *Formidable* did suffer structural damage that led them to be written off and scrapped, as beyond economic repair, but Britain's dire post war finances and the constantly declining size of the Royal Navy undoubtedly played a role in deciding not to repair damaged carriers. By contrast, even the most seriously damaged American carriers such USS *Bunker Hill* were successfully repaired to good condition, although they saw no service after WWII as they were considered surplus.

The number of ships sunk is a matter of debate. According to a wartime Japanese propaganda announcement, the missions sank 81 ships and damaged 195, and according to a Japanese tally, suicide attacks accounted for up to 80% of the U.S. losses in the final phase of the war in the Pacific. In a 2004 book, *World War II*, the historians Wilmott, Cross and Messenger stated that more than 70 U.S. vessels were "sunk or damaged beyond repair" by *kamikazes*.

According to a U.S Air Force webpage:

> Approximately 2,800 Kamikaze attackers sunk 34 Navy ships, damaged 368 others, killed 4,900 sailors, and wounded over 4,800. Despite radar detection and cuing, airborne interception and attrition, and massive anti-aircraft barrages, a distressing 14 percent of Kamikazes survived to score a hit on a ship; nearly 8.5 percent of all ships hit by Kamikazes sank.

Australian journalists Denis and Peggy Warner, in a 1982 book with Japanese naval historian Seno Sadao (*The Sacred Warriors: Japan's Suicide Legions*), arrived at a total of 57 ships sunk by *kamikazes*. However, Bill Gordon, an American Japanologist who specialises in *kamikazes*, states in a 2007 article that 47 ships were sunk by *kamikaze* aircraft. Gordon says that the Warners and Seno included ten ships that did not sink. His list consists of:

- three escort carriers: *St. Lo*, *Ommaney Bay*, *Bismarck Sea*
- 14 destroyers, including the last ship to be sunk, *Callaghan* on July 29, 1945, off Okinawa
- three high-speed transport ships
- five Landing Ship, Tank
- four Landing Ship Medium
- three Landing Ship Medium (Rocket)
- one auxiliary tanker
- three Canadian Victory ships
- three Liberty ships
- two high-speed minesweepers
- one Auk class minesweeper
- one submarine chaser
- two PT boats
- two Landing Craft Support

Recruitment

Japanese Yokosuka MXY-7 *Ohka* ("cherry blossom"), a specially built rocket-powered *kamikaze* aircraft used towards the end of the war. The U.S. called them *Baka* ("idiot").

The establishment of *kamikaze* forces required recruiting men for the task; this proved easier than the commanders had expected. Qualifications were simple: "youth, alertness and zeal. Flight experience was of minimal importance and expertise in landing a luxury". Captain Motoharu Okamura commented that "there were so many volunteers for suicide missions that he referred to them as a swarm of bees," explaining: "Bees die after they have stung." Okamura is credited with being the first to propose the *kamikaze* attacks. He had expressed his desire to lead a volunteer group of suicide attacks some four months before Admiral Takijiro Ohnishi, commander of the Japanese naval air forces in the Philippines, presented the idea to his staff. While Vice Admiral Shigeru Fukudome, commander of the second air fleet, was inspecting the 341st Air Group, Captain Okamura took the chance to express his ideas on crash-dive tactics. "In our present situation I firmly believe that the only way to swing the war in our favor is to resort to crash-dive attacks with our planes. There is no other way. There will be more than enough volunteers for this chance to save our country, and I would like to command such an operation. Provide me with 300 planes and I will turn the tide of war."

When the volunteers arrived for duty in the corps there were twice as many persons as aircraft. "After the war, some commanders would express regret for allowing superfluous crews to accompany sorties, sometimes squeezing themselves aboard bombers and fighters so as to encourage the suicide pilots and, it seems, join in the exultation of sinking a large enemy vessel." Many of the *kamikaze* pilots believed their death would pay the debt they owed and show the love they had for their families, friends, and emperor. "So eager were many minimally trained pilots to take part in suicide missions that when their sorties were delayed or aborted, the pilots became deeply despondent. Many of those who were selected for a bodycrashing mission were described as being extraordinarily blissful immediately before their final sortie."

Training

> When you eliminate all thoughts about life and death, you will be able to totally disregard your earthly life. This will also enable you to concentrate your attention on eradicating the enemy with unwavering determination, meanwhile reinforcing your excellence in flight skills.
>
> —An excerpt from a kamikaze pilots' manual.

Tokkōtai pilot training, as described by Kasuga Takeo,[citation needed] generally "consisted of incredibly strenuous training, coupled with cruel and torturous corporal punishment as a daily routine." Irokawa Daikichi, who trained at Tsuchiura Naval Air Base, recalled that he "was struck on the face so hard and frequently that [his] face was no longer recognizable." He also wrote: "I was hit so hard that I could no longer see and fell on the floor. The minute I got up, I was hit again by a club so that I would confess." This brutal "training" was justified by the idea that it would instill a "soldier's fighting spirit." However, daily beatings and corporal punishment eliminated patriotism among many pilots.

Pilots were given a manual which detailed how they were supposed to think, prepare, and attack. From this manual, pilots were told to "attain a high level of spiritual training," and to "keep [their] health in the very best condition." These things, among others, were meant to put the pilot into the mindset in which he would be mentally ready to die.

The *tokkōtai* pilot's manual also explained how a pilot may turn back if the pilot could not locate a target and that "[a pilot] should not waste [his] life lightly." However, one pilot who continually came back to base was shot after his ninth return.

We tried to live with 120 percent intensity, rather than waiting for death. We read and read, trying to understand why we had to die in our early twenties. We felt the clock ticking away towards our death, every sound of the clock shortening our lives.

Irokawa Daikichi, *Kamikaze Diaries: Reflections of Japanese Student Soldiers*

The manual was very detailed in how a pilot should attack. A pilot would dive towards his target and "aim for a point between the bridge tower and the smoke stacks". Entering a smoke stack was also said to be "effective". Pilots were told not to aim at a ship's bridge tower or gun turret but instead to look for elevators or the flight deck to crash into. For horizontal attacks, the pilot was to "aim at the middle of the vessel, slightly higher than the waterline" or to "aim at the entrance to the aircraft hangar, or the bottom of the stack" if the former was too difficult.

The *tokkōtai* pilot's manual told pilots never to close their eyes. This was because if a pilot closed his eyes he would lower the chances of hitting his target. In the final moments before the crash, the pilot was to yell "*Hissatsu*" at the top of his lungs which roughly translates to "sink without fail".

Cultural background

In 1944–45, the Japanese were heavily influenced by Shinto beliefs. Among other things, Emperor worship was stressed after Shinto was established as a state religion during the Meiji Restoration. As time went on, Shinto was used increasingly in the promotion of nationalist sentiment. In 1890, the Imperial Rescript on Education was passed, under which students were required to ritually recite its oath to offer themselves "courageously to the State" as well as protect the Imperial family. The ultimate offering was to give up one's life. It was an honor to die for Japan and the Emperor. Axell and Kase pointed out: "The fact is that innumerable soldiers, sailors and pilots were determined to die, to become eirei, that is 'guardian spirits' of the country. [...] Many Japanese felt that to be enshrined at Yasukuni was a special honour because the Emperor twice a year visited the shrine to pay homage. Yasukuni is the only shrine, deifying common men, which the Emperor would visit to pay his respects". Young

Japanese people were indoctrinated from an earliest age with these ideals.

Following the commencement of the *kamikaze* tactic, newspapers and books ran advertisements, articles, and stories regarding the suicide bombers, to aid in recruiting and support. In October 1944, the *Nippon Times* quoted Lieutenant Sekio Nishina: "The spirit of the Special Attack Corps is the great spirit that runs in the blood of every Japanese.... The crashing action which simultaneously kills the enemy and oneself without fail is called the Special Attack.... Every Japanese is capable of becoming a member of the Special Attack Corps". Publishers also played up the idea that the *kamikaze* were enshrined at Yasukuni and ran exaggerated stories of *kamikaze* bravery – there were even fairy tales for little children that promoted the *kamikaze*. A Foreign Office official named Toshikazu Kase said: "It was customary for GHQ [in Tokyo] to make false announcements of victory in utter disregard of facts, and for the elated and complacent public to believe them".

While many stories were falsified, some were true, such as the story of Kiyu Ishikawa who saved a Japanese ship when he crashed his plane into a torpedo that an American submarine had launched. The sergeant major was posthumously promoted to second lieutenant by the emperor and was enshrined at Yasukuni. Stories like these, which showed the kind of praise and honor death produced, encouraged young Japanese to volunteer for the Special Attack Corps and instilled a desire in the youth to die as a *kamikaze*.

Ceremonies were carried out before *kamikaze* pilots departed on their final mission. They were given the flag of Japan or the rising sun flag (Japanese naval ensign), inscribed with inspirational and spiritual words, Nambu pistol or katana and drank sake before they took off generally. They put on a *hachimaki* headband with the rising sun, and a *senninbari*, a "belt of a thousand stitches" sewn by a thousand women who made one stitch each. They also composed and read a death poem, a tradition stemming from the samurai, who did it before committing *seppuku*. Pilots carried prayers from their families and were given military decorations.

While commonly perceived that volunteers signed up in droves for *kamikaze* missions, it has also been contended that there was extensive coercion and peer pressure involved in recruiting soldiers for the sacrifice. Their motivations in "volunteering" were complex and not simply about patriotism or bringing honour to their families. And at least one of these pilots was a conscripted Korean with a Japanese name, adopted under the pre-war *Soshi-kaimei* ordinance that compelled Koreans to take Japanese personal names. Out of the 1,036 IJA *kamikaze* pilots who died in sorties from Chiran and other Japanese air bases, during the Battle of Okinawa, 11 were Koreans.

Chiran high school girls wave farewell with cherry blossom branches to departing *kamikaze* pilot in a Ki-43-II *Hayabusa*.

According to legend, young pilots on *kamikaze* missions often flew southwest from Japan over the 922 m (3025 ft) Mount Kaimon. The mountain is also called "*Satsuma Fuji*" (meaning a mountain like

Mount Fuji but located in the Satsuma Province region). Suicide mission pilots looked over their shoulders to see this, the most southern mountain on the Japanese mainland, while they were in the air, said farewell to their country, and saluted the mountain.

Residents on Kikaishima Island, east of Amami Ōshima, say that pilots from suicide mission units dropped flowers from the air as they departed on their final missions. According to legend, the hills above Kikaishima airport have beds of cornflower that bloom in early May.

With the passing of time, some prominent Japanese military figures who survived the war became critical of the policy. Saburo Sakai, an IJN ace said:

> "A kamikaze is a surprise attack, according to our ancient war tactics. Surprise attacks will be successful the first time, maybe two or three times. But what fool would continue the same attacks for ten months? Emperor Hirohito must have realized it. He should have said 'Stop.'
>
> "Even now, many faces of my students come up when I close my eyes. So many students are gone. Why did headquarters continue such silly attacks for ten months! Fools! Genda, who went to America—all those men lied that all men volunteered for kamikaze units. They lied."

In 2006, Tsuneo Watanabe, Editor-in-Chief of the *Yomiuri Shimbun*, criticized Japanese nationalists' glorification of *kamikaze* attacks:

> "It's all a lie that they left filled with braveness and joy, crying, 'Long live the emperor!' They were sheep at a slaughterhouse. Everybody was looking down and tottering. Some were unable to stand up and were carried and pushed into the plane by maintenance soldiers."

Quotations

> I cannot predict the outcome of the air battles but you will be making a mistake if you should regard Special Attack operations as normal methods. The right way is to attack the enemy with skill and return to the base with good results. A plane should be utilized over and over again. That's the way to fight a war. The current thinking is skewed. Otherwise you cannot expect to improve air power. There will be no progress if flyers continue to die.
>
> —Lieutenant Commander Iwatani, Taiyo (Ocean) magazine, March 1945.

> *Zwei Seelen wohnen auch in mein[em] Herz*!! (Ah, two souls [tamashi'i] reside in my heart [kokoro]!!) After all I am just a human being. Sometimes my chest pounds with excitement when I think of the day I will fly into the sky. I trained my mind and body as hard as I could and am anxious for the day I can use them to their full capacity in fighting. I think my life and death belong to the mission. Yet, at other times, I envy those science majors who remain at home [exempt from the draft]. ... One of my souls looks to heaven, while the other is attracted to the

earth. I wish to enter the Navy as soon as possible so that I can devote myself to the task. I hope that the days when I am tormented by stupid thoughts will pass quickly.

—Sasaki Hachiro

It is easy to talk about death in the abstract, as the ancient philosophers discussed. But it is real death I fear, and I don't know if I can overcome the fear. Even for a short life, there are many memories. For someone who had a good life, it is very difficult to part with it. But I reached a point of no return. I must plunge into an enemy vessel.

To be honest, I cannot say that the wish to die for the emperor is genuine, coming from my heart. However, it is decided for me that I die for the emperor.

—Hayashi Ichizo

Film

Saigo no Tokkotai aka The Last Kamikaze (1970) - Directed by Yahagi Toshihiko and Starring Koji Tsuruta, Ken Takakura and Shinichi Chiba

See also

- Banzai charge
- Bushidō
- Giretsu
- Living torpedoes
- Ramming
- Suicide weapon
- "*Umi yukaba*"
- Vehicle explosion

References

Bibliography

- Axell, Albert; Hideaki, Kase (2002). *Kamikaze: Japan's suicide gods*. New York: Longman. ISBN 0-582-77232-X.
- Brown, David (1990). *Fighting Elites: Kamikaze*. New York: Gallery Books. ISBN 9780831726713.
- Hobbes, Nicholas (2003). *Essential militaria*. London: Atlantic Books. ISBN 9781843542292.
- Hoyt, Edwin P. (1993). *The Last Kamikaze*. Praeger. ISBN 0-275-94067-5.
- Inoguchi, Rikihei; Nakajima, Tadashi and Pineau, Roger (1959). *The Divine Wind*. London: Hutchinson & Co. (Publishers) Ltd..
- Mahon, John K. (May 1959). *The Pacific Historical Review*. Vol. 28, No. 2.

- Millot, Bernard (1971). *Divine Thunder: The life and death of the Kamikazes*. Macdonald. OCLC 8142990 [1]. ISBN 0-356-03856-4.
- Ohnuki-Tierney, Emiko. (2006). *Kamikaze Diaries: Reflections of Japanese Student Soldiers*. Chicago and London: The University of Chicago Press. ISBN 9780226619507
- Sheftall, Mordecai G. (2005). *Blossoms in the Wind: Human Legacies of the Kamikaze*. NAL Caliber. ISBN 0-451-21487-0.
- Toland, John (1970). *The rising sun; the decline and fall of the Japanese Empire, 1936-1945.*. New York: Random House. OCLC 105915 [2].
- Ugaki, Matome; Masataka Chihaya (Translator) (1991). *Fading Victory: The Diary of Admiral Matome Ugaki, 1941-1945* [3]. University of Pittsburgh Press. ISBN 0-8229-3665-8.
- Warner, Denis & Peggy; Sadao Seno (1984; first published 1982). *The Sacred Warriors: Japan's Suicide Legions* [4]. Avon Books (previously Van Nostrand Reinhold). ISBN 0-380-67678-8.
- Willmott, H.P; Cross, Robin & Messenger, Charles (2004). *World War II*. London: Dorling Kindersley. ISBN 9781405305877.

Further reading

- Ohnuki-Tierney, Emiko (2006). *Kamikaze Diaries: Reflections of Japanese Student Soldiers*. University of Chicago Press. ISBN 9780226619514.
- Ohnuki-Tierney, Emiko (2002). *Kamikaze, Cherry Blossoms, and Nationalisms: The Militarization of Aesthetics in Japanese History*. University of Chicago Press. ISBN 9780226620916.

External links

- Kamikaze Images [5] – Explores different Western and Japanese portrayals and perceptions of kamikaze pilots.
- Personal website of Mr Nobu [6]
- Dayofthekamikaze.com [7]
- An ex-kamikaze pilot creates a new world [8]
- "Gyokusai" [9]
- "Who became Kamikaze Pilots..." [10]
- www.tokkotai.or.jp [11]
- "The kamikaze pilot who chose life before empire" [12]
- Excerpt from *Kamikaze Diaries* [13]
- The End of Kamikaze [14] (Japanese)
- Day of the Kamikaze, Smithsonian Networks [15]
- "Ascent of the Fireflies" [16], TIME about Tome Torihama called "Kamikaze Mom"
- TOEI movie "I will die only for you above all" [17] (Orewa Kimi no tamenikoso Shiniyuku / 俺は、君のためにこそ死ににいく) about Tome Torihama ("Kamikaze Mom"), the Chiran high

school girls and young Army kamikaze pilots flying Ki-43 Hayabusa fighters, DVD [18] (2007)
- WW2DB: Kamikaze Doctrine [19]
- What motivated the Kamikazes? [20] on WW2History.com
- The Rising Sun Pins Its Hope on Jap Suicide Killers [21] propaganda article in June 1945 Popular Science in attempt to downplay the Kamikazes

Shinyo (suicide boat)

The *Shin'yō* (Japanese: 震洋, "Sea Quake") were Japanese suicide boats developed during World War II. They were part of the wider Japanese Special Attack Units program.

Characteristics

These fast motorboats were driven by one man, to speeds of around 30 knots. They were typically equipped with two depth charges as explosives or a bow-mounted explosive charge. Those equipped with depth charges were not actually suicide boats, as the idea was to drop the depth charges and then turn around before the explosion took place. However, the wave from the explosion would probably have killed the crew, or at least swamped the boat.

Japanese *Shin'yō* suicide boat, 1945

A *Shin'yō* under way, being tested by Lt Col James F. Doyle USA commanding officer 2nd Bn. 305th Inf. 77th Div.

Approximately 6,200 *Shin'yō* were produced for the Imperial Japanese Navy and 3,000 *Maru-ni* for the Imperial Japanese Army. Around 400 boats were transported to Okinawa and Formosa, and the rest were stored on the coast of Japan for the ultimate defense against the expected invasion of the Home islands.

Operational results

- January 10, 1945: Sinking of American ships USS LCI(G)-365 (Landing Craft Infantry - Gunboat), USS LCI(M)-974 (Landing Craft Infantry - Mortar) and crippling of USS *War Hawk* (an auxiliary transport) in Lingayen Gulf, Luzon, Philippines.
- January 31, 1945: Sinking of USS PC-1129 (Submarine chaser) off Nasugbu in Luzon, Philippines.
- February 16, 1945. Sinking of USS LCS(L)-7 (Landing Craft Support - Large), LCS(L)-26, and LCS(L)-49 off Mariveles, Corregidor Channel, Luzon.
- April 4, 1945. Sinking of USS LCI(G)-82 (Landing Craft Infantry - Gunboat) and USS LSM-12 (Landing Ship Medium) off Okinawa.
- April 27, 1945. Crippling of USS Hutchins (DD-476) in Buckner Bay, Okinawa.

External links

- Japanese suicide weapons [1]
- *Grave markers at sea: Record of sea-based special attack shinyo boats* [2] - review of memoir written by former *Shin'yō* pilot

Suicide weapon

A **suicide weapon** is a weapon that is specially designed for a suicide attack. It is typically based on explosives.

In a wider sense, a suicide weapon is any weapon used in a suicide attack, and any object used as such, for example an aircraft.

Examples:

- Suicide bombs
- Kamikaze air attacks by Japan in WWII
- Kaiten human-steered torpedo, used by Japan in WWII

It might also be argued that the doctrine of mutual assured destruction has turned nuclear weapons into suicide weapons. The idea of a Doomsday weapon took this to its logical extreme.

Today, the most common suicide weapons are antipersonnel bombs carried by a single person. Such bombs are typically used to carry out terrorist attacks (suicide bombings are less common, although not unknown, in conventional warfare). Suicide bombers strap explosives (often covered with nails, screws, or other items intended to act as fragments) to their bodies (see explosive belt) or otherwise carry them into populated areas and detonate them. The Tamil Tigers of Sri Lanka invented and refined this method, which was adopted by (among others) Palestinian terrorist groups in the Israeli-Palestinian conflict.

The Pacific War of World War II bore witness to the Japanese Kamikaze suicide attack pilots. Late in the war, as the tide turned against Japan, Kamikaze pilots were deployed to attempt to crash their aircraft into American ships in the Pacific. The Japanese even developed specialized aircraft (the Ohka) for the tactic. (Nazi Germany also developed suicide planes (the Selbstopfer), although their designs included a feature for the pilot to escape, and it is unlikely that they ever saw combat.) A successful Kamikaze attack would both kill the plane's pilot and sink the target ship. Related tactics included the Kaiten suicide minisub, which a single Japanese pilot would steer into an American ship.

Kamikaze attacks were mimicked in the September 11, 2001 attacks, in which terrorists destroyed the World Trade Center and part of The Pentagon by flying hijacked civilian aircraft into them.

See also
- Suicide attack tactics
- Japanese Special Attack Units

External links
- *Suicide Squads: The Men and Machines of World War II Special Operations* [1] - book review
- Japanese suicide weapon: Human torpedo *Kaiten* and Human Bomb *Ohoka* [2] (Japanese)

Mass Suicide

Mass suicide

Suicide
Social aspects
Legislation · Philosophy Religious views · Euthanasia Assisted suicide · Right to die Benevolent suicide
Suicide crisis
Assessment of risk · Crisis hotline · Intervention · Prevention · Suicide watch
Suicide types
Copycat · Cult · Euthanasia · Familicide · Forced · Honor · Internet · Mass · Murder–suicide · Parasuicide · Suicide attack · By cop · Pact
Epidemiology
Gender · Suicide rate
History
List of suicides · Suicide methods
Related phenomena
Ideation · Self-harm · Suicide note · Locations · Failed suicide attempt
By country
China · Japan · South Korea · United States

Mass suicide occurs when a number of people kill themselves together for the same reason.

Examples

Mass suicide sometimes occurs in religious or cultic settings. Suicide missions, suicide bombers, and kamikazes are military or paramilitary forms of mass suicide. Defeated groups may resort to mass suicide rather than being captured. Suicide pacts are a form of mass suicide unconnected to cults or war that are sometimes planned or carried out by small groups of frustrated people, typically lovers [citation needed]. Mass suicides have been used as a form of political protest.

Notable mass suicides

- During the late 2nd century BC, the Teutons are recorded as marching south through Gaul along with their neighbors, the Cimbri, and attacking Roman Italy. After several victories for the invading armies, the Cimbri and Teutones were then defeated by Gaius Marius in 102 BC at the Battle of Aquae Sextiae (near present-day Aix-en-Provence). Their King, Teutobod, was taken in irons. The captured women committed mass suicide, which passed into Roman legends of Germanic heroism: by the conditions of the surrender three hundred of their married women were to be handed over to the Romans. When the Teuton matrons heard of this stipulation, they first begged the consul that they might be set apart to minister in the temples of Ceres and Venus; then, when they failed to obtain their request and were removed by the lictors, they slew their children and next morning were all found dead in each other's arms having strangled themselves in the night.
- At the end of the fifteen months of the siege of Numantia in summer 133 BC most of the defeated Numantines, instead of surrendering, preferred to commit suicide and set fire to the city.
- The 960 members of the Sicarii Jewish community at Masada, who collectively committed suicide in 73 AD, rather than be conquered and enslaved by the Romans. Each man killed his wife and children, then the men drew lots and killed each other until the last man killed himself.
- The occasional practice of mass suicide known as Jauhar was carried out in medieval times by Rajput communities in India, when the fall of a city besieged by Muslim invaders was certain, in order to avoid capture and dishonour. The best known cases of Jauhar are the three occurrences at the fort of Chittaur in Rajasthan, in 1303, in 1535, and 1568.
- In 1336, when the castle of Pilėnai (in Lithuania) was besieged by the army of the Teutonic Knights, the defenders, led by the Duke Margiris, realized that it was impossible to defend themselves any longer and made the decision to commit mass suicide, as well as to set the castle on fire in order to destroy all of their possessions, and anything of value to the enemy.
- During the Turkish rule of Greece and shortly before the Greek War of Independence, women from Souli, pursued by the Ottomans, ascended the mount Zalongo, threw their children over the precipice and then jumped themselves, to avoid capture.
- On 1 May 1945, about 1,000 residents of Demmin, Germany, committed mass suicide after the Red Army had sacked the town.

- A Balinese mass ritual suicide is called a puputan. Major puputan occurred in 1906-1908 when Balinese kingdoms faced overwhelming Dutch colonial forces. The root of the Balinese term *puputan* is *puput*, meaning 'finishing' or 'ending'. It is an act that is more symbolic than strategic; the Balinese are "a people whose genius for theatre is unsurpassed" and a puputan is viewed as "the last act of a tragic dance-drama".
- Japan is known for its centuries of suicide tradition, from seppuku ceremonial self-disemboweling to kamikaze warriors flying their aircraft into Allied warships during World War II. During this same war, the Japanese falsely stated to the people of Saipan that the invading American troops were going to torture and murder anyone on the island. In a desperate effort to avoid this, the people of Saipan committed suicide, mainly by jumping off the nearby cliffsides.
- The Jonestown suicides in Guyana, where 909 members of the Peoples Temple, led by Jim Jones, died in 1978. Of the 918 dead (including four in Georgetown and five non-members at an airstrip), 276 were children. On a tape of their final meeting, Jones tells Temple members that the Soviet Union, with whom the Temple had been negotiating a potential exodus for months, would not take them after the Temple had murdered Congressman Leo Ryan, NBC reporter Don Harris and three others at a nearby airstrip. When members apparently cried during what the Temple called "revolutionary suicide," Jones counseled "Stop this hysterics. This is not the way for people who are Socialists or Communists to die. No way for us to die. We must die with some dignity."
- The Order of the Solar Temple mass suicide killed 74 people in two towns in Switzerland and one in Canada in October 1994. About two thirds of the deaths were murders, including the ritual murder of a newborn child.
- The Heaven's Gate mass suicide occurred in a hilltop mansion near San Diego, California, in 1997. They were mistakenly reported to believe an alien spaceship was following in the tail of the Comet Hale-Bopp and that killing themselves was necessary to reach it. They were cited on their website as wishing to reach the next plane of existence. The victims were self-drugged and then suffocated by other members in a series of suicides over a period of three days. Thirty-nine died, from a wide range of backgrounds.
- The 778 deaths of members of the Ugandan group Movement for the Restoration of the Ten Commandments of God, on March 17, 2000, is considered to be a mass murder and suicide orchestrated by leaders of the group.
- In April 2009, about 1,500 Indian farmers committed a large number of individual suicides due to crop debts.

See also

- Cult suicide
- The Lemming Suicide Myth
- Mass hysteria
- Suicide epidemic

References

- Pringle, Robert (2004). *Bali: Indonesia's Hindu Realm; A short history of*. Short History of Asia Series. Allen & Unwin. ISBN 1-86508-863-3.

External links

- Cult Mass Suicide [1]
- 39 men die in mass suicide near San Diego [2] - CNN, March 26, 1997
- Near-Death Experience [3] Time.com January 19, 1998

Suicide mission

The term **suicide mission** commonly refers to a task which is so dangerous for the people involved that they are not expected to survive. The term is sometimes extended to, but is not limited to, suicide attacks such as kamikaze and suicide bombings, where the people involved actively commit suicide during the execution. The risks involved with suicide missions are not always apparent to those participating in them or to those who plan them. However, for an action to be considered a suicide mission someone involved must be aware of the risks. A mission that goes horribly wrong is not a suicide mission. An individual or group taking part in a mission may perceive the risks involved to be far greater than what they believe to be acceptable, while those planning or commanding the mission may think otherwise. These situations can often lead to refusals to participate in missions on the basis that they are "suicide missions". Similarly, planners or commanders may be well aware of the risks involved with missions while those participating in them may not.

In a military context, soldiers can be ordered to perform very dangerous tasks or can undertake them on their own initiative. In October 2004, during the Iraq War, 19 soldiers in the US Army refused orders to drive unarmored fuel trucks near Baghdad, calling the task a "suicide mission". Those soldiers faced investigations for breakdown of discipline. In the First World War, French soldiers mutinied en masse in 1917 after appalling losses convinced them that their participation at the front would inevitably lead to their deaths. At the same time, many groups voluntarily undertake suicide missions in times of war. Both the Waffen SS and the Imperial Japanese Army were known for executing what could be labeled as suicide missions throughout the Second World War. Suicide missions can also be an act of desperation, such as a last stand. The latter end of the Battle of Stalingrad could be seen as a suicide mission from the German perspective, as they were ordered to fight to the death with no option of surrendering and no chance of escape.

Special Forces groups are often sent on missions that are exceedingly dangerous with the hope that their superior training and abilities will allow them to complete them successfully and survive. An example is the desperate attempt by two U.S. Delta Force snipers to protect a downed helicopter pilot from being killed or captured by masses of Somali militia during the Battle of Mogadishu in 1993. While the sniper team held off overwhelming numbers of Somalis long enough for the pilot to survive, both were killed and the pilot was eventually captured but then later released. However, even special forces groups refuse to participate in some missions. During the 1982 Falklands War, a plan for an SAS raid on Río Grande, Tierra del Fuego was ultimately not executed, due in part to significant hostility from members of the SAS who saw the mission as exceedingly risky.

Armed hostage takings, particularly those planned (e.g. by a terrorist group) for political purposes, could be considered suicide missions. As most governments have a policy of refusing to negotiate with terrorists, such incidents usually end with a bloody confrontation between the hostage takers and an armed force (police, military etc.) attempting to free the hostages. In addition, such hostage takings often occur in a country foreign to those participating in it, making their chances of escape very limited. Notable examples include the 1972 Munich massacre, the 1980 Iranian Embassy Siege and the Beslan school hostage crisis. All of these high profile hostage takings ended with the hostage takers being engaged by the military forces of the country in which the incident occurred, with the vast majority of the hostage takers being killed in the aftermath. The extent to which the hostage takers in each incident expected to survive or simply desired to capitalize on their publicity to send a message is a matter of speculation.

See also

- Forlorn hope

Suicide epidemic

Suicide
Social aspects
Legislation · Philosophy Religious views · Euthanasia Assisted suicide · Right to die Benevolent suicide
Suicide crisis
Assessment of risk · Crisis hotline · Intervention · Prevention · Suicide watch
Suicide types
Copycat · Cult · Euthanasia · Familicide · Forced · Honor · Internet · Mass · Murder–suicide · Parasuicide · Suicide attack · By cop · Pact
Epidemiology
Gender · Suicide rate
History
List of suicides · Suicide methods
Related phenomena
Ideation · Self-harm · Suicide note · Locations · Failed suicide attempt
By country
China · Japan · South Korea · United States

A **suicide epidemic** is an epidemic of suicides. Such epidemics have occurred in the former Soviet Union in the 1990s; among police officers; on Indian reservations; in Micronesia; The Werther effect occurs when suicides that are made publicly known encourage others to imitate them. It has been suggested that the teaching of stories such as *Romeo and Juliet* may encourage suicide among young people.

See also

- Mass suicide
- Epidemiology of suicide

Peer pressure

Peer pressure refers to the influence exerted by a peer group in encouraging a person to change his or her attitudes, values, or behavior in order to conform to group norms. Social groups affected include *membership groups*, when the individual is "formally" a member (for example, political party, trade union), or a social clique. A person affected by peer pressure may or may not want to belong to these groups. They may also recognize *dissociative groups* with which they would *not* wish to associate, and thus they behave adversely concerning that group's behaviors.[citation needed]

In young people

Youth peer pressure is one of the most frequently referred to forms of peer pressure. It is particularly common because most young people spend large amounts of time in fixed groups (schools and subgroups within them) regardless of their opinion of those groups. In addition to this, they may lack the maturity to handle pressure from 'friends'. Also, young people are more willing to behave negatively towards those who are not members of their own peer groups. However, youth peer pressure can also have positive effects. For example, if one is involved with a group of people that are ambitious and working to succeed, one might feel pressured to follow suit to avoid feeling excluded from the group. Therefore, the youth would be pressured into improving themselves, bettering them in the long run. This is most commonly seen in youths that are active in sports or other extracurricular activities where conformity with one's peer group is strongest. .

Risk behavior

While socially accepted children fare the best in high school due to having the most resources, the most opportunities and the most positive experiences, research shows that being in the popular crowd may also be a risk factor for mild to moderate deviant behavior. Popular adolescents are the most socialized into their peer groups and thus are vulnerable to peer pressures, such as behaviors usually reserved for those of a greater maturity and understanding, such as the use of drugs. Adolescence is a time of experimentation with new identities and experiences. The culture of high school often has its own social norms that are different from the outside culture. Some of these norms may not be especially positive or beneficial. Socially accepted kids are often accepted for the sheer fact that they conform well to the norms of teen culture, good and bad aspects included. Popular adolescents are more strongly associated with their peer groups in which they may together experiment with things like alcohol, cigarettes and drugs. Although there are a few risk factors correlated with popularity, deviant behavior is often only mild to moderate. Regardless, social acceptance provides more overall protective factors than risk factors.

The Third Wave was an experiment to demonstrate the appeal of fascism undertaken by history teacher Ron Jones with sophomore high school students attending his Contemporary History as part of a study of Nazi Germany. The experiment took place at Cubberley High School in Palo Alto, California, during the first week of April 1967. Jones, unable to explain to his students how the German populace could claim ignorance of the extermination of the Jewish people, decided to show them instead. Jones started a movement called "The Third Wave" and convinced his students that the movement is to eliminate democracy. The fact that democracy emphasizes individuality was considered as a drawback of democracy, and Jones emphasized this main point of the movement in its motto: "Strength through discipline, strength through community, strength through action, strength through pride". The Third Wave experiment is an example of risk behavior in authoritarian and peer pressure situations.

Benign peer pressure

Management

In management, benign peer pressure refers to a technique used to boost team members' motivation, proactiveness and self goal settings. It's one useful tool in leadership. Instead of direct delegation of tasks and results demanding, employees are in this case, induced into a behaviour of self propelled performance and innovation, by comparison feelings towards their peers. There are several ways peer pressure can be induced in a working environment. Examples are: training, team meetings. *Training* since the team member is in contact with people with comparable roles in other organizations. Team meetings since there will be an implicit comparison between every team member especially if the meeting agenda is the presentation of results and goal status.

School

In school, benign peer pressure refers to the achieving of school discipline and internal self-discipline (inner discipline within each individual) by democratic means. It is adduced that appropriate school learning theory and educational philosophy is decisive in preventing violence, and promoting learning, order, and discipline in schools. Children should be accorded the same human rights and freedoms as adults; they should be granted responsibility for the conduct of their affairs; and they should be full participants in the life of their community. Children of all ages are entitled to participate in all decisions affecting the school, without exception. They have a full and equal vote in deciding expenditures, in hiring and firing all employees (including teachers), and in making and enforcing the rules of the community. Typically, rules are made and business is handled at a weekly School Meeting, where each student, like each staff member, has one vote: freedom on individual rights' matters and peer justice.

Neural mechanisms

Neuroimaging identifies the anterior insula and anterior cingulate as key areas in the brain determining whether people conform in their preferences in regard to its being popular with their peer group.

External links

- Beating Peer Pressure at About.com [1]
- Info on alcohol and resisting peer pressure [2]
- [3]

Metaphorical Suicide

Political suicide

Political suicide is the concept that a politician or political party would lose widespread support and confidence from the voting public by proposing actions that are seen as unfavourable or that might threaten the status quo. A politician who committed political suicide might be forced to resign. A political party could stand to lose followers by deviating greatly from its core values and policies. Another term for such policies are "the third rail".

Cynics may blame this concept as a reason for a lack of real change or progress in society and that actions described as political suicide are usually sound intentions shot down by reactionism and fear of change.

External links

- BBC News - "Fowler warns of Tory 'political suicide'" [1]

Suicide Methods

Suicide methods

Suicide
Social aspects
Legislation · Philosophy Religious views · Euthanasia Assisted suicide · Right to die Benevolent suicide
Suicide crisis
Assessment of risk · Crisis hotline · Intervention · Prevention · Suicide watch
Suicide types
Copycat · Cult · Euthanasia · Familicide · Forced · Honor · Internet · Mass · Murder–suicide · Parasuicide · Suicide attack · By cop · Pact
Epidemiology
Gender · Suicide rate
History
List of suicides · Suicide methods
Related phenomena
Ideation · Self-harm · Suicide note · Locations · Failed suicide attempt
By country
China · Japan · South Korea · United States

A **suicide method** is any means by which one or more persons purposely kills themselves. Examples of methods that have been used to commit suicide are listed below. Though individuals with suicidal feelings may consider these methods, most do not ultimately act upon them.

Suicide methods can be classified according to two modes of interrupting life processes: physical or chemical. Physical modes of interruption typically act by incapacitating the respiratory system or the central nervous system, usually by destruction of one or more key components. Chemical modes focus on interrupting biologically significant processes such as cellular respiration or diffusion capacity. Chemical methods of suicide produce latent evidence of action, whereas physical methods provide direct evidence.

Whether or not exposure to suicide is a risk factor for suicide is controversial. A 1996 study was unable to find a relationship between suicides among friends, while a 1986 study found clusters of suicide among teenagers following the televisation of news stories regarding suicide. These clusters account for 5% of teenage suicides. There is some concern in the medical community that certain suicide methods described on the Internet, that can be easily found through online searches, are potentially more lethal than methods people might otherwise consider.

Bleeding

See also: Self-injury

Suicide by exsanguination involves reducing the volume and pressure of the blood to below critical levels by inducing massive blood loss. It is usually the result of damage inflicted on arteries. The carotid, radial, ulnar or femoral arteries may be targeted. Death may occur directly as a result of the desanguination of the body or via hypovolemia, wherein the blood volume in the circulatory system becomes too low and results in the body shutting down.

Wrist cutting

Wrist cutting is usually due to deliberate self harm rather than attempted suicide. People who engage in self harm however are at a 30 times greater risk of future suicide.

The subject may or may not experience a noticeable release of adrenaline and endorphins. As the bleeding continues cardiac arrhythmia is likely to ensue as the body is eventually unable to compensate. If the exsanguination is allowed to continue, the resulting severe hypovolemia will cause shock, followed by cardiovascular collapse, cardiac arrest and death.

In the case of a failed suicide attempt, the person may experience injury of the tendons of the extrinsic flexor muscles, or the ulnar and median nerves which control the muscles of the hand, both of which can result in temporary or permanent reduction in the victim's sensory and/or motor ability and/or also cause chronic somatic or autonomic pain. As in any class IV hemorrhage, aggressive resuscitation is required to prevent death of the patient; standard emergency bleeding control applies for pre-hospital treatment.

Arterial bleeding is identified by the rhythmic gush of blood (in unison with the heartbeat) that is bright red in color. Venous bleeding, on the other hand, produces a continuous stream of blood of a darker red color. Arterial bleeding is more difficult to control and usually more life-threatening. The bleeding may be further controlled by indirect arterial pressure—for example, pressure on the brachial artery can reduce bleeding from the arm; however, pressure points should be used with caution as inadequate blood flow may cause severe damage to a limb. Tourniquets, if used at all, should be reserved for professionals.

Drowning

Main article: Drowning

Suicide by drowning is the act of deliberately submerging oneself in water or other liquid to prevent breathing and deprive the brain of oxygen. Due to the body's natural tendency to come up for air, drowning attempts often involve the use of a heavy object to overcome this reflex. Drowning involves physical and mental anguish.

Drowning is among the least common methods of suicide, typically accounting for less than 2% of all reported suicides in the United States.

A homeless girl contemplates drowning herself.

Suffocation

Main article: Suicide bag

Suicide by suffocation is the act of inhibiting one's ability to breathe or limiting oxygen uptake while breathing, causing hypoxia and eventually asphyxia. This may involve an exit bag (a plastic bag fixed over the head) or confinement in an enclosed space without oxygen. These attempts involve using depressants to make the user pass out due to the oxygen deprivation before the instinctive panic and the urge to escape due to the hypercapnic alarm response.

Helium, argon and nitrogen are commonly used in suicides by suffocation. Breathing inert gas quickly renders a person unconscious and may cause death within minutes.

Hypothermia

Main article: Hypothermia

Suicide by hypothermia or by cold, is a slow death that goes through several stages. Hypothermia begins with mild symptoms, gradually leading to moderate and severe penalties. This may involve shivering, delirium, hallucinations, lack of coordination, sensations of warmth, then finally death. One's organs literally shut down, though clinical brain death can be prolonged.

Electrocution

Main article: Electrocution

Suicide by electrocution involves using a lethal electric shock to kill oneself. This would cause arrythmias of the heart, meaning that the heart would not contract in synchrony between the different chambers causing essentially elimination of blood flow. Furthermore, depending on the amount of electrical current, burns may also occur.

> "The evidence here shows that electrocution inflicts intense pain and agonizing suffering," (Justice William M. Connolly, Nebraska Supreme Court)

Jumping from height

Main articles: Jumper (suicide) and Self-defenestration

Jumping from height is the act of jumping from high altitudes, for example, from a window (self-defenestration or autodefenestration), balcony or roof of a high rise building, cliff, dam or bridge.

In the United States, jumping is among the least common methods of committing suicide (less than 2% of all reported suicides in the United States for 2005).

In Hong Kong, jumping is the most common method of committing suicide, accounting for 52.1% of all reported suicide cases in 2006 and similar rates for the years prior to that. The Centre for Suicide Research and Prevention of the University of Hong Kong believes that it may be due to the abundance of easily accessible high rise buildings in Hong Kong.

Firearms

A common suicide method is to use a firearm. Generally, the bullet will be aimed at point-blank range, often at the head or, less commonly, into the mouth, under the chin or pointed at the chest. In the United States, firearms remain the most common method of suicide, accounting for 53.7% of all suicides committed during 2003.

What happens when a human gets shot will be a function of at least the missile velocity, the available energy in the projectile and the *tissue interaction*. A high energy firearm and proper barrel orientation to the head is likely to create devastating damage; high class haemorrhage, severe physical brain damage with permanent partial or complete tissue destruction of multiple lobes, nerve destruction and obvious skull fracture with potential bone fragments embedded in the brain; structures likely to be affected are intracranial, vascular, middle or inner ear, cranial nerve and external canal structures. With low caliber and low powered weapons, despite optimal orientation of the barrel the firearm may not be effective in killing the victim.[*citation needed*]

A failed suicide attempt by firearm may result in severe chronic pain for the patient as well as reduced cognitive abilities and motor function, subdural hematoma, foreign bodies in the head, pneumocephalus and cerebrospinal fluid leaks. For temporal bone directed bullets, temporal lobe abscess, meningitis, aphasia, hemianopsia, and hemiplegia are common late intracranial complications. As many as 50% of people who survive gunshots wounds directed at the temporal bone suffer facial nerve damage, usually due to a severed nerve.

As for treatment, the patient should first be treated for critical life-threatening injuries. If dural injury is suspected, antibiotic prophylaxis is often employed, intracranial injuries are treated by intravenous steroids and osmotic diuretics. Craniotomy and lumbar drainage are utilized as needed. An important notion is that the surgeon should treat the wound, not the weapon—i.e. that wound management is difficult to be based on the characteristics of the weapon.

Research published in the New England Journal of Medicine and the National Academy of Science found an association between household firearm ownership and gun suicide rates, though a study by one researcher did not find a statistically significant association between household firearms and gun suicide rates, except in the suicides of children aged 5–14. During the 1980s and early 1990s, there was a strong upward trend in adolescent suicides with a gun, as well as a sharp overall increase in suicides among those age 75 and over.

Two separate studies, in Canada and Australia, conducted in conjunction with more restrictive firearms legislation, demonstrated that while said legislation showed a decrease in firearms suicide, other methods such as hanging increased. In Australia, the overall rate of suicide actually increased (following a trend that had been moving upwards for some time), and did not decrease until measures specifically aimed at providing support to would-be suicide victims was enacted.

Research also indicates no association *vis-à-vis* safe-storage laws of guns that *are* owned, and gun suicide rates, and studies that attempt to link gun ownership to likely victimology often fail to account for the presence of guns owned by other people. Researchers have shown that *safe-storage laws* do not appear to affect gun suicide rates or juvenile accidental gun death.

Shotgun suicides tend to be extremely messy, and can cause body matter to go under closed doors. Suicides committed with some hollow point bullets can essentially cause the head to explode.

Hanging

Main article: Hanging

With this technique, the patient attempts to use some form of device around the throat to strangle and/or break the neck. In the event of death, the actual cause of death depends upon the type of hanging used, where type usually refers to the length of the drop.

In a short drop the victim may die from strangulation—in which the death may result from a lack of air asphyxiating the brain; if the former is true the patient is likely to experience hypoxia, skin tingling, dizziness, vision narrowing, convulsions, shock and acute respiratory acidosis; if the latter is true one or both carotid arteries and/or the jugular vein may be compressed sufficiently to cause cerebral ischemia and a hypoxic condition in the brain which will eventually result in or contribute to the death. In the case of a sufficiently long drop, the patient is likely to suffer a fractured 2nd and 3rd and/or 4th and 5th cervical vertebrae which may cause paralysis or death.

Suicide by hanging.

The patient should be supported and removed from the entrapment with standard emergency procedures applied for resuscitation when necessary; in the event of suspected neck injury complete immobilization of the head and neck should be done as early as possible and before moving the patient to minimize or prevent further spinal cord injury—in the event of neck injuries only medical professionals should handle the patient post release from the choking device and only critical, life saving help should be administered by non-professionals.

Hanging is the prevalent means of suicide in pre-industrial societies and is more common in rural areas than in urban areas. It is also a common means of suicide in situations where materials are not readily at hand (such as in prisons).

Vehicular impact

Some people commit suicide by deliberately placing themselves in the path of a large and fast-moving vehicle, resulting in a fatal impact.

Rail

Main line systems

Some may throw themselves directly in front of an oncoming train, or drive a car onto the tracks and sit inside while they wait for the train to arrive. Suicide by being hit by a train has a 10% survival rate; a failed attempt typically results in severe injuries, including massive fractures, amputations and concussion, possibly leading to permanent brain damage and physical disability. Even when death occurs, it is not always painless and immediate.

In some European countries with highly developed rail networks and very strict gun control laws, such as Germany and Sweden, railway-related suicide is considered a social problem, and extensive research has been carried out into this type of suicide. According to these studies, most suicides occur not in densely populated areas, but away from rail stations and terminal points. Wooded areas, curves and tunnels are especially plagued. Most suicides occur at evening or night time when the driver's visibility is reduced, reducing the chance of a failed suicide. [citation needed]

People who commit suicide in this manner usually stay at or around the place for the suicide for an extended period of time before the actual suicide.[citation needed] Unlike on underground railways, in suicides involving above ground railway lines the victim will often simply stand or lie on the tracks, waiting for the arrival of the train. As the trains usually travel at high speeds (usually between 80 and 200 km/h), the driver is usually unable to bring the train to a halt before the collision. This type of suicide may be traumatizing to the driver of the train and may lead to post-traumatic stress disorder. The sound of a train striking a person has been likened to that of hitting a pumpkin.

In Germany, 7% of all suicides occur in this manner, making this type account for the largest share of overall suicides in the country.

Methods to reduce the number of rail-related suicides include CCTV surveillance of stretches where suicides frequently occur, often with direct links to the local police or surveillance companies. This enables the police or guards to be on the scene within minutes after the trespassing was noted. Public access to the tracks is also made more difficult by erecting fences. Trees and bushes are cut down around the tracks in order to increase driver visibility.

According to the Federal Railroad Administration, in the U.S., there are 300 to 500 train suicides a year.

Metro systems

Jumping in front of an oncoming subway train has a 67% survival rate, much higher than the 10% survival rate for rail-related suicides. This is most likely because trains traveling on open tracks travel relatively quickly, whereas trains arriving at a subway station are decelerating so that they can stop and board passengers.

Different methods have been used in order to decrease the number of suicide attempts in the underground: a deep drainage pit halves the likelihood of fatality. Separation of the passengers from the track by means of a partition with sliding-doors is being introduced in some stations, but is expensive.

Traffic collisions

Some car crashes are in fact suicides. This especially applies to single-occupant, single-vehicle accidents. "The automobile lends itself admirably to attempts at self-destruction because of the frequency of its use, the generally accepted inherent hazards of driving, and the fact that it offers the individual an opportunity to imperil or end his life without consciously confronting himself with his suicidal intent." There is always the risk that a car accident will affect other road users, for example a car that brakes abruptly or swerves to avoid a suicidal pedestrian may get into a collision with something else on the road.

The real percentage of suicides among car accidents is not reliably known; studies by suicide researchers tell that "vehicular fatalities that are suicides vary from 1.6% to 5%". Some suicides are misclassified as accidents because suicide must be proven; "It is noteworthy that even when suicide is strongly suspected but a suicide note is not found, the case will be classified an 'accident.'"

Some researchers believe that suicides disguised as traffic accidents are far more prevalent than previously thought. One large-scale community survey (in Australia) among suicidal persons provided the following numbers: "Of those who reported planning a suicide, 14.8% (19.1% of male planners and 11.8% of female planners) had conceived to have a motor vehicle "accident"... Of all attempters, 8.3% (13.3% of male attempters) had previously attempted via motor vehicle collision."

Aircraft

There have been instances of suicides involving intentionally crashing aircraft:

- EgyptAir Flight 990
- SilkAir Flight 185
- 2010 Austin plane crash

Poisoning

Suicide can be committed by using fast-acting poisons, such as hydrogen cyanide, or substances which are known for their high levels of toxicity to humans. For example, most of the people of Jonestown, in northwestern Guyana, died when Jim Jones, the leader of a religious sect, organized a mass suicide by drinking a cocktail of diazepam and cyanide in 1978. Sufficient doses of some plants like the belladonna family, castor beans, *Jatropha curcas* and others, are also toxic. Poisoning through the means of toxic plants however is usually less quick and relatively painful.

Pesticide poisoning

Worldwide, 30% of suicides are from pesticide poisonings. The use of this method however varies markedly in different areas of the world from 4% in Europe to more than 50% in the Pacific region. Poisoning by farm chemicals is very common among females in the Chinese countryside, and is regarded as a major social problem in the country. In Finland, the highly lethal pesticide Parathion was commonly used for suicide in the 1950s. When access to the chemical was restricted, other methods replaced it, leading researchers to conclude that restricting certain suicide methods does little to impact the overall suicide rate.

Drug overdosing

Main article: Drug overdose

Overdosing is a method of suicide which involves taking medication in doses greater than the indicated levels, or in a combination that will interact to either cause harmful effects or increase the potency of one or other of the substances.

A peaceful overdose is the preferred method of dignified dying among members of right to die societies. A poll among members of right to die society Exit International has shown that 89% would prefer to take a pill, rather than use a plastic exit bag, a CO generator or use 'slow euthanasia'.

Reliability of this method highly depends on chosen drugs and additional measures like use of antiemetics to prevent vomiting. Average fatality rate for overdoses in the US is estimated to be 1.8% only. At the same time, assisted suicide group Dignitas reported no single failure among 840 cases (fatality rate 100%), where an overdose of a former sleeping pill active agent Nembutal was used in combination with antiemetic drugs.

While barbiturates (such as Seconal or Nembutal) have long been considered a safe option for suicide, they are becoming increasingly difficult for potential suicide victims to acquire. Dutch right to die society WOZZ proposed several safe alternatives to barbiturates for use in euthanasia. *The Peaceful Pill Handbook* mentions the still easy availability of solutions containing pentobarbital in Mexico where they are available over the counter from veterinarians for animal euthanasia.

However, a typical drug overdose uses random prescription and over-the-counter substances. In this case death is uncertain, and an attempt may leave a person alive but with severe organ damage, although that itself may in turn eventually prove fatal. Drugs taken orally may also be vomited back out before being absorbed. Considering the very high doses needed, vomiting or losing consciousness before taking enough of the active agent is often a major problem for people attempting this.

Analgesic overdose attempts are among the most common, due to easy availability of over-the-counter substances. Overdosing may also be performed by mixing medications in a cocktail with one another, or with alcohol or illegal drugs. This method may leave confusion over whether the death was a suicide or accidental, especially when alcohol or other judgment-impairing substances are also involved and no suicide note was left behind.

Carbon monoxide poisoning

Main article: Carbon monoxide poisoning#Suicide

A particular type of poisoning involves inhalation of high levels of carbon monoxide. Death usually occurs through hypoxia. In most cases carbon monoxide (CO) is used because it is easily available as a product of incomplete combustion; for example it is released by cars and some types of heaters.

Carbon monoxide is a colorless and odorless gas, so its presence cannot be detected by sight or smell. It acts by binding preferentially to the hemoglobin in the victim's blood, displacing oxygen molecules and progressively deoxygenating the blood, eventually resulting in the failure of cellular respiration, and death.

In the past, before air-quality regulations and catalytic converters, suicide by carbon monoxide poisoning would often be achieved by running a car's engine in a closed space such as a garage, or by redirecting a running car's exhaust back inside the cabin with a hose. Motor car exhaust may have contained up to 25% carbon monoxide. However, catalytic converters found on all modern automobiles eliminate over 99% of carbon monoxide produced. As a further complication, the amount of unburned gasoline in emissions can make exhaust unbearable to breathe well before losing consciousness.

The incidence of suicide by carbon monoxide poisoning through burning charcoal, such as a barbecue in a sealed room, appears to have risen. This has been referred to by some as "death by hibachi".

Carbon monoxide is extremely dangerous to bystanders and people who may discover the body, so "Right to Die" advocates like Philip Nitschke recommend the use of safer alternatives like nitrogen, for example in his EXIT euthanasia device.

Other toxins

Detergent-related suicide involves mixing household chemicals to produce hydrogen sulfide or other poisonous gases. The suicide rates by domestic gas fell from 1960 to 1980.

Several creatures such as spiders, snakes, scorpions, carry venoms that can easily and quickly kill a person. These substances can be used to conduct suicide. For example, Cleopatra supposedly had an asp bite her when she heard of Marc Antony's death.

Immolation

Main article: Self-immolation

Immolation usually refers to suicide by fire. It has been used as a protest tactic, most famously by Thích Quảng Đức in 1963 to protest the South Vietnamese government; and by Malachi Ritscher in 2006 to protest the United States' involvement in the Iraq War.

Self immolation was also carried out as a ritual in certain parts of India known as *sati*, where a wife "voluntarily" immolated herself in her dead husband's funeral pyre.

The Latin root of "immolate" means "sacrifice", and is not restricted to the use of fire, though common media usage uses the term immolation to refer to suicide by fire.

This method of suicide is relatively rare due to the long and painful experience one has to go through before death sets in. This is also contributed to the ever present risk that the fire is extinguished before death sets in, and in that way causes one to live with severe burnings, scar tissue and the emotional impact of such horrific injuries.

Seppuku

Main article: Seppuku

Seppuku (colloquially *harakiri* "belly slitting") is a Japanese ritual method of suicide, practiced mostly in the medieval era, though some isolated cases appear in modern times. For example, Yukio Mishima committed seppuku in 1970 after a failed *coup d'etat* intended to restore full power to the Japanese emperor.

Unlike other methods of suicide, this was regarded as a way of preserving one's honor. The ritual is part of *bushido*, the code of the *samurai*.

As originally performed solely by an individual it was an extremely painful method by which to die. Dressed ceremonially, with his sword placed in front of him and sometimes seated on special cloth, the warrior would prepare for death by writing a death poem. The samurai would open his *kimono*, take up his *wakizashi* (short sword), fan, or a *tantō* and plunge it into his abdomen, making first a left-to-right cut and then a second slightly upward stroke. As the custom evolved a selected attendant (*kaishakunin*, his second) standing by who, on the second stroke, would perform *daki-kubi*, where the warrior is all but decapitated, leaving a slight band of flesh attaching the head to the body, so as to not let the head fall off the body and roll on the floor/ground; which was considered dishonorable in feudal Japan. The act eventually became so highly ritualistic that the samurai would only have to reach for his sword and his *kaishakunin* would execute the killing stroke. Later still, there would be no sword but something like a fan for which the samurai would reach.

Apocarteresis (suicide by starvation)

Main article: Starvation

A hunger strike may ultimately lead to death. Starvation has been used by Hindu and Jain monks as a ritual method of penance, and Albigensians or Cathars also fasted after receiving the 'consolamentum' sacrament, in order to die while in a morally perfect state.

This method of death is often associated with political protest, such as the 1981 Irish Hunger Strike during which 7 IRA and 3 INLA POWs died in H-Blocks of Long Kesh prison. The explorer Thor Heyerdahl refused to eat or take medication for the last month of his life, after having been diagnosed with cancer.

Dehydration

Main article: Terminal dehydration

Dehydration can be hard to bear, and requires patience and determination, since it takes from several days to a few weeks. This means that unlike many other suicide methods, it cannot be accomplished impulsively. Those who die by terminal dehydration typically lapse into unconsciousness before death, and may also experience delirium and deranged serum sodium. Discontinuation of hydration does not produce true thirst, although a sensation of dryness of the mouth often is reported as "thirst." The evidence this is not true thirst is extensive and shows the ill feeling is not relieved by giving fluids intravenously but is relieved by wetting the tongue and lips and proper care of the mouth. Patients with edema tend to take longer to die of dehydration because of the excess fluid in their bodies.

Terminal dehydration has been described as having substantial advantages over physician-assisted suicide with respect to self-determination, access, professional integrity, and social implications. Specifically, a patient has a right to refuse treatment and it would be a personal assault for someone to force water on a patient, but such is not the case if a doctor merely refuses to provide lethal medication. But it also has distinctive drawbacks as a humane means of voluntary death. One survey of hospice nurses found that nearly twice as many had cared for patients who chose voluntary refusal of food and fluids to hasten death as had cared for patients who chose physician-assisted suicide. They also rated fasting and dehydration as causing less suffering and pain and being more peaceful than physician-assisted suicide. Other sources, however, have noted very painful side effects of dehydration, including seizures, skin cracking and bleeding, blindness, nausea, vomiting, cramping and severe headaches. There can be a fine line between terminal sedation that results in death by dehydration and euthanasia.

Explosion

Another method is death by explosion. High-explosives that are certain to explode and release an extreme amount of energy are often used to avoid unnecessary pain.

Suicide attack

Main article: Suicide attack

A suicide attack is an attack in which the attacker (*attacker* being either an individual or a group) intends to kill others and intends to die in the process of doing so (e.g. Columbine, Virginia Tech). In a suicide attack, in the strictest sense, the attacker dies by the attack itself, for example in an explosion or crash caused by the attacker. The term is sometimes loosely applied to an incident in which the intention of the attacker is not clear though he is almost sure to die by the defense or retaliation of the attacked party, e.g., "suicide by cop", that is, menacing or assaulting an armed police officer with a weapon or apparent or proclaimed harmful intent which all but insures that the cop will use deadly force to terminate the attack. This can also be referred to as murder/suicide.

Such attacks are typically motivated by religious or political ideologies and have been carried out using numerous methods. For example, attackers might attach explosives directly to their bodies before detonating themselves close to their target also known as suicide attack. They may use a car bomb or other machinery to cause maximum damage (e.g. Japanese *kamikaze* pilots during World War II).

Additionally, teenage students (most often in the US, and recently in Finland and Germany) have committed several notable suicide attacks in recent years, in the form of school shooting massacres. Often, these suicide attacks involve guns or homemade bombs brought into high schools or college campuses. After the attack, the perpetrator will commit suicide before being apprehended.

Indirect suicide

Indirect suicide is the act of setting out on an obviously fatal course without directly committing the act upon oneself. Indirect suicide is differentiated from legally defined suicide by the fact that the actor does not pull the figurative (or literal) trigger. Examples of indirect suicide include a soldier enlisting in the army with the express intention and expectation of being killed in combat. Another example would be provoking an armed officer into using lethal force against them. This is generally called "suicide by cop". In some instances the subject commits a capital crime in hope of being sentenced to death. This state-assisted suicide was extremely popular in Enlightenment Era Scandinavia, where law and religion forbade suicide.[*citation needed*] Today, this type of suicide is relatively rare.

Further reading

- Humphry, Derek. *Final Exit: The Practicalities of Self-Deliverance and Assisted Suicide for the Dying.* Dell. 1997.
- Philip Nitschke. The Peaceful Pill Handbook. Exit International US, 2007. ISBN 0-9788-7882-5
- Stone, Geo. *Suicide and Attempted Suicide: Methods and Consequences* [1]. New York: Carroll & Graf, 2001. ISBN 0-7867-0940-5
- Guide to a Humane Self-Chosen Death by Dr. Pieter Admiraal et al. WOZZ Foundation, Delft, The Netherlands. ISBN 9-0785-8101-8. 112 pages
- Departing Drugs by Chris Docker, Cheryl Smith, and the International Drugs Consensus Working Party, 1993, 68 pages. Published by *Exit* [2] and others.
- Docker, Chris *Five Last Acts* 2nd edition 2010. ISBN 9781453869376. 414 pages.
- The Complete Manual of Suicide

Prevention and Intervention

Suicide prevention

Suicide
Social aspects
Legislation · Philosophy Religious views · Euthanasia Assisted suicide · Right to die Benevolent suicide
Suicide crisis
Assessment of risk · Crisis hotline · Intervention · Prevention · Suicide watch
Suicide types
Copycat · Cult · Euthanasia · Familicide · Forced · Honor · Internet · Mass · Murder–suicide · Parasuicide · Suicide attack · By cop · Pact
Epidemiology
Gender · Suicide rate
History
List of suicides · Suicide methods
Related phenomena
Ideation · Self-harm · Suicide note · Locations · Failed suicide attempt
By country
China · Japan · South Korea · United States

Suicide prevention is an umbrella term for the collective efforts of local citizen organizations, mental health practitioners and related professionals to reduce the incidence of suicide through prevention and proactive measures. One of the first exclusively professional research centers was established 1958 in Los Angeles. The first crisis hotline service in the U.S. run by selected, trained citizen volunteers was established 1961 in San Francisco.

Various suicide prevention strategies have been used:

- Selection and training of volunteer citizen groups offering confidential referral services.
- Promoting mental resilience through optimism and connectedness.
- Education about suicide, including risk factors, warning signs and the availability of help.
- Increasing the proficiency of health and welfare services at responding to people in need. This includes better training for health professionals and employing crisis counseling organizations.
- Reducing domestic violence and substance abuse are long-term strategies to reduce many mental health problems.
- Reducing access to convenient means of suicide (e.g. toxic substances, handguns).
- Reducing the quantity of dosages supplied in packages of non-prescription medicines e.g. aspirin.
- Interventions targeted at high-risk groups.
- Research. (see below)

It has also been suggested that news media can help prevent suicide by linking suicide with negative outcomes such as pain for the suicide and his survivors, conveying that the majority of people choose something other than suicide in order to solve their problems, avoiding mentioning suicide epidemics, and avoiding presenting authorities or sympathetic, ordinary people as spokespersons for the reasonableness of suicide.

Research

Under the theory of four humors, Hippocrates attributed melancholia to an excess of black bile, a view still propagated by Robert Burton to explain suicide in his 1621 *Anatomy of Melancholy*. Sociologist Emile Durkheim's 1897 book *On Suicide* identified four different motives for suicide, asserting that anomie or the "normlessness" of social connection strongly correlated with suicide. Psychoanalysts such as Harry Stack Sullivan saw suicide as "hostility turned inward" while Karl Menninger's 1936 *Man Against Himself* connected suicide with masturbation. Edwin Shneidman followed Henry Murray in attributing suicide to the emotional pain of unmet needs, asserting that "lethality" was what separated suicides from other frustrated individuals. Aaron T. Beck emphasized the importance of hopelessness as contributing factor. Roy Baumeister posits an "escape theory" of suicidal ideation where a numbed state of "cognitive deconstruction" precedes suicidal acts, wherein they are falsely perceived as the only logical action. Marsha Linehan identifies a number of factors that contribute to suicidal behavior, including certain biological deficits, exposure to trauma and a lack of adaptive coping skills.

In his 2005 book *Why People Die by Suicide,* Thomas Joiner posits a three-part explanation of suicide which focuses on ability and desire. The desire to commit suicide comes from a sense of disconnection from others and lack of belonging, combined with a belief that one is a burden on others. The ability to commit suicide comes from a gradual desensitization to violence and a decreased fear of pain, combined with technical competence in one or more suicide methods. This combination of desire and ability will precede the most serious suicide attempts under Joiner's model.

Interventions

Group psychotherapy strategy

A psychosocial-psychoeducational group therapeutic intervention for recurrent suicide attempters is being developed which involves a combination of open discussion of the daily lived experience of individuals who have made repeated suicide attempts, and teaching new skills that can be used to "stay safe". The goal outcome of skill use, staying "safe", means avoiding making an attempt or engaging in behaviour that is harmful to the person. Participants in this program are taught skills which they can reasonably apply in their everyday lives, from "basic personal rights" to self-soothing, setting boundaries in interpersonal relationships, distraction tactics, problem-solving strategies, and the idea that distress felt in the moment, no matter how seemingly unendurable, is not permanent but an experience that will pass. The goal of the program is to provide a supportive environment in which skill use is discussed each week, and successful skill use is consistently met with praise from other participants and the facilitators.

As a suicide prevention initiative, this sign promotes a special telephone available on the bridge that connects to a crisis hotline.

Basic personal rights

Many individuals who make recurrent suicide attempts come from backgrounds that were abusive or otherwise detrimental. Often individuals with such backgrounds have been given the message that they have no rights. Teaching basic personal rights, such as "I have the right to say no to a request" and "I have the right to make choices that take care of ME." helps to promote a sense of self-efficacy among participants. This can help set the stage for teaching skills that require participants actively to choose to care for themselves. Though a flaw may arise, when they think that they have the right to choose the personal course of the life they want, including whether or not they should die; this approach is known as the right to die.

Self-soothing

Self-soothing, a skill that is taught in suicide prevention groups and also in Dialectical Behavior Therapy, involves using one of the five senses to provide some sort of stimulation that is calming to the individual. For example, many find a hot beverage such as tea or coffee to be comforting. Other self-soothing activities might include a warm or cool bath or shower, putting on favourite comfortable clothes, stroking a pet, burning incense, or listening to music. The goal of self-soothing is to lessen the person's current level of distress by providing stimulation that feels positive.

Interpersonal boundaries

Individuals who make recurrent suicide attempts often feel that they have very little control over their lives, or that their lives are controlled by other people rather than themselves. The goal of teaching boundary-setting skills is to make the participants aware that it is okay for them to have needs and wants and to go about getting these needs and wants met. Boundary-setting also encourages participants to be aware of when other people in their lives are asking for things the participant would rather not give/share, or acting in a way that makes the participant feel unsafe. Boundary-setting means choosing actively which things will be shared and which will not, when someone is welcome to visit and when not, and so on.

Distraction tactics

Another skill that this particular therapeutic intervention and DBT have in common is the use of distraction tactics. The goal of using a distraction is to survive the period of distress by doing things that take one's mind off it. Distraction tactics may range anything from a quiet task like reading a favorite book, to an active task like going for a run. Distraction does not act to lessen the emotional pain, but it can take the mind off it long enough for it to recede, which may prevent a suicide attempt that is made to escape seemingly unendurable pain.

Problem-solving strategies

Crisis intervention, a technique used at Parkland Hospital Psychiatric Emergency Department in Dallas, asks: Is this patient suicidal? Is he or she at high risk? What is the problem—and what can be done about it? What would it take to help this patient become non-suicidal? Examples of how crisis intervention works are given by Doug Puryear, MD, in his March 18, 2010, article in *Psychiatric Times*.

Police officers are trained in suicide prevention, such as for cases where a person attempts to jump from a height. In this instance, a Dallas officer manages to convince the young woman not to jump.

Support groups

Many non-profit organizations exist, such as the American Foundation for Suicide Prevention in the United States, which serve as crisis hotlines. In addition, some groups like To Write Love on Her Arms have been promoted using social media to reach more people.

Further reading

- Bergmans, Yvonne; Links, Paul S. (December 2002). "A description of a psychosocial/psychoeducational intervention for persons with recurrent suicide attempts". *Crisis: the Journal of Crisis Intervention and Suicide Prevention* **23**: 156–160. doi:10.1027//0227-5910.23.4.156 [1].
- Suicide Prevention Action Network
- Suicide & Life-Threatening Behavior; New York - Guilford Publications, Inc
- American Foundation for Suicide Prevention

See also

- Living Is For Everyone

External links

- Stamp Out Suicide! [9] promotes suicide awareness and supports suicide prevention
- Suicide prevention [2] at the Open Directory Project
- American Foundation for Suicide Prevention [10] is the leading not-for-profit dedicated to preventing suicide through research, education and advocacy.
- Suicide Prevention Resource Center (SPRC) Online Library [3]
- International Association for Suicide Prevention [4] Organization co-sponsors World Suicide Prevention Day on September 10 every year with the World Health Organization (WHO).

Journals of suicide prevention research

- Crisis: The Journal of Crisis Intervention and Suicide Prevention [5]
- U.S. Surgeon General - Suicide Prevention [6]

Suicide intervention

Suicide
Social aspects
Legislation · Philosophy Religious views · Euthanasia Assisted suicide · Right to die Benevolent suicide
Suicide crisis
Assessment of risk · Crisis hotline · Intervention · Prevention · Suicide watch
Suicide types
Copycat · Cult · Euthanasia · Familicide · Forced · Honor · Internet · Mass · Murder–suicide · Parasuicide · Suicide attack · By cop · Pact
Epidemiology
Gender · Suicide rate
History
List of suicides · Suicide methods
Related phenomena
Ideation · Self-harm · Suicide note · Locations · Failed suicide attempt
By country
China · Japan · South Korea · United States

Suicide intervention or **suicide crisis intervention** is direct effort to stop or prevent persons attempting or contemplating suicide from killing themselves. Current medical advice concerning people who are attempting or seriously considering suicide is that they should immediately go or be taken to the nearest emergency room, or emergency services should be called immediately by them or anyone aware of the problem. Modern medicine treats suicide as a mental health issue. According to medical practice, severe suicidal ideation, that is, serious contemplation or planning of suicide, is a medical emergency and that the condition requires immediate emergency medical treatment.

In the United States, individuals who express the intent to harm themselves are automatically determined to lack the *present mental capacity* to refuse treatment, and can be transported to an emergency department against their will.[citation needed] An emergency physician there will determine whether or not inpatient care at a mental health care facility is warranted. This is sometimes referred to as being "committed." If the doctor determines involuntary commitment is needed, the patient is hospitalized and kept under observation until a court hearing is held to determine the patient's *competence*.

Individuals suffering from depression are considered a high-risk group for suicidal behavior. When depression is a major factor, successful treatment of the depression usually leads to the disappearance of suicidal thoughts.[citation needed] However, medical treatment of depression is not always successful, and lifelong depression can contribute to recurring suicide attempts.

Medical personnel frequently receive special training to look for suicidal signs in patients. Suicide hotlines are widely available for people seeking help. However, the negative and often too clinical reception that many suicidal people receive after relating their feelings to health professionals (e.g. threats of institutionalization, increased dosages of medication, the social stigma) may cause patients to remain more guarded about their mental health history or suicidal urges and ideation.[citation needed]

First aid for suicide ideation

Medical professionals advise that people who have expressed plans to kill themselves be encouraged to seek medical attention immediately. This is especially relevant if the means (weapons, drugs, or other methods) are available, or if the patient has crafted a detailed plan for executing the suicide. Mental health professionals suggest that people who know a person whom they suspect to be suicidal can assist him or her by asking directly if the person has contemplated committing suicide and made specific arrangements, has set a date, etc. Posing such a question *does not* render a previously non-suicidal person suicidal[citation needed]. According to this advice, the person questioning should seek to be understanding and empathetic above all else since a suicidal person will often already feel ashamed or guilty about contemplating suicide so care should be taken not to exacerbate that guilt.

Mental health professionals suggest that an affirmative response to these questions should motivate the immediate seeking of medical attention, either from that person's doctor, or, if unavailable, the emergency room of the nearest hospital.

If the prior interventions fail, mental health professionals suggest involving law enforcement officers. While the police do not always have the authority to stop the suicide attempt itself, in some countries including some jurisdictions in the US, killing oneself is illegal.

In most cases law enforcement does have the authority to have people involuntarily committed to mental health wards. Usually a court order is required, but if an officer feels the person is in immediate danger he/she can order an involuntary commitment without waiting for a court order. Such commitments are for a limited period, such as 72 hours – which is intended to be enough time for a doctor to see the person and make an evaluation. After this initial period, a hearing is held in which a judge can decide to order the person released or can extend the treatment time. Afterwards, the court is kept informed of the person's condition and can release the person when they feel the time is right to do so. Legal punishment for suicide attempts is extremely rare[citation needed].

Mental health treatment

Treatment, often including medication, counseling and psychotherapy, is directed at the underlying causes of suicidal thinking. Clinical depression is the most common treatable cause, with alcohol or drug abuse being the next major categories[citation needed].

Other psychiatric disorders associated with suicidal thinking include bipolar disorder, schizophrenia, Borderline personality disorder, Gender identity disorder and eating disorders. Suicidal thoughts provoked by crises will generally settle with time and counseling. Severe depression can continue throughout life even with treatment and repetitive suicide attempts or suicidal ideation can be the result.

Methods for disrupting suicidal thinking include having family members or friends tell the person contemplating suicide about who else would be hurt by the loss, citing valuable and productive aspects of the patient's life, and provoking simple curiosity about the victim's own future[citation needed].

During the acute phase, the safety of the person is one of the prime factors considered by doctors, and this can lead to admission to a psychiatric ward or even involuntary commitment.

According to a 2005 randomized controlled trial by Gregory Brown, Aaron Beck and others, cognitive therapy can reduce repeat suicide attempts by 50%.

Suicide prevention

Main article: Suicide prevention

Various suicide prevention strategies are suggested by Mental Health professionals[citation needed]:

- Promoting mental resilience through optimism and connectedness.
- Education about suicide, including risk factors, warning signs, and the availability of help.
- Increasing the proficiency of health and welfare services in responding to people in need. This includes better training for health professionals and employing crisis counseling organizations.
- Reducing domestic violence, substance abuse, and divorce are long-term strategies to reduce many mental health problems.
- Reducing access to convenient means of suicide (e.g., toxic substances, handguns).
- Reducing the quantity of dosages supplied in packages of non-prescription medicines e.g., aspirin.
- Interventions targeted at high-risk groups.

Research on suicide prevention

Research into suicide is published across a wide spectrum of journals dedicated to the biological, economic, psychological, medical and social sciences. In addition to those, a few journals are exclusively devoted to the study of suicide (suicidology), most notably, *Crisis*, *Suicide and Life Threatening Behavior*, and the *Archives of Suicide Research*.

External links

- Stamp Out Suicide [9] Promoting suicide awareness and supporting suicide prevention
- Suicide Prevention Help [1] A portal for texts, hot-lines, and other websites designed for the sufferer and care-provider of suicidal crises.
- National Suicide Prevention Lifeline [2]
- National (U.S) Suicide Prevention Hot-lines [3] provides telephone numbers for access to crisis intervention counselors, and brief helping texts for people in crisis situations

Epidemiology of Suicide

Epidemiology of suicide

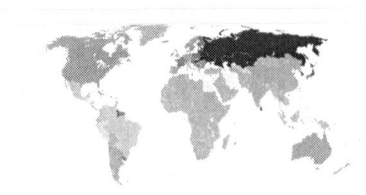

Suicide rate per 100,000 males (data from 1978–2008)   no data   < 1   1–5   5–5.8   5.8–8.5   8.5–12   12–19   19–22.5   22.5–26   26–29.5   29.5–33   33–36.5   >36.5

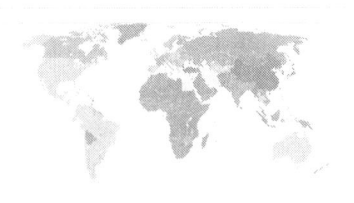

Suicide rate per 100,000 females (data from 1978–2008)   no data   < 1   1–5   5–5.8   5.8–8.5   8.5–12   12–19   19–22.5   22.5–26   26–29.5   29.5–33   33–36.5   >36.5

Incidence of suicide is under-reported due to both religious and social pressures, and possibly completely unreported in some areas. Nevertheless, from reported cases, certain trends are apparent. Since the data is skewed, comparing suicide rates between nations is statistically unsound. The trends themselves are not the cause, but may be indicative of a root cause.Wikipedia:Please clarify

Epidemiology

See also: List of countries by suicide rate

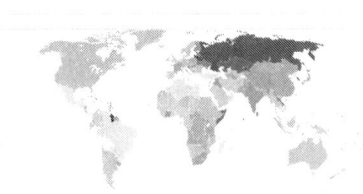

Deaths for self inflicted injuries per 100,000 inhabitants in 2004. "Mortality and Burden of Disease Estimates for WHO Member States in 2002" (xls). World Health Organization. 2002. . Retrieved 2009-12-13.   no data   less than 3   3-6   6-9   9-12   12-15   15-18   18-21   21-24   24-27   27-30   30-33   more than 33

Suicides per 100,000 people per year:

Rank	Country	Year	Males	Females	Total
1.	Lithuania	2005	68.1	12.9	38.6
2.	Belarus	2003	63.3	10.3	35.1
3.	Russia	2004	61.6	10.7	34.3
4.	Kazakhstan	2003	51.0	8.9	29.2
5.	Slovenia	2003	45.0	12.0	28.1
6.	Hungary	2003	44.9	12.0	27.7
7.	Latvia	2004	42.9	8.5	24.3
8.	Japan	2004	35.6	12.8	24.0
9.	Ukraine	2004	43.0	7.3	23.8
10.	Sri Lanka	1996	NA	NA	21.6

A 2006 report by the World Health Organisation (WHO) states that nearly a million people take their own lives every year, more than those murdered or killed in war. WHO figures show a suicide takes place somewhere in the world every 40 seconds. Suicide rates are highest in Europe's Baltic states, where around 40 people per 100,000 die by suicide each year, second in line is in the Sub-Saharan Africa where 32 people per 100,000 die by suicide each year. The lowest rates are found mainly in Latin America and a few countries in Asia.

In 1998, the World Health Organization ranked suicide as the twelfth leading cause of death worldwide.

In most countries the incidence of suicides is higher than the incidence of intentional homicides.

As many as 60,000 people commit suicide in Russia every year; approximately 30,000 people die by suicide each year in the United States; over 30,000 kill themselves in Japan; and about 250,000 commit suicide each year in China. In western countries men commit suicide at four times the rate of women. Women are more likely to attempt suicide than men. The countries of the former Soviet Bloc have the highest suicide rate in the world. The region with the lowest suicide rate is Latin America. Up to at least the 1950s, it was the Republic of Ireland which had the lowest suicide rate in the world, as reported by an Irish TV news report in 2007. In India, suicide rates for women are nearly three times higher than those for men. Higher suicide rates among women have been reported in China.

According to the National Institute of Mental Health, suicide contagion is a serious problem, especially for young people. Suicide can be facilitated in vulnerable teens by exposure to real or fictional accounts of suicide, including media coverage of suicide, such as intensive reporting of the suicide of a celebrity or idol.

Gender and suicide

Main article: Gender and suicide

In the United States, males are four times more likely to die by suicide than females. Male suicide rates are higher than females in all age groups (the ratio varies from 3:1 to 10:1). In other western countries, males are also much more likely to die by suicide than females (usually by a factor of 3–4:1). It was the 8th leading cause of death for males, and 19th leading cause of death for females. Excess male mortality from suicide is also evident from data from non-Western countries.

Race and suicide

In 2003, in the United States, whites were nearly 2.5 times more likely to kill themselves than were blacks or Hispanics. There is a marked divergence by age as seen in the chart below. In the eastern portion of the world (primarily in Asian or Pacific-Island countries) the growing numbers of reported suicides is growing every year. Of all ethnic groups in the United States, Native Americans, Multiracial Americans, and Filipino Americans have the highest risk of suicide.[citation needed]

Sexual orientation and suicide

See also: Homosexuality and psychology

The likelihood of suicide attempts are increased in both gay males and lesbians, as well as bisexuals of both sexes when compared to their heterosexual counterparts. The trend of having a higher incident rate among females is no exception with lesbians or bisexual females and when compared with homosexual males, lesbians are more likely to attempt than gay or bisexual males.

Studies vary with just how increased the risk is compared to heterosexuals with a low of 0.8-1.1 times more likely for females and 1.5-2.5 times more likely for males. The highs reach 4.6 more likely in females and 14.6 more likely in males.

Race and age play a factor in the increased risk. The highest ratios for males are attributed to caucasians when they are in their youthhood. By the age of 25, their risk is down to less than half of what it was however black gay males risk steadily increases to 8.6 times more likely. Through a lifetime the risks are 5.7 for white and 12.8 for black gay and bisexual males. Lesbian and bisexual females have opposite effects with less attempts in youthhood when compared to heterosexual females. Through a lifetime the likelihood to attempt nearly triple the youth 1.1 ratio for caucasion females, however for black females the rate is affected very little (less than 0.1 to 0.3 difference) with heterosexual black females having a slightly higher risk throughout most of the age-based study.

Gay and lesbian youth who attempt suicide are disproportionately subject to anti-gay attitudes, and have weaker skills for coping with discrimination, isolation, and loneliness, and were more likely to experience family rejection than those who do not attempt suicide. Another study found that gay and bisexual youth who attempted suicide had more feminine gender roles, adopted an LGB identity at a young age and were more likely than peers to report sexual abuse, drug abuse, and arrests for misconduct.

One study found that same-sex sexual behavior, but not homosexual attraction or homosexual identity, was significantly predictive of suicide among Norwegian adolescents. In Denmark, the age-adjusted suicide mortality risk for men in registered domestic partnerships was nearly eight times greater than for men with positive histories of heterosexual marriage and nearly twice as high for men who had never married.

Social factors and suicide

Higher levels of social and national cohesion reduce suicide rates. Suicide levels are highest among the retired, unemployed, impoverished, divorced, the childless, urbanites, empty nesters, and other people who live alone. Suicide rates also rise during times of economic uncertainty (although poverty is not a direct cause, it can contribute to the risk of suicide). Epidemiological studies generally show a relationship between suicide or suicidal behaviors and socio-economic disadvantage, including limited educational achievement, homelessness, unemployment, economic dependence and contact with the police or justice system. War is traditionally believed to be associated with a fall in suicide rates, however this has been questioned in recent studies, showing a more complex picture than previously conceived.

Health and suicide

Depression, either unipolar or as part of bipolar disorder, is an especially common cause. Substance abuse, severe physical disease or infirmity are also recognized causes.

An unknown amount of suicide fatalities are misdiagnosed as consequences of severe illness.

Season and suicide

The idea that suicide is more common during the winter holidays (including Christmas in the northern hemisphere) is actually a myth, generally reinforced by media coverage associating suicide with the holiday season. The National Center for Health Statistics found that suicides drop during the winter months, and peak during spring and early summer. Considering that there is a correlation between the winter season and rates of depression, there are theories that this might be accounted for by capability to commit suicide and relative cheerfulness. Suicide has also been linked to other seasonal factors.

The variation in suicides by day of week is actually greater than any seasonal variation. In the United States, more people die by suicide on Monday than any other day; Saturday is the day with the least number of suicides.

Suicide trends

Certain time trends can be related to the type of death. In the United Kingdom, for example, the steady rise in suicides from 1945 to 1962-63 was probably to some extent curtailed following the removal of carbon monoxide from domestic gas supplies which occurred with the change from coal gas to natural gas during the sixties. Methods vary across cultures, and the easy availability of lethal agents and materials plays a role.

It is estimated that global annual suicide fatalities could rise to 1.5 million by 2020. Worldwide, suicide ranks among the three leading causes of death among those aged 15–44 years. Suicide attempts are up to 20 times more frequent than completed suicides.

Suicide and body mass index

Risk of suicide decreases with increased weight and is low in obese persons.

Suicide and religion

Suicide rates are shown to be higher in low religious environments.

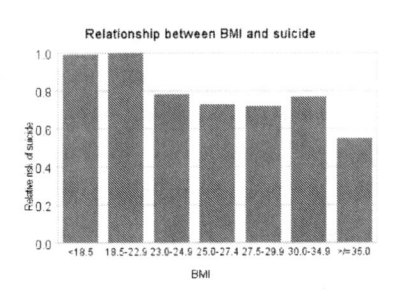

Risk of suicide decreases with increased body mass index in the United States.

See also

- Copycat suicide
- Suicide epidemic

List of countries by suicide rate

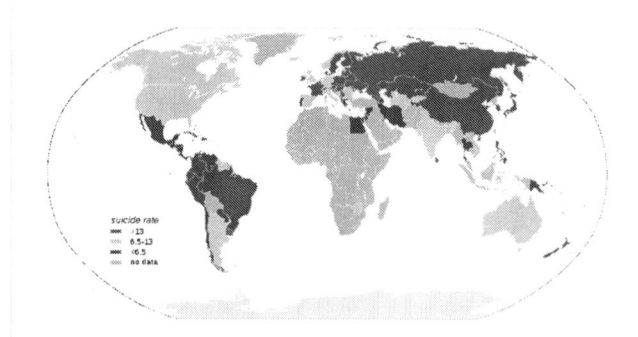

World map of suicide rates per 100,000. Red: >13, yellow: 6.5-13, blue: <6.5.

Suicide
Social aspects
Legislation · Philosophy Religious views · Euthanasia Assisted suicide · Right to die Benevolent suicide
Suicide crisis
Assessment of risk · Crisis hotline · Intervention · Prevention · Suicide watch
Suicide types
Copycat · Cult · Euthanasia · Familicide · Forced · Honor · Internet · Mass · Murder–suicide · Parasuicide · Suicide attack · By cop · Pact
Epidemiology
Gender · Suicide rate
History
List of suicides · Suicide methods
Related phenomena
Ideation · Self-harm · Suicide note · Locations · Failed suicide attempt
By country

List of countries by suicide rate

China · Japan · South Korea · United States

The following is a **list of suicide rates by country** according to data from the World Health Organization from 2008 in which a country's rank is determined by its total rate deaths officially recorded as suicides.[citation needed] Male and female suicide rates are out of total male population and total female population, respectively (i.e. total number of male suicides divided by total male population). The total rate of suicides is based on the total number of suicides divided by the total population rather than merely the average of the male and female suicide rates, because the gender ratio in most countries is not 1:1. *Year* refers to the most recent year that data was available for a particular country.

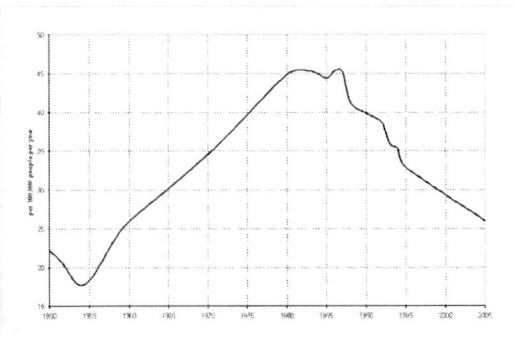

Suicide rate in Hungary (1950-2005), 1983: 45.3 suicides per 100,000 people, it was the second highest rate (after Lithuania, 1995: 45.6) in recorded human history

List

Suicides per 100,000 people per year

Position	Country	Male	Female	Total pop.	Year
1	Belarus	63.3	10.3	35.1	2003
2	South Korea *See: Suicide in South Korea*	N/A	N/A	31.0	2009
3	Lithuania	55.9	9.1	30.7	2008
4	Kazakhstan	46.2	9.0	26.9	2007
5	Japan *See: Suicide in Japan*	35.8	13.7	24.4	2007
6	Russia	37.2	9.0	23.1	2010
7	Guyana	33.8	11.6	22.9	2005
8	Ukraine	40.9	7.0	22.6	2005
9	Sri Lanka	N/A	N/A	21.6	1996
10	Hungary	37.1	8.6	21.5	2008
11	Latvia	34.1	7.7	19.9	2007
12	Slovenia	32.1	7.9	19.8	2008

List of countries by suicide rate

13		Serbia and Montenegro	28.4	11.1	19.5	2006
14		Finland	28.9	9.0	18.8	2007
15		Belgium	27.2	9.5	18.2	1999
16		Croatia	26.9	9.7	18.0	2006
17		Switzerland	23.5	11.7	17.5	2006
18		France	25.5	9.0	17.0	2006
19		Uruguay	26.0	6.3	15.8	2004
20		Moldova	28.0	4.3	15.7	2007
21		Austria	23.8	7.4	15.4	2007
22		South Africa	25.3	5.6	15.4	2005
23		Hong Kong	19.3	11.5	15.2	2006
24		Poland	26.8	4.4	15.2	2006
25		Suriname	23.9	4.8	14.4	2005
26		Estonia	29.1	6.2	16.5	2008
27		New Zealand	20.3	6.5	13.2	2008
28		Sweden	18.1	8.3	13.2	2006
29		Seychelles	N/A	N/A	13.2	1998
30		Slovakia	22.3	3.4	12.6	2005
31		Cuba	19.6	4.9	12.3	2006
32		Trinidad and Tobago	20.4	4.0	12.0	2002
33		Czech Republic	20.2	4.2	11.8	2008
34		Bosnia and Herzegovina	20.3	3.3	11.8	1991
35		Canada	17.9	5.4	11.6	2005
36		Portugal	17.9	5.5	11.5	2004
37		Norway	16.8	6.0	11.4	2006
38		Romania	18.9	4.0	11.3	2007
39		Iceland	17.9	4.5	11.3	2009
40		United States *See: Suicide in the United States*	17.7	4.5	11.1	2005
41		Luxembourg	17.7	4.3	11.0	2005
42		Denmark	16.0	5.7	10.6	2006

List of countries by suicide rate

43	India	12.2	9.1	10.6	1998
44	Australia	16.7	4.4	10.5	2004
45	Mauritius	16.0	4.8	10.4	2007
46	Singapore	12.9	7.7	10.3	2006
47	Chile	17.4	3.4	10.3	2005
48	Bulgaria	15.3	4.7	9.5	2007
49	Germany	14.9	4.4	9.4	2007
50	Ireland	14.5	4.2	9.3	2008
51	Kyrgyzstan	14.4	3.7	9.0	2006
52	Turkmenistan	13.8	3.5	8.6	1998
53	Netherlands	11.6	5.0	8.3	2007
54	Costa Rica	13.2	2.5	8.0	2006
55	Argentina	12.7	3.4	7.9	2005
56	Zimbabwe	10.6	5.2	7.9	1990
57	Thailand	12.0	3.8	7.8	2002
58	Saint Lucia	10.4	5.0	7.7	2002
59	Belize	13.4	1.6	7.6	2001
60	Puerto Rico	13.2	2.0	7.4	2005
61	Nicaragua	11.1	3.3	7.2	2005
62	Ecuador	9.1	4.5	6.8	2006
63	El Salvador	10.2	3.7	6.8	2006
64	Republic of Macedonia	9.5	4.0	6.8	2003
65	People's Republic of China	-	-	6.6	2008
66	United Kingdom	17.7	5.4	9.2	2008
67	Malta	12.3	0.5	6.4	2007
68	Spain	9.6	3.0	6.1	2007
69	Israel	9.9	2.1	5.8	2007
70	Grenada	9.8	1.9	5.9	2005
71	Panama	10.4	0.8	5.7	2006
72	Italy	8.4	2.3	5.2	2007

List of countries by suicide rate

73		Colombia	7.8	2.1	4.9	2005
74		Uzbekistan	7.0	2.3	4.7	2005
75		Brazil	7.3	1.9	4.6	2005
76		Cyprus	7.0	1.7	4.3	2008
77		Paraguay	5.5	2.7	4.1	2004
78		Albania	4.7	3.3	4.0	2008
79		Mexico	6.8	1.3	4.0	2008
80		Turkey	5.36	2.50	3.94	2008
81		Venezuela	6.1	1.4	3.8	2005
82		Saint Vincent and the Grenadines	7.3	0.0	3.7	2004
83		Bahrain	4.9	0.5	3.1	1988
84		Greece	4.8	1.0	2.8	2008
85		Tajikistan	2.9	2.3	2.6	2001
86		Armenia	3.9	1.0	2.4	2006
87		Guatemala	3.6	1.1	2.3	2006
88		Georgia	3.4	1.1	2.2	2001
89		Philippines	2.5	1.7	2.1	1993
90		Kuwait	2.5	1.4	2.0	2002
91		Dominican Republic	2.6	0.6	1.6	2004
92		The Bahamas	1.9	0.0	1.0	2002
93		Peru	1.1	0.6	0.9	2000
94		São Tomé and Príncipe	0.0	1.8	0.9	1987
95		Barbados	1.4	0.0	0.7	2001
96		Azerbaijan	1.0	0.3	0.6	2007
97		Maldives	0.7	0.0	0.3	2005
98		Iran	0.3	0.1	0.2	1991
99		Jamaica	0.3	0.0	0.1	1990
100		Syria	0.2	0.0	0.1	1985
101		Egypt	0.1	0.0	0.0	1987
102		Honduras	0.0	0.0	0.0	1978
103		Jordan	0.0	0.0	0.0	1979

104	Saint Kitts and Nevis	0.0	0.0	0.0	1995
105	Antigua and Barbuda	0.0	0.0	0.0	1995
106	Haiti	0.0	0.0	0.0	2003

See also

- List of OECD countries by suicide rate

Gender and suicide

Main article: Suicide

Suicide rate per 100,000 males (left) and per 100,000 females (right) (data from 1978–2008)

no data   < 1   1–5   5–5.8   5.8–8.5   8.5–12   12–19   19–22.5   22.5–26   26–29.5   29.5–33   33–36.5   >36.5

The relationship between **gender and suicide** has been extensively researched by Western sociologists, given that males die much more often by means of suicide than do females, although reported suicide attempts are more common among females.

Some medical professionals Wikipedia:Avoid weasel words believe this stems from the fact that males are more likely to end their lives through effective violent means (guns, knives, hanging, etc.), while women primarily use less severe methods such as overdosing on medications [citation needed].

The incidence of successful suicide is vastly higher among males than females among all age groups in most of the world. In the United States, the ratio varies between 3:1 to 10:1.

Some Wikipedia:Avoid weasel words ascribe the disparity to inherent differences in male/female psychology. Greater social stigma against male depression and a lack of social networks of support and help with depression are often identified as key reasons for men's disproportionately higher level of suicides, since suicide as a "cry for help" is not seen by men as an equally viable option. [citation needed]

Typically males die from suicide three to four times more often as females, and not unusually five or more times as often. CALM, the Campaign Against Living Miserably is a charity in the UK that attempts to highlight this issue for public discussion.

Excess male mortality from suicide is also evident from data from non-Western countries. In 1979-81, out of 74 countries with a non-zero suicide rate, two reported equal rates for the sexes (Seychelles and Kenya), three reported female rates exceeding male rates (Papua-New Guinea, Macau, and French Guiana), while the remaining 69 countries had male suicide rates greater than female suicide rates.

Barraclough found that the female rates of those aged 5–14 equaled or exceeded the male rates only in 14 countries, mainly in South America and Asia.

China is the only country in the world where more women than men take their own lives, with female suicides representing 58 percent of the total.

Suicides per 100,000 people per year

Rank	Country	Males	Females	Total	Year
1	Lithuania	68.1	12.9	38.6	2005
2	Belarus	63.3	10.3	35.1	2003
3	Russia	58.1	9.8	32.2	2005
4	Slovenia	42.1	11.1	26.3	2006
5	Hungary	42.3	11.2	26.0	2005
6	Kazakhstan	45.0	8.1	25.9	2005
7	Latvia	42.0	9.6	24.5	2005

Homosexuality and psychology

Psychology was one of the first disciplines to study **homosexuality** as a discrete phenomenon. In the late 19th century, and throughout most of the 20th century, it was standard for psychology to view homosexuality in terms of pathological models as a mental illness. That classification began to be subjected to critical scrutiny in research which consistently failed to produce any empirical or scientific basis for regarding homosexuality as a disorder or abnormality. As results from such research accumulated, professionals in medicine, mental health, and the behavioral and social sciences reached the conclusion that it was inaccurate to classify homosexuality as a mental disorder and that the DSM classification reflected untested assumptions based on once-prevalent social norms and clinical impressions from unrepresentative samples comprising patients seeking therapy and individuals whose conduct brought them into the criminal justice system. The research and clinical literature demonstrate that same-sex sexual and romantic attractions, feelings, and behaviors are normal and positive variations of human sexuality. Since the 1970s, the consensus of the behavioral and social sciences and the health and mental health professions is that homosexuality is a normal variation of human sexual orientation. In 1973 the American Psychiatric Association declassified homosexuality as a mental disorder. The American Psychological Association Council of Representatives followed in 1975.

Major areas of psychological research

Major psychological research into homosexuality is divided into five categories:

1. What causes some people to be attracted to their own sex?
2. What causes discrimination against people with a homosexual orientation and how can this be influenced?
3. Does having a homosexual orientation affect one's health status, psychological functioning or general well-being?
4. What determines successful adaptation to rejecting social climates? Why is homosexuality central to the identity of some people, but peripheral to the identity of others?
5. How do the children of homosexual people develop?

Psychological research in these areas has been important to counteracting prejudicial attitudes and actions, and to the gay and lesbian rights movement generally.

Etiology of homosexuality

See also: Biology and sexual orientation

See also: Environment and sexual orientation

Numerous different theories have been proposed to explain the development of homosexuality, but there is so far no universally accepted account of the origins of a sexual preference for persons of one's own sex.

Discrimination

See also: Homophobia and Societal attitudes toward homosexuality

Anti-gay attitudes and behaviors (sometimes called *homophobia* or *heterosexism*) have been objects of psychological research. Such research usually focuses on attitudes hostile to gay men, rather than attitudes hostile to lesbians. Anti-gay attitudes are often found in those who do not know gay people on a personal basis. There is also a high risk for anti-gay bias in psychotherapy with lesbian, gay, and bisexual clients.

One study found that "families with a strong emphasis on traditional values – implying the importance of religion, an emphasis on marriage and having children – were less accepting of homosexuality than were low-tradition families." One study found that parents who respond negatively to their child's sexual orientation tended to have lower self-esteem and negative attitudes toward women, and that "negative feelings about homosexuality in parents decreased the longer they were aware of their child's homosexuality."

One study found that nearly half of its sample had been the victim of verbal or physical violence because of their sexual orientation, usually committed by men. Such victimization is related to higher levels of depression, anxiety, anger, and symptoms of post-traumatic stress.

Mental health issues

Psychological research in this area includes examining mental health issues (including stress, depression, or addictive behavior) faced by gay and lesbian people as a result of the difficulties they experience because of their sexual orientation, physical appearance issues, eating disorders, or gender atypical behavior.

- **Drug and alcohol use**: Gay men are not at a higher risk for drug or alcohol abuse than heterosexual men, but lesbian women may be at a higher risk than heterosexual women. This finding is contrary to a common assumption that, because of the issues people face relating to coming out and anti-gay attitudes, drug and alcohol use is higher among lesbian, gay, and bisexual people than heterosexuals. Several clinical reports address methods of treating alcoholism in lesbian, gay, and bisexual clients specifically, including fostering greater acceptance of the client's sexual orientation.

- **Psychiatric disorders**: In a Dutch study, gay men reported significantly higher mood and anxiety disorders than straight men, and lesbians were significantly more likely to experience depression (but not other mood or anxiety disorders) than straight women.
- **Physical appearance and eating disorders**: Gay men tend to be more concerned about their physical appearance than straight men. Lesbian women are at a lower risk for eating disorders than heterosexual women.
- **Gender atypical behavior**: While this is not a disorder, gay men may face difficulties due to being more likely to display gender atypical behavior than heterosexual men. The difference is less pronounced between lesbians and straight women.
- **Minority Stress**: Stress caused from a sexual stigma, manifested as prejudice and discrimination, is a major source of stress for people with a homosexual orientation. Sexual-minority affirming groups and gay peer groups help counteract and buffer minority stress.
- **Ego-dystonic sexual orientation**: Conflict between religious identity and sexual orientation identity can cause severe stress, causing some people to want to change their sexual orientation. Sexual orientation identity exploration can help individuals evaluate the reasons behind the desire to change and help them resolve the conflict between their religious and sexual identity, either through sexual orientation identity reconstruction or affirmation therapies. Therapists are to offer acceptance, support, and understanding of clients and the facilitation of clients' active coping, social support, and identity exploration and development, without imposing a specific sexual orientation identity outcome. Ego-dystonic sexual orientation is a disorder where a person wishes their sexual orientation were different because of associated psychological and behavioral disorders.
- **Sexual relationship disorder**: People with a homosexual orientation in mixed-orientation marriages may struggle with the fear of the loss their marriage. Therapists should focus exploring the underlying personal and contextual problems, motivations, realities, and hopes for being in, leaving, or restructuring the relationship and should not focus solely on one outcome such as divorce or marriage. Sexual relationship disorder is a disorder where the gender identity or sexual orientation interferes with maintaining or forming of a relationship.

Suicide

See also: Suicide

The likelihood of suicide attempts are increased in both gay males and lesbians, as well as bisexuals of both sexes when compared to their heterosexual counterparts. The trend of having a higher incident rate among females is no exception with lesbians or bisexual females and when compared with homosexual males, lesbians are more likely to attempt than gay or bisexual males.

Studies vary with just how increased the risk is compared to heterosexuals with a low of 0.8–1.1 times more likely for females and 1.5–2.5 times more likely for males. The highs reach 4.6 more likely in females and 14.6 more likely in males.

Race and age play a factor in the increased risk. The highest ratios for males are attributed to caucasians when they are in their youthhood. By the age of 25, their risk is down to less than half of what it was however black gay males risk steadily increases to 8.6 times more likely. Through a lifetime the risks are 5.7 for white and 12.8 for black gay and bisexual males. Lesbian and bisexual females have opposite effects with less attempts in youthhood when compared to heterosexual females. Through a lifetime the likelihood to attempt nearly triple the youth 1.1 ratio for caucasian females, however for black females the rate is affected very little (less than 0.1 to 0.3 difference) with heterosexual black females having a slightly higher risk throughout most of the age-based study.

Gay and lesbian youth who attempt suicide are disproportionately subject to anti-gay attitudes, and have weaker skills for coping with discrimination, isolation, and loneliness, and were more likely to experience family rejection than those who do not attempt suicide. Another study found that gay and bisexual youth who attempted suicide had more feminine gender roles, adopted an LGB identity at a young age and were more likely than peers to report sexual abuse, drug abuse, and arrests for misconduct. One study found that same-sex sexual behavior, but not homosexual attraction or homosexual identity, was significantly predictive of suicide among Norwegian adolescents.

Sexual orientation identity development

Main article: Sexual orientation identity

- **Coming out**: Many gay and lesbian people go through a "coming out" experience at some point in their lives. Psychologists often say this process includes several stages "in which there is an awareness of being different from peers ('sensitization'), and in which people start to question their sexual identity ('identity confusion'). Subsequently, they start to explore practically the option of being gay or lesbian and learn to deal with the stigma ('identity assumption'). In the final stage, they integrate their sexual desires into a position understanding of self ('commitment')." However, the process is not always linear and it may differ for lesbians and gay men.
- **Different degrees of coming out**: One study found that gay men are more likely to be out to friends and siblings than co-workers, parents, and more distant relatives.
- **Coming out and well-being**: Same-sex couples who are openly gay are more satisfied in their relationships. For women who self-identify as lesbian, the more people know about her sexual orientation, the less anxiety, more positive affectivity, and greater self-esteem she has.
- **Rejection of gay identity**: Various studies report that for some religious people, rejecting a gay identity appears to relieve the distress caused by conflicts between religious values and sexual orientation. After reviewing the research, Dr. Glassgold of the American Psychological Association said some people are content in denying a gay identity and there is no clear evidence of harm.

Fluidity of sexual orientation

The American Psychiatric Association (APA) states that "some people believe that sexual orientation is innate and fixed; however, sexual orientation develops across a person's lifetime". In a statement issued jointly with other major American medical organizations, the American Psychological Association states that "different people realize at different points in their lives that they are heterosexual, gay, lesbian, or bisexual". A report from the Centre for Addiction and Mental Health states that, "For some people, sexual orientation is continuous and fixed throughout their lives. For others, sexual orientation may be fluid and change over time". Lisa Diamond's study "Female bisexuality from adolescence to adulthood" suggests that there is "considerable fluidity in bisexual, unlabeled, and lesbian women's attractions, behaviors, and identities".

Parenting

See also: LGBT parenting

LGBT parenting is when lesbian, gay, bisexual, and transgender (LGBT) people are parents to one or more children, either as biological or non-biological parents. Gay men face options which include: "foster care, variations of domestic and international adoption, diverse forms of surrogacy (whether "traditional" or gestational), and kinship arrangements, wherein they might coparent with a woman or women with whom they are intimately but not sexually involved." LGBT parents can also include single people who are parenting; to a lesser extent, the term sometimes refers to families with LGBT children.

In the 2000 U.S. Census, 33 percent of female same-sex couple households and 22 percent of male same-sex couple households reported at least one child under eighteen living in their home. Some children do not know they have an LGB parent; coming out issues vary and some parents may never come out to their children. LGBT parenting in general, and adoption by LGBT couples may be controversial in some countries. In January 2008, the European Court of Human Rights ruled that same-sex couples have the right to adopt a child. In the U.S., LGB people can legally adopt in all states except for Florida.

Although it is sometimes asserted in policy debates that heterosexual couples are inherently better parents than same-sex couples, or that the children of lesbian or gay parents fare worse than children raised by heterosexual parents, those assertions find no support in the scientific research literature. There is ample evidence to show that children raised by same-gender parents fare as well as those raised by heterosexual parents. More than 25 years of research have documented that there is no relationship between parents' sexual orientation and any measure of a child's emotional, psychosocial, and behavioral adjustment. These data have demonstrated no risk to children as a result of growing up in a family with 1 or more gay parents. No research supports the widely held conviction that the gender of parents matters for child well-being. If gay, lesbian, or bisexual parents were inherently less capable than otherwise comparable heterosexual parents, their children would evidence problems regardless of the type of sample. This pattern clearly has not been observed. Given the consistent failures in this research literature to disprove the null hypothesis, the burden of empirical proof is on those who argue that the children of sexual minority parents fare worse than the children of heterosexual parents.

Professor Judith Stacey, of New York University, stated: "Rarely is there as much consensus in any area of social science as in the case of gay parenting, which is why the American Academy of Pediatrics and all of the major professional organizations with expertise in child welfare have issued reports and resolutions in support of gay and lesbian parental rights". These organizations include the American Academy of Pediatrics, the American Academy of Child and Adolescent Psychiatry, the American Psychiatric Association, the American Psychological Association, the American Psychoanalytic Association, the National Association of Social Workers, the Child Welfare League of America, the North American Council on Adoptable Children, and Canadian Psychological Association (CPA). CPA is concerned that some persons and institutions are mis-interpreting the findings of psychological research to support their positions, when their positions are more accurately based on other systems of belief or values.

The vast majority of families in the United States today are not the "middle class family with a bread-winning father and a stay-at-home mother, married to each other and raising their biological children" that has been viewed as the norm. Since the end of the 1980s, it has been well established that children and adolescents can adjust just as well in nontraditional settings as in traditional settings.

Psychotherapy

Most people with a homosexual orientation who seek psychotherapy do so for the same reasons as straight people (stress, relationship difficulties, difficulty adjusting to social or work situations, etc.); their sexual orientation may be of primary, incidental, or no importance to their issues and treatment. Whatever the issue, there is a high risk for anti-gay bias in psychotherapy with lesbian, gay, and bisexual clients.

Relationship counseling

See also: Relationship counseling

Most relationship issues are shared equally among couples regardless of sexual orientation, but LGB clients additionally have to deal with homophobia, heterosexism, and other societal oppressions. Individuals may also be at different stages in the coming out process. Often, same-sex couples do not have as many role models of successful relationships as opposite-sex couples. There may be issues with gender-role socialization that does not affect opposite-sex couples.

A significant number of men and women experience conflict surrounding homosexual expression within a mixed-orientation marriage. Therapy may include helping the client feel more comfortable and accepting of same-sex feelings and to explore ways of incorporating same-sex and opposite-sex feelings into life patterns. Although a strong homosexual identity was associated with difficulties in marital satisfaction, viewing the same-sex activities as compulsive facilitated commitment to the marriage and to monogamy.

Gay affirmative psychotherapy

Main article: Gay affirmative psychotherapy

Gay affirmative psychotherapy is a form of psychotherapy for gay and lesbian clients which encourages them to accept their sexual orientation, and does not attempt to change their sexual orientation to heterosexual, or to eliminate or diminish their same-sex desires and behaviors. The American Psychological Association (APA) offers guidelines and materials for gay affirmative psychotherapy. Practitioners of gay affirmative psychotherapy states that homosexuality or bisexuality is not a mental illness, and that embracing and affirming gay identity can be a key component to recovery from other mental illnesses or substance abuse. Some people may find neither gay affirmative therapy nor conversion therapy appropriate, however. Clients whose religious beliefs are inconsistent with homosexual behavior may require some other method of integrating their conflicting religious and sexual selves.

Sexual orientation identity exploration

See also: Ego-dystonic sexual orientation

The APA recommends that if a client wants treatment to change his sexual orientation, the therapist should explore the reasons behind the desire, without favoring any particular outcome. The therapist should neither promote nor reject the idea of celibacy, but help the client come to their own decisions by evaluating the reasons behind the patient's goals. One example of sexual orientation identity exploration is Sexual Identity Therapy.

After exploration, a patient may proceed with Sexual orientation identity reconstruction, which helps a patient reconstruct sexual orientation identity. Psychotherapy, support groups, and life events can influence identity development; similarly, self-awareness, self-conception, and identity may evolve during treatment. It can change sexual orientation identity (private and public identification, and group belonging), emotional adjustment (self-stigma and shame reduction), and personal beliefs, values and norms (change of religious and moral belief, behavior and motivation). Some therapies include Gender Wholeness Therapy. Participation in an ex-gay groups can also help a patient develop a new sexual orientation identity.

Developments in Individual Psychology

In contemporary Adlerian thought homosexuals are not considered within the problematic discourse of the "failures of life". Christopher Shelley (1998), an Adlerian psychotherapist, published a volume of essays in the 1990s that feature Freudian, (post)Jungian and Adlerian contributions that demonstrate affirmative shifts in the depth psychologies. These shifts show how depth psychology can be utilized to support rather than pathologise gay and lesbian psychotherapy clients. The Journal of Individual Psychology, the English language flagship publication of Adlerian Psychology, released a volume in the summer of 2008 that reviews and corrects Adler's previously held beliefs on the homosexual community.

See also

- Association of Gay and Lesbian Psychiatrists
- Ego-dystonic sexual orientation

Resources and external links

American Psychological Association

- Answers to Your Questions About Sexual Orientation and Homosexuality [1]
- A Selected Bibliography of Lesbian, Gay, and Bisexual Concerns in Psychology [2]
- Guidelines for Psychotherapy with Lesbian, Gay, & Bisexual Clients [3]
- Avoiding Heterosexual Bias in Psychological Research [4]
- Being Gay Is Just as Healthy as Being Straight [5]
- Resolution on Sexual Orientation and Marriage [6]
- Resolution on Sexual Orientation, Parents, and Children [7]

American Academy of Pediatrics

- Sexual Orientation and Adolescents [8]

National Mental Health Association

- Factsheet: Bullying and Gay Youth [9]
- What Does Gay Mean? How to Talk with Kids about Sexual Orientation and Prejudice [10]

Copycat suicide

Suicide
Social aspects
Legislation · Philosophy Religious views · Euthanasia Assisted suicide · Right to die Benevolent suicide
Suicide crisis
Assessment of risk · Crisis hotline · Intervention · Prevention · Suicide watch
Suicide types
Copycat · Cult · Euthanasia · Familicide · Forced · Honor · Internet · Mass · Murder–suicide · Parasuicide · Suicide attack · By cop · Pact
Epidemiology
Gender · Suicide rate
History
List of suicides · Suicide methods
Related phenomena
Ideation · Self-harm · Suicide note · Locations · Failed suicide attempt
By country
China · Japan · South Korea · United States

A **copycat suicide** is defined as an emulation of another suicide that the person attempting suicide knows about either from local knowledge or due to accounts or depictions of the original suicide on television and in other media.

The massive wave of emulation suicides after a widely publicized suicide is known as the **Werther effect**, following the Werther novel of Goethe.

The well-known suicide serves as a model, in the absence of protective factors, for the next suicide. This is referred to as **suicide contagion**. They occasionally spread through a school system, through a community, or in terms of a celebrity suicide wave, nationally. This is called a **suicide cluster**. Examples of celebrities whose suicides have inspired suicide clusters include the Japanese musicians

Yukiko Okada and hide.

To prevent this type of suicide, it is customary in some countries for the media to discourage suicide reports except in special cases.

History

One of the earliest known associations between the media and suicide arose from Goethe's novel *Die Leiden des jungen Werthers* (*The Sorrows of Young Werther*), published in 1774. In that work the hero shoots himself after an ill-fated love, and shortly after its publication there were many reports of young men using the same method to commit suicide. This resulted in a ban of the book in several places. Hence the term "Werther effect", used in the technical literature to designate copycat suicides. The term was coined by researcher David Phillips in 1974. Copycat suicide is mostly blamed on the media.

Factors in suicide reporting

The Werther effect not only predicts an increase in suicide, but the majority of the suicides will take place in the same or a similar way as the one publicized. The more similar the person in the publicized suicide is to the people exposed to the information about it, the more likely the age group or demographic is to commit suicide. Upon learning of someone else's suicide, many people decide that action is appropriate for them as well, especially if the publicized suicide was of someone in a similar situation as them.

Publishing the means of suicides, romanticized and sensationalized reporting, particularly about celebrities, suggestions that there is an epidemic, glorifying the deceased and simplifying the reasons all lead to increases in the suicide rate. Increased rate of suicides has been shown to occur up to ten days after a television report. Studies in Japan and Germany have replicated findings of an imitative effect. Etzersdorfer et al. in an Austrian study showed a strong correlation between the number of papers distributed in various areas and the number of subsequent firearm suicides in each area after a related media report. Higher rates of copycat suicides have been found in those with similarities in race, age, and gender to the victim in the original report. Stack analyzed the results from 42 studies and found that those measuring the effect of a celebrity suicide story were 14.3 times more likely to find a copycat effect than studies that did not. Studies based on a real as opposed to fictional story were 4.03 times more likely to uncover a copycat effect and research based on televised stories was 82% less likely to report a copycat effect than research based on newspapers. Other scholars have been less certain about whether copycat suicides truly happen or are selectively hyped. For instance, fears of a suicide wave following the death of Kurt Cobain never materialized in an actual increase in suicides. Similarly the researcher Gerard Sullivan has critiqued research on copycat suicides, suggesting that data analyses have been selective and misleading, and that the evidence for copycat suicides are much less consistent than suggested by some researchers.

Many people interviewed after the suicide of a relative or friend have a tendency to simplify the issues; their grief can lead to their minimizing or ignoring significant factors. Studies show a high incidence of psychiatric disorders in suicide victims at the time of their death with the total figure ranging from 98% to 87.3% with mood disorders and substance abuse being the two most common. These are often undiagnosed or untreated and treatment can result in reductions in the suicide rate. Reports that minimize the impact of psychiatric disorders contribute to copycat suicides whereas reports that mention this factor and provide help-line contact numbers and advice for where sufferers may gain assistance can reduce suicides.

Social proof model

An alternate model to explain copycat suicide, called "social proof" by Cialdini, goes beyond the theories of glorification and simplification of reasons to look at why copycat suicides are so similar, demographically and in actual methods, to the original publicized suicide. In the social proof model, people imitate those who seem similar, despite or even because of societal disapproval. This model is important because it has nearly opposite ramifications for what the media ought to do about the copycat suicide effect than the standard model does.

Journalism codes

Various countries have national journalism codes which range from one extreme of, "Suicide and attempted suicide should in general never be given any mention" (Norway) to a more moderate, "In cases of suicide, publishing or broadcasting information in an exaggerated way that goes beyond normal dimensions of reporting with the purpose of influencing readers or spectators should not occur. Photography, pictures, visual images or film depicting such cases should not be made public" (Turkey) Many countries do not have national codes but do have in-house guidelines along similar lines. In the US there are no industrywide standards and a survey of inhouse guides of 16 US daily newspapers showed that only three mentioned the word *suicide* and none gave guidelines about publishing the method of suicide. Craig Branson, online director of the American Society of News Editors (ASNE), has been quoted as saying, "Industry codes are very generic and totally voluntary. Most ethical decisions are left to individual editors at individual papers. The industry would fight any attempt to create more specific rules or standards, and editors would no doubt ignore them." Guidelines on the reporting of suicides in Ireland were introduced recently which attempt to remove any positive connotations the act might have (e.g. using the term "completed" rather than "successful" when describing a suicide attempt which resulted in a death).

Journalist training

Australia is one of the few countries where there is a concerted effort to teach journalism students about this subject. The Mindframe national media initiative followed an ambivalent response by the Australian Press Council to an earlier media resource kit issued by Suicide Prevention Australia and the Australian Institute for Suicide Research and Prevention. The UK-based media ethics charity MediaWise [1] provides training for journalists on reporting suicide related issues.

See also

- Epidemiology of suicide
- Herd behavior
- Synchronicity
- Meme
- Badfinger A band of which 2 members committed suicide by hanging.

In art

- *Heathers*, a 1989 black comedy film in which the ostensible suicides of popular high school students spur copycat attempts.
- *Suicide Club (film)*, a 2002 Japanese horror film which revolves largely around a string of nationwide copycat suicides.

Further reading

- *The Copycat Effect* (ISBN 0-7434-8223-9)
- *Suicide Clusters* (ISBN 0-571-12991-9)

External links

- *Copycat Effect* [2] (Article that discusses the how the sensational coverage of violent events tends to provoke similar events and the journalistic ethics involved).
- Reporting on Suicide: Recommendations for the Media [3] - American Foundation for Suicide Prevention
- Suicide and the media [4] Links, resources and articles from The MediaWise Trust
- Gregor S, *Copycat suicide: The influence of the media* [5] 2004, Australian Psychological Society
- Stack S, *Media coverage as a risk factor in suicide* [6] Journal of Epidemiology and Community Health 2003;**57**:238-240
- Herman J, *Reporting on suicide* [7] Australian Press Council news, February 1998
- *Suicide and the media* [8] New Zealand youth suicide prevention strategy

- "Suicide and the Media: Recommendations on Suicide Reporting for Media Professionals (in Chinese)" [9], The Hong Kong Jockey Club Centre for Suicide Research and Prevention, The University of Hong Kong

Article Sources and Contributors

Suicide *Source*: http://en.wikipedia.org/?oldid=390081504 *Contributors*: Froid

Self-harm *Source*: http://en.wikipedia.org/?oldid=388750634 *Contributors*: Jdrewitt

Self-inflicted wound *Source*: http://en.wikipedia.org/?oldid=377432711 *Contributors*: Woohookitty

Attention seeking *Source*: http://en.wikipedia.org/?oldid=384157296 *Contributors*: Maurice Carbonaro

Psychological pain *Source*: http://en.wikipedia.org/?oldid=378452828 *Contributors*: Robert Daoust

Self-injury Awareness Day *Source*: http://en.wikipedia.org/?oldid=373319087 *Contributors*: Santryl

Enucleation of the eye *Source*: http://en.wikipedia.org/?oldid=389038319 *Contributors*: Graham87

Major depressive disorder *Source*: http://en.wikipedia.org/?oldid=390649055 *Contributors*: 1 anonymous edits

Euthanasia *Source*: http://en.wikipedia.org/?oldid=389035163 *Contributors*: Alan Liefting

Voluntary euthanasia *Source*: http://en.wikipedia.org/?oldid=389039018 *Contributors*: Alan Liefting

Non-voluntary euthanasia *Source*: http://en.wikipedia.org/?oldid=384708801 *Contributors*:

Involuntary euthanasia *Source*: http://en.wikipedia.org/?oldid=371564841 *Contributors*:

Legality of euthanasia *Source*: http://en.wikipedia.org/?oldid=390611673 *Contributors*: 1 anonymous edits

Murder–suicide *Source*: http://en.wikipedia.org/?oldid=383294552 *Contributors*:

Suicide pact *Source*: http://en.wikipedia.org/?oldid=389899348 *Contributors*: 1 anonymous edits

School shooting *Source*: http://en.wikipedia.org/?oldid=390575281 *Contributors*: 1 anonymous edits

Cult suicide *Source*: http://en.wikipedia.org/?oldid=390415845 *Contributors*: Bilby

Crime of passion *Source*: http://en.wikipedia.org/?oldid=372562902 *Contributors*: Zifnab

Suicide attack *Source*: http://en.wikipedia.org/?oldid=390579961 *Contributors*: Ewe Fokker

Kamikaze *Source*: http://en.wikipedia.org/?oldid=390199813 *Contributors*: Damwiki1

Shinyo (suicide boat) *Source*: http://en.wikipedia.org/?oldid=379597233 *Contributors*: Hoary

Suicide weapon *Source*: http://en.wikipedia.org/?oldid=324751098 *Contributors*: 1 anonymous edits

Mass suicide *Source*: http://en.wikipedia.org/?oldid=388467689 *Contributors*: 1 anonymous edits

Suicide mission *Source*: http://en.wikipedia.org/?oldid=383315459 *Contributors*:

Suicide epidemic *Source*: http://en.wikipedia.org/?oldid=386926485 *Contributors*: Xezbeth

Peer pressure *Source*: http://en.wikipedia.org/?oldid=390423817 *Contributors*: 1 anonymous edits

Political suicide *Source*: http://en.wikipedia.org/?oldid=366920503 *Contributors*: Mahanga

Suicide methods *Source*: http://en.wikipedia.org/?oldid=390674542 *Contributors*: GB fan

Suicide prevention *Source*: http://en.wikipedia.org/?oldid=390189794 *Contributors*: Rorybowman

Suicide intervention *Source*: http://en.wikipedia.org/?oldid=387252354 *Contributors*:

Epidemiology of suicide *Source*: http://en.wikipedia.org/?oldid=389455966 *Contributors*: 1 anonymous edits

List of countries by suicide rate *Source*: http://en.wikipedia.org/?oldid=388816554 *Contributors*: Diannaa

Gender and suicide *Source*: http://en.wikipedia.org/?oldid=384357756 *Contributors*: 1 anonymous edits

Homosexuality and psychology *Source*: http://en.wikipedia.org/?oldid=390055647 *Contributors*: Tijfo098

Copycat suicide *Source*: http://en.wikipedia.org/?oldid=387127520 *Contributors*:

Image Sources, Licenses and Contributors

File:Chatterton.jpg *Source*: http://bibliocm.bibliolabs.com/mwAnon/index.php?title=File:Chatterton.jpg *License*: Public Domain *Contributors*: Henry Wallis (1830 - 1916)

Image:David_-_The_Death_of_Socrates_crop.jpg *Source*: http://bibliocm.bibliolabs.com/mwAnon/index.php?title=File:David_-_The_Death_of_Socrates_crop.jpg *License*: Public Domain *Contributors*: Jacques-Louis David

File:Euthanasia machine (Australia).JPG *Source*: http://bibliocm.bibliolabs.com/mwAnon/index.php?title=File:Euthanasia_machine_(Australia).JPG *License*: Public Domain *Contributors*: ABF, Badseed, Bjarki S, Gaius Cornelius, Túrelio, 10 anonymous edits

File:USS White Plains attack by Tokkotai unit 25.10.1945 kk1a.jpg *Source*: http://bibliocm.bibliolabs.com/mwAnon/index.php?title=File:USS_White_Plains_attack_by_Tokkotai_unit_25.10.1945_kk1a.jpg *License*: Public Domain *Contributors*: Emijrp, GeorgHH, Ian Dunster, Joshbaumgartner, Makthorpe, 1 anonymous edits

File:Suicides by firearm 1999-2005.png *Source*: http://bibliocm.bibliolabs.com/mwAnon/index.php?title=File:Suicides_by_firearm_1999-2005.png *License*: GNU Free Documentation License *Contributors*: Original uploader was Citynoise at en.wikipedia (Original text : Citynoise (talk))

File:Self-inflicted injuries world map - Death - WHO2004.svg *Source*: http://bibliocm.bibliolabs.com/mwAnon/index.php?title=File:Self-inflicted_injuries_world_map_-_Death_-_WHO2004.svg *License*: Creative Commons Attribution-Sharealike 2.5 *Contributors*: User:Lokal_Profil

Image:Suicide world map - 2009 Male.svg *Source*: http://bibliocm.bibliolabs.com/mwAnon/index.php?title=File:Suicide_world_map_-_2009_Male.svg *License*: Creative Commons Attribution-Sharealike 2.5 *Contributors*: User:Lokal_Profil

Image:Suicide world map - 2009 Female,2.svg *Source*: http://bibliocm.bibliolabs.com/mwAnon/index.php?title=File:Suicide_world_map_-_2009_Female,2.svg *License*: Creative Commons Attribution-Sharealike 2.5 *Contributors*: User:Lokal_Profil

File:Wakisashi-sepukku-p1000699.jpg *Source*: http://bibliocm.bibliolabs.com/mwAnon/index.php?title=File:Wakisashi-sepukku-p1000699.jpg *License*: Creative Commons Attribution-Sharealike 2.0 *Contributors*: User:Rama

File:The way out.jpg *Source*: http://bibliocm.bibliolabs.com/mwAnon/index.php?title=File:The_way_out.jpg *License*: GNU Free Documentation License *Contributors*: George Grie

File:Schnittwunden.JPG *Source*: http://bibliocm.bibliolabs.com/mwAnon/index.php?title=File:Schnittwunden.JPG *License*: GNU Free Documentation License *Contributors*: user:Hendrike

File:DrugOverdose.jpg *Source*: http://bibliocm.bibliolabs.com/mwAnon/index.php?title=File:DrugOverdose.jpg *License*: Public Domain *Contributors*: Sam Metsfan

Image:Orange ribbon.svg *Source*: http://bibliocm.bibliolabs.com/mwAnon/index.php?title=File:Orange_ribbon.svg *License*: GNU Free Documentation License *Contributors*: user:MesserWoland

Image:Self-inflicted injuries world map - DALY - WHO2004.svg *Source*: http://bibliocm.bibliolabs.com/mwAnon/index.php?title=File:Self-inflicted_injuries_world_map_-_DALY_-_WHO2004.svg *License*: Creative Commons Attribution-Sharealike 2.5 *Contributors*: User:Lokal_Profil

Image:Moluccan Cockatoo (Cacatua moluccensis) -feather plucking.jpg *Source*: http://bibliocm.bibliolabs.com/mwAnon/index.php?title=File:Moluccan_Cockatoo_(Cacatua_moluccensis)_-feather_plucking.jpg *License*: Creative Commons Attribution 2.0 *Contributors*: julie corsi

File:Vincent Willem van Gogh 002.jpg *Source*: http://bibliocm.bibliolabs.com/mwAnon/index.php?title=File:Vincent_Willem_van_Gogh_002.jpg *License*: Public Domain *Contributors*: EDUCA33E, Emijrp, Ilse@, Rlbberlin, Tokorokoko, Vincent Steenberg, W., Wst, 2 anonymous edits

Image:Synapse Illustration2 tweaked.svg *Source*: http://bibliocm.bibliolabs.com/mwAnon/index.php?title=File:Synapse_Illustration2_tweaked.svg *License*: GNU Free Documentation License *Contributors*: Nrets

Image:Biological clock human.PNG *Source*: http://bibliocm.bibliolabs.com/mwAnon/index.php?title=File:Biological_clock_human.PNG *License*: GNU Free Documentation License *Contributors*: User:YassineMrabet

File:Unipolar depressive disorders world map - DALY - WHO2002.svg *Source*: http://bibliocm.bibliolabs.com/mwAnon/index.php?title=File:Unipolar_depressive_disorders_world_map_-_DALY_-_WHO2002.svg *License*: Creative Commons Attribution-Sharealike 2.5 *Contributors*: User:Lokal_Profil

Image:Abraham Lincoln head on shoulders photo portrait.jpg *Source*: http://bibliocm.bibliolabs.com/mwAnon/index.php?title=File:Abraham_Lincoln_head_on_shoulders_photo_portrait.jpg *License*: Public Domain *Contributors*: Bkell, Closeapple, Cwbm (commons), Daderot, Howcheng, Infrogmation, Jatkins, Mxn, Outriggr, Selket, Shizhao, Tharnton345, Tom, UpstateNYer, Wutsje, Zzyzx11, 8 anonymous edits

File:Euthanasia and the Law.png *Source*: http://bibliocm.bibliolabs.com/mwAnon/index.php?title=File:Euthanasia_and_the_Law.png *License*: Public Domain *Contributors*: User:Jrockley

Image:Euthanasia machine (Australia).JPG *Source*: http://bibliocm.bibliolabs.com/mwAnon/index.php?title=File:Euthanasia_machine_(Australia).JPG *License*: Public Domain *Contributors*: ABF, Badseed, Bjarki S, Gaius Cornelius, Túrelio, 10 anonymous edits

File:Hydrocephalus-baby.jpg *Source*: http://bibliocm.bibliolabs.com/mwAnon/index.php?title=File:Hydrocephalus-baby.jpg *License*: GNU Free Documentation License *Contributors*: Unknown

Image:Scale of justice 2.svg *Source*: http://bibliocm.bibliolabs.com/mwAnon/index.php?title=File:Scale_of_justice_2.svg *License*: Public Domain *Contributors*: User:DTR

Image:Ajax suicide.jpg *Source*: http://bibliocm.bibliolabs.com/mwAnon/index.php?title=File:Ajax_suicide.jpg *License*: unknown *Contributors*: .:Ajvol:., Bibi Saint-Pol, Filos96, Wolfmann

File:Gianciotto Discovers Paolo and Francesca Jean Auguste Dominique Ingres.jpg *Source*: http://bibliocm.bibliolabs.com/mwAnon/index.php?title=File:Gianciotto_Discovers_Paolo_and_Francesca_Jean_Auguste_Dominique_Ingres.jpg *License*: Public Domain *Contributors*: Juanpdp, Kilom691, Lotsofissues, Mattes, Sailko, Superm401, Tsui, Wst, 1 anonymous edits

Image:USS Bunker Hill burning.jpg *Source*: http://bibliocm.bibliolabs.com/mwAnon/index.php?title=File:USS_Bunker_Hill_burning.jpg *License*: Public Domain *Contributors*: U.S. Navy

Image Sources, Licenses and Contributors

Image:USS White Plains attack by Tokkotai unit 25.10.1945 kk1a.jpg *Source*: http://bibliocm.bibliolabs.com/mwAnon/index.php?title=File:USS_White_Plains_attack_by_Tokkotai_unit_25.10.1945_kk1a.jpg *License*: Public Domain *Contributors*: Emijrp, GeorgHH, Ian Dunster, Joshbaumgartner, Makthorpe, 1 anonymous edits

File:Kamikaze zero.jpg *Source*: http://bibliocm.bibliolabs.com/mwAnon/index.php?title=File:Kamikaze_zero.jpg *License*: Public Domain *Contributors*: Cave cattum, Get It, Ian Dunster, Makthorpe, Methem, Michael Reschke, Prüm, TOR, W.wolny, たね, 2 anonymous edits

Image:USS Bunker Hill hit by two Kamikazes.jpg *Source*: http://bibliocm.bibliolabs.com/mwAnon/index.php?title=File:USS_Bunker_Hill_hit_by_two_Kamikazes.jpg *License*: Public Domain *Contributors*: U.S. Navy; Original uploader was Quercusrobur at en.wikipedia.

File:Loudspeaker.svg *Source*: http://bibliocm.bibliolabs.com/mwAnon/index.php?title=File:Loudspeaker.svg *License*: Public Domain *Contributors*: Bayo, Gmaxwell, Husky, Iamunknown, Myself488, Nethac DIU, Omegatron, Rocket000, The Evil IP address, Wouterhagens, 9 anonymous edits

Image:Ensign Kiyoshi Ogawa hit Bunker Hill (new).png *Source*: http://bibliocm.bibliolabs.com/mwAnon/index.php?title=File:Ensign_Kiyoshi_Ogawa_hit_Bunker_Hill_(new).png *License*: Public Domain *Contributors*: User:JustDerek

Image:MokoShurai.jpg *Source*: http://bibliocm.bibliolabs.com/mwAnon/index.php?title=File:MokoShurai.jpg *License*: unknown *Contributors*: Kikuchi Yoosai / (of the reproduction) Tokyo National Museum

Image:D4Y Yoshinori Yamaguchi col.jpg *Source*: http://bibliocm.bibliolabs.com/mwAnon/index.php?title=File:D4Y_Yoshinori_Yamaguchi_col.jpg *License*: Public Domain *Contributors*: Original uploader was Felix c at en.wikipedia

File:CV09 Essex USG-80-G-273032-.jpg *Source*: http://bibliocm.bibliolabs.com/mwAnon/index.php?title=File:CV09_Essex_USG-80-G-273032-.jpg *License*: Public Domain *Contributors*: U.S. Naval Historical Center #80-G-80-G-273032

Image:A6M5 52c Kyushu.jpg *Source*: http://bibliocm.bibliolabs.com/mwAnon/index.php?title=File:A6M5_52c_Kyushu.jpg *License*: Public Domain *Contributors*: unlisted

File:Arima Masafumi.jpg *Source*: http://bibliocm.bibliolabs.com/mwAnon/index.php?title=File:Arima_Masafumi.jpg *License*: Public Domain *Contributors*: MChew, Reggaeman

Image:D4Y tail kitkun.jpg *Source*: http://bibliocm.bibliolabs.com/mwAnon/index.php?title=File:D4Y_tail_kitkun.jpg *License*: unknown *Contributors*: Original uploader was Felix c at en.wikipedia

Image:HMAS Australia bridge.jpg *Source*: http://bibliocm.bibliolabs.com/mwAnon/index.php?title=File:HMAS_Australia_bridge.jpg *License*: unknown *Contributors*: Bukvoed, Gsl, Makthorpe, Moroboshi, PMG, Pibwl, Rcbutcher, STB-1, Schekinov Alexey Victorovich, Thuresson, W.wolny

Image:USS Columbia attacked by kamikaze.jpg *Source*: http://bibliocm.bibliolabs.com/mwAnon/index.php?title=File:USS_Columbia_attacked_by_kamikaze.jpg *License*: Public Domain *Contributors*: Felix Stember, Hirurg, Makthorpe, STB-1, 1 anonymous edits

Image:USS Columbia hit by kamikaze.jpg *Source*: http://bibliocm.bibliolabs.com/mwAnon/index.php?title=File:USS_Columbia_hit_by_kamikaze.jpg *License*: Public Domain *Contributors*: Felix Stember, Hirurg, Makthorpe, STB-1, 1 anonymous edits

Image:USS Louisville hit by kamikaze.jpg *Source*: http://bibliocm.bibliolabs.com/mwAnon/index.php?title=File:USS_Louisville_hit_by_kamikaze.jpg *License*: Public Domain *Contributors*: Claus Ableiter, 2 anonymous edits

File:HMS Victorious on fire.jpg *Source*: http://bibliocm.bibliolabs.com/mwAnon/index.php?title=File:HMS_Victorious_on_fire.jpg *License*: unknown *Contributors*: User:W.wolny

Image:USS Intrepid CV-11 kamikaze strike.jpg *Source*: http://bibliocm.bibliolabs.com/mwAnon/index.php?title=File:USS_Intrepid_CV-11_kamikaze_strike.jpg *License*: Public Domain *Contributors*: U.S. Navy Photo

File:Kamikaze-ManchesterMSI crop.jpg *Source*: http://bibliocm.bibliolabs.com/mwAnon/index.php?title=File:Kamikaze-ManchesterMSI_crop.jpg *License*: Creative Commons Attribution-Sharealike 2.5 *Contributors*: User:Ed Fitzgerald, User:Error

Image:Chiran high school girls wave kamikaze pilot.jpg *Source*: http://bibliocm.bibliolabs.com/mwAnon/index.php?title=File:Chiran_high_school_girls_wave_kamikaze_pilot.jpg *License*: Public Domain *Contributors*: Bukvoed, Cave cattum, Joshbaumgartner, PMG, 5 anonymous edits

Image:ShinyoBoat.jpg *Source*: http://bibliocm.bibliolabs.com/mwAnon/index.php?title=File:ShinyoBoat.jpg *License*: Public Domain *Contributors*: Makthorpe, World Imaging

Image:ShinyoUnderWay.jpg *Source*: http://bibliocm.bibliolabs.com/mwAnon/index.php?title=File:ShinyoUnderWay.jpg *License*: Public Domain *Contributors*: Makthorpe, World Imaging

File:Street Girl's End.jpg *Source*: http://bibliocm.bibliolabs.com/mwAnon/index.php?title=File:Street_Girl's_End.jpg *License*: Public Domain *Contributors*: Jorva, Mattes, Origamiemensch, Sherurcij

File:Giotto - Scrovegni - -47- - Desperation.jpg *Source*: http://bibliocm.bibliolabs.com/mwAnon/index.php?title=File:Giotto_-_Scrovegni_-_-47-_-_Desperation.jpg *License*: Public Domain *Contributors*: Andreagrossmann, AndreasPraefcke, Eusebius, G.dallorto, Goldfritha, Hekerui, Mattes, Oldrydalian, Olivier2, Petrusbarbygere, Wst, 2 anonymous edits

Image:suicidemessageggb01252006.JPG *Source*: http://bibliocm.bibliolabs.com/mwAnon/index.php?title=File:Suicidemessageggb01252006.JPG *License*: Creative Commons Attribution 2.5 *Contributors*: Ies, Infrogmation, Man vyi, Miskatonic, Pfctdayelise, 4 anonymous edits

File:Jumper (suicide) in Dallas.jpg *Source*: http://bibliocm.bibliolabs.com/mwAnon/index.php?title=File:Jumper_(suicide)_in_Dallas.jpg *License*: Creative Commons Attribution 2.0 *Contributors*: Dieselgeek

File:Suicide world map - 2009 Male.svg *Source*: http://bibliocm.bibliolabs.com/mwAnon/index.php?title=File:Suicide_world_map_-_2009_Male.svg *License*: Creative Commons Attribution-Sharealike 2.5 *Contributors*: User:Lokal_Profil

File:Suicide world map - 2009 Female,2.svg *Source*: http://bibliocm.bibliolabs.com/mwAnon/index.php?title=File:Suicide_world_map_-_2009_Female,2.svg *License*: Creative Commons Attribution-Sharealike 2.5 *Contributors*: User:Lokal_Profil

Image:Relationship between bmi and suicide.png *Source*: http://bibliocm.bibliolabs.com/mwAnon/index.php?title=File:Relationship_between_bmi_and_suicide.png *License*: Creative Commons Attribution-Sharealike 3.0 *Contributors*: User:Jmh649

Image:Suicide rates map-en.svg *Source*: http://bibliocm.bibliolabs.com/mwAnon/index.php?title=File:Suicide_rates_map-en.svg *License*: Creative Commons Attribution-Sharealike 2.5 *Contributors*: User:Bamse

Image:Hungarian suicide rate.png *Source*: http://bibliocm.bibliolabs.com/mwAnon/index.php?title=File:Hungarian_suicide_rate.png *License*: GNU Free Documentation License *Contributors*: Rovibroni (Barna Rovács)

Image Sources, Licenses and Contributors

File:Flag of Belarus.svg *Source*: http://bibliocm.bibliolabs.com/mwAnon/index.php?title=File:Flag_of_Belarus.svg *License*: Public Domain *Contributors*: User:Zscout370

File:Flag of South Korea.svg *Source*: http://bibliocm.bibliolabs.com/mwAnon/index.php?title=File:Flag_of_South_Korea.svg *License*: Public Domain *Contributors*: Various

File:Flag of Lithuania.svg *Source*: http://bibliocm.bibliolabs.com/mwAnon/index.php?title=File:Flag_of_Lithuania.svg *License*: Public Domain *Contributors*: User:SKopp

File:Flag of Kazakhstan.svg *Source*: http://bibliocm.bibliolabs.com/mwAnon/index.php?title=File:Flag_of_Kazakhstan.svg *License*: unknown *Contributors*: -xfi-

File:Flag of Japan.svg *Source*: http://bibliocm.bibliolabs.com/mwAnon/index.php?title=File:Flag_of_Japan.svg *License*: Public Domain *Contributors*: Various

File:Flag of Russia.svg *Source*: http://bibliocm.bibliolabs.com/mwAnon/index.php?title=File:Flag_of_Russia.svg *License*: Public Domain *Contributors*: Zscout370

File:Flag of Guyana.svg *Source*: http://bibliocm.bibliolabs.com/mwAnon/index.php?title=File:Flag_of_Guyana.svg *License*: Public Domain *Contributors*: User:SKopp

File:Flag of Ukraine.svg *Source*: http://bibliocm.bibliolabs.com/mwAnon/index.php?title=File:Flag_of_Ukraine.svg *License*: Public Domain *Contributors*: User:Jon Harald Søby, User:Zscout370

File:Flag of Sri Lanka.svg *Source*: http://bibliocm.bibliolabs.com/mwAnon/index.php?title=File:Flag_of_Sri_Lanka.svg *License*: Public Domain *Contributors*: Zscout370

File:Flag of Hungary.svg *Source*: http://bibliocm.bibliolabs.com/mwAnon/index.php?title=File:Flag_of_Hungary.svg *License*: Public Domain *Contributors*: User:SKopp

File:Flag of Latvia.svg *Source*: http://bibliocm.bibliolabs.com/mwAnon/index.php?title=File:Flag_of_Latvia.svg *License*: Public Domain *Contributors*: User:SKopp

File:Flag of Slovenia.svg *Source*: http://bibliocm.bibliolabs.com/mwAnon/index.php?title=File:Flag_of_Slovenia.svg *License*: Public Domain *Contributors*: User:SKopp, User:Vzb83, User:Zscout370

File:Flag of Serbia and Montenegro.svg *Source*: http://bibliocm.bibliolabs.com/mwAnon/index.php?title=File:Flag_of_Serbia_and_Montenegro.svg *License*: Public Domain *Contributors*: User:Zscout370

File:Flag of Finland.svg *Source*: http://bibliocm.bibliolabs.com/mwAnon/index.php?title=File:Flag_of_Finland.svg *License*: Public Domain *Contributors*: User:SKopp

File:Flag of Belgium (civil).svg *Source*: http://bibliocm.bibliolabs.com/mwAnon/index.php?title=File:Flag_of_Belgium_(civil).svg *License*: Public Domain *Contributors*: Bean49, David Descamps, Dbenbenn, Denelson83, Fry1989, Gabriel trzy, Howcome, Ms2ger, Nightstallion, Oreo Priest, Rocket000, Sir Iain, ThomasPusch, Warddr, Zscout370, 4 anonymous edits

File:Flag of Croatia.svg *Source*: http://bibliocm.bibliolabs.com/mwAnon/index.php?title=File:Flag_of_Croatia.svg *License*: Public Domain *Contributors*: AnyFile, Argo Navis, Denelson83, Denniss, Dijxtra, Klemen Kocjancic, Kseferovic, Minestrone, Multichill, Neoneo13, Nightstallion, O, PatríciaR, Platonides, R-41, Rainman, Reisio, Rocket000, Suradnik13, Zicera, ZooFari, Zscout370, 5 anonymous edits

File:Flag of Switzerland.svg *Source*: http://bibliocm.bibliolabs.com/mwAnon/index.php?title=File:Flag_of_Switzerland.svg *License*: Public Domain *Contributors*: User:-xfi-, User:Marc Mongenet, User:Zscout370

File:Flag of France.svg *Source*: http://bibliocm.bibliolabs.com/mwAnon/index.php?title=File:Flag_of_France.svg *License*: Public Domain *Contributors*: User:SKopp, User:SKopp, User:SKopp, User:SKopp, User:SKopp, User:SKopp

File:Flag of Uruguay.svg *Source*: http://bibliocm.bibliolabs.com/mwAnon/index.php?title=File:Flag_of_Uruguay.svg *License*: Public Domain *Contributors*: CommonsDelinker, Fry1989, Homo lupus, Huhsunqu, Kineto007, Klemen Kocjancic, Kookaburra, Lorakesz, Mattes, Neq00, Nightstallion, Pumbaa80, Reisio, ThomasPusch, Zscout370, 6 anonymous edits

File:Flag of Moldova.svg *Source*: http://bibliocm.bibliolabs.com/mwAnon/index.php?title=File:Flag_of_Moldova.svg *License*: unknown *Contributors*: User:Nameneko

File:Flag of Austria.svg *Source*: http://bibliocm.bibliolabs.com/mwAnon/index.php?title=File:Flag_of_Austria.svg *License*: Public Domain *Contributors*: User:SKopp

File:Flag of South Africa.svg *Source*: http://bibliocm.bibliolabs.com/mwAnon/index.php?title=File:Flag_of_South_Africa.svg *License*: unknown *Contributors*: Adriaan, Anime Addict AA, AnonMoos, BRUTE, Daemonic Kangaroo, Dnik, Duduziq, Dzordzm, Fry1989, Homo lupus, Jappalang, Juliancolton, Kam Solusar, Klemen Kocjancic, Klymene, Lexxyy, Mahahahaneapneap, Manuelt15, Moviedefender, Ninane, Poznaniak, SKopp, ThePCKid, ThomasPusch, Tvdm, Ultratomio, Vzb83, Zscout370, 33 anonymous edits

File:Flag of Hong Kong.svg *Source*: http://bibliocm.bibliolabs.com/mwAnon/index.php?title=File:Flag_of_Hong_Kong.svg *License*: Public Domain *Contributors*: Designed by

File:Flag of Poland.svg *Source*: http://bibliocm.bibliolabs.com/mwAnon/index.php?title=File:Flag_of_Poland.svg *License*: Public Domain *Contributors*: User:Mareklug, User:Wanted

File:Flag of Suriname.svg *Source*: http://bibliocm.bibliolabs.com/mwAnon/index.php?title=File:Flag_of_Suriname.svg *License*: Public Domain *Contributors*: ALE!, Anime Addict AA, Fry1989, Homo lupus, Klemen Kocjancic, Kookaburra, Krun, Mattes, Mikewazhere, Mmxx, Nightstallion, Pfctdayelise, Reisio, ThomasPusch, Vzb83, Zscout370, 16 anonymous edits

File:Flag of Estonia.svg *Source*: http://bibliocm.bibliolabs.com/mwAnon/index.php?title=File:Flag_of_Estonia.svg *License*: Public Domain *Contributors*: User:PeepP, User:SKopp

File:Flag of New Zealand.svg *Source*: http://bibliocm.bibliolabs.com/mwAnon/index.php?title=File:Flag_of_New_Zealand.svg *License*: Public Domain *Contributors*: Adambro, Arria Belli, Avenue, Bawolff, Bjankuloski06en, ButterStick, Denelson83, Donk, Duduziq, EugeneZelenko, Fred J, Fry1989, Hugh Jass, Ibagli, Jusjih, Klemen Kocjancic, Mamndassan, Mattes, Nightstallion, O, Peeperman, Poromiami, Reisio, Rfc1394, Shizhao, Tabasco, Transparent Blue, Väsk, Xufanc, Zscout370, 35 anonymous edits

File:Flag of Sweden.svg *Source*: http://bibliocm.bibliolabs.com/mwAnon/index.php?title=File:Flag_of_Sweden.svg *License*: Public Domain *Contributors*: User:Jon Harald Søby

File:Flag of the Seychelles.svg *Source*: http://bibliocm.bibliolabs.com/mwAnon/index.php?title=File:Flag_of_the_Seychelles.svg *License*: Public Domain *Contributors*: Denniss, Emijrp, Fry1989, Gabbe, Homo lupus, Klemen Kocjancic, Nightstallion, Porao, Sertion, ThomasPusch, Vzb83, Zscout370, 2 anonymous edits

File:Flag of Slovakia.svg *Source*: http://bibliocm.bibliolabs.com/mwAnon/index.php?title=File:Flag_of_Slovakia.svg *License*: Public Domain *Contributors*: User:SKopp

File:Flag of Cuba.svg *Source*: http://bibliocm.bibliolabs.com/mwAnon/index.php?title=File:Flag_of_Cuba.svg *License*: Public Domain *Contributors*: see below

File:Flag of Trinidad and Tobago.svg *Source*: http://bibliocm.bibliolabs.com/mwAnon/index.php?title=File:Flag_of_Trinidad_and_Tobago.svg *License*: Public Domain *Contributors*: AnonMoos, Boricuaeddie, Duduziq, Enbéká, Fry1989, Homo lupus, Klemen Kocjancic, Madden, Mattes, Nagy, Neq00, Nightstallion, Pumbaa80, SKopp, Tomia, 10 anonymous edits

File:Flag of the Czech Republic.svg *Source*: http://bibliocm.bibliolabs.com/mwAnon/index.php?title=File:Flag_of_the_Czech_Republic.svg *License*: Public Domain *Contributors*: special commission (of code): SVG version by cs:-xfi-. Colors according to Appendix No. 3 of czech legal Act 3/1993. cs:Zirland.

Image Sources, Licenses and Contributors

File:Flag of Bosnia and Herzegovina.svg *Source*: http://bibliocm.bibliolabs.com/mwAnon/index.php?title=File:Flag_of_Bosnia_and_Herzegovina.svg *License*: Public Domain *Contributors*: User:Kseferovic

File:Flag of Canada.svg *Source*: http://bibliocm.bibliolabs.com/mwAnon/index.php?title=File:Flag_of_Canada.svg *License*: Public Domain *Contributors*: User:E Pluribus Anthony, User:Mzajac

File:Flag of Portugal.svg *Source*: http://bibliocm.bibliolabs.com/mwAnon/index.php?title=File:Flag_of_Portugal.svg *License*: Public Domain *Contributors*: User:Nightstallion

File:Flag of Norway.svg *Source*: http://bibliocm.bibliolabs.com/mwAnon/index.php?title=File:Flag_of_Norway.svg *License*: Public Domain *Contributors*: User:Dbenbenn

File:Flag of Romania.svg *Source*: http://bibliocm.bibliolabs.com/mwAnon/index.php?title=File:Flag_of_Romania.svg *License*: Public Domain *Contributors*: User:AdiJapan

File:Flag of Iceland.svg *Source*: http://bibliocm.bibliolabs.com/mwAnon/index.php?title=File:Flag_of_Iceland.svg *License*: Public Domain *Contributors*: User:Zscout370, User:Ævar Arnfjörð Bjarmason

File:Flag of the United States.svg *Source*: http://bibliocm.bibliolabs.com/mwAnon/index.php?title=File:Flag_of_the_United_States.svg *License*: Public Domain *Contributors*: User:Dbenbenn, User:Indolences, User:Jacobolus, User:Technion, User:Zscout370

File:Flag of Luxembourg.svg *Source*: http://bibliocm.bibliolabs.com/mwAnon/index.php?title=File:Flag_of_Luxembourg.svg *License*: Public Domain *Contributors*: User:SKopp

File:Flag of Denmark.svg *Source*: http://bibliocm.bibliolabs.com/mwAnon/index.php?title=File:Flag_of_Denmark.svg *License*: Public Domain *Contributors*: User:Madden

File:Flag of India.svg *Source*: http://bibliocm.bibliolabs.com/mwAnon/index.php?title=File:Flag_of_India.svg *License*: Public Domain *Contributors*: User:SKopp

File:Flag of Australia.svg *Source*: http://bibliocm.bibliolabs.com/mwAnon/index.php?title=File:Flag_of_Australia.svg *License*: Public Domain *Contributors*: Ian Fieggen

File:Flag of Mauritius.svg *Source*: http://bibliocm.bibliolabs.com/mwAnon/index.php?title=File:Flag_of_Mauritius.svg *License*: Public Domain *Contributors*: User:Gabbe, User:SKopp

File:Flag of Singapore.svg *Source*: http://bibliocm.bibliolabs.com/mwAnon/index.php?title=File:Flag_of_Singapore.svg *License*: Public Domain *Contributors*: Various

File:Flag of Chile.svg *Source*: http://bibliocm.bibliolabs.com/mwAnon/index.php?title=File:Flag_of_Chile.svg *License*: Public Domain *Contributors*: User:SKopp

File:Flag of Bulgaria.svg *Source*: http://bibliocm.bibliolabs.com/mwAnon/index.php?title=File:Flag_of_Bulgaria.svg *License*: Public Domain *Contributors*: Avala, Denelson83, Fry1989, Homo lupus, Ikonact, Kallerna, Klemen Kocjancic, Martyr, Mattes, Neq00, Pumbaa80, SKopp, Scroch, Spacebirdy, Srtxg, Ultratomio, Vonvon, Zscout370, Викимонетчик, 9 anonymous edits

File:Flag of Germany.svg *Source*: http://bibliocm.bibliolabs.com/mwAnon/index.php?title=File:Flag_of_Germany.svg *License*: Public Domain *Contributors*: User:Madden, User:Pumbaa80, User:SKopp

File:Flag of Ireland.svg *Source*: http://bibliocm.bibliolabs.com/mwAnon/index.php?title=File:Flag_of_Ireland.svg *License*: Public Domain *Contributors*: User:SKopp

File:Flag of Kyrgyzstan.svg *Source*: http://bibliocm.bibliolabs.com/mwAnon/index.php?title=File:Flag_of_Kyrgyzstan.svg *License*: Public Domain *Contributors*: Made by Andrew Duhan for the Sodipodi SVG flag collection, and is public domain.

File:Flag of Turkmenistan.svg *Source*: http://bibliocm.bibliolabs.com/mwAnon/index.php?title=File:Flag_of_Turkmenistan.svg *License*: Public Domain *Contributors*: User:Vzb83

File:Flag of the Netherlands.svg *Source*: http://bibliocm.bibliolabs.com/mwAnon/index.php?title=File:Flag_of_the_Netherlands.svg *License*: Public Domain *Contributors*: User:Zscout370

File:Flag of Costa Rica.svg *Source*: http://bibliocm.bibliolabs.com/mwAnon/index.php?title=File:Flag_of_Costa_Rica.svg *License*: Public Domain *Contributors*: User:Gabbe, User:SKopp

File:Flag of Argentina.svg *Source*: http://bibliocm.bibliolabs.com/mwAnon/index.php?title=File:Flag_of_Argentina.svg *License*: Public Domain *Contributors*: User:Dbenbenn

File:Flag of Zimbabwe.svg *Source*: http://bibliocm.bibliolabs.com/mwAnon/index.php?title=File:Flag_of_Zimbabwe.svg *License*: Public Domain *Contributors*: User:Madden

File:Flag of Thailand.svg *Source*: http://bibliocm.bibliolabs.com/mwAnon/index.php?title=File:Flag_of_Thailand.svg *License*: Public Domain *Contributors*: Andy Dingley, Chaddy, Duduziq, Emerentia, Fry1989, Gabbe, Gurch, Homo lupus, Juiced lemon, Klemen Kocjancic, Mattes, Neq00, Paul 012, Rugby471, Sahapon-krit hellokitty, TOR, Teetaweepo, Xiengyod, Zscout370, Δ, 24 anonymous edits

File:Flag of Saint Lucia.svg *Source*: http://bibliocm.bibliolabs.com/mwAnon/index.php?title=File:Flag_of_Saint_Lucia.svg *License*: Public Domain *Contributors*: User:SKopp

File:Flag of Belize.svg *Source*: http://bibliocm.bibliolabs.com/mwAnon/index.php?title=File:Flag_of_Belize.svg *License*: Public Domain *Contributors*: Caleb Moore

File:Flag of Puerto Rico.svg *Source*: http://bibliocm.bibliolabs.com/mwAnon/index.php?title=File:Flag_of_Puerto_Rico.svg *License*: Public Domain *Contributors*: User:Madden

File:Flag of Nicaragua.svg *Source*: http://bibliocm.bibliolabs.com/mwAnon/index.php?title=File:Flag_of_Nicaragua.svg *License*: Public Domain *Contributors*: User:Nightstallion

File:Flag of Ecuador.svg *Source*: http://bibliocm.bibliolabs.com/mwAnon/index.php?title=File:Flag_of_Ecuador.svg *License*: Public Domain *Contributors*: President of the Republic of Ecuador, Zscout370

File:Flag of El Salvador.svg *Source*: http://bibliocm.bibliolabs.com/mwAnon/index.php?title=File:Flag_of_El_Salvador.svg *License*: Public Domain *Contributors*: user:Nightstallion

File:Flag of Macedonia.svg *Source*: http://bibliocm.bibliolabs.com/mwAnon/index.php?title=File:Flag_of_Macedonia.svg *License*: Public Domain *Contributors*: User:Gabbe, User:SKopp

File:Flag of the People's Republic of China.svg *Source*: http://bibliocm.bibliolabs.com/mwAnon/index.php?title=File:Flag_of_the_People's_Republic_of_China.svg *License*: Public Domain *Contributors*: User:Denelson83, User:SKopp, User:Shizhao, User:Zscout370

File:Flag of the United Kingdom.svg *Source*: http://bibliocm.bibliolabs.com/mwAnon/index.php?title=File:Flag_of_the_United_Kingdom.svg *License*: Public Domain *Contributors*: User:Zscout370

Image Sources, Licenses and Contributors

File:Flag of Malta.svg *Source*: http://bibliocm.bibliolabs.com/mwAnon/index.php?title=File:Flag_of_Malta.svg *License*: Public Domain *Contributors*: Fry1989, Gabbe, Homo lupus, Klemen Kocjancic, Liftarn, Mattes, Nightstallion, Peeperman, Pumbaa80, Ratatosk, Zscout370, 3 anonymous edits

File:Flag of Spain.svg *Source*: http://bibliocm.bibliolabs.com/mwAnon/index.php?title=File:Flag_of_Spain.svg *License*: Public Domain *Contributors*: Pedro A. Gracia Fajardo, escudo de Manual de Imagen Institucional de la Administración General del Estado

File:Flag of Israel.svg *Source*: http://bibliocm.bibliolabs.com/mwAnon/index.php?title=File:Flag_of_Israel.svg *License*: Public Domain *Contributors*: AnonMoos, Bastique, Bobika, Brown spite, Captain Zizi, Cerveaugenie, Drork, Etams, Fred J, Fry1989, Geagea, Himasaram, Homo lupus, Humus sapiens, Klemen Kocjancic, Kookaburra, Luispihormiguero, Madden, Neq00, NielsF, Nightstallion, Oren neu dag, Patstuart, PeeJay2K3, Pumbaa80, Ramiy, Reisio, SKopp, Technion, Typhix, Valentinian, Yellow up, Zscout370, 31 anonymous edits

File:Flag of Grenada.svg *Source*: http://bibliocm.bibliolabs.com/mwAnon/index.php?title=File:Flag_of_Grenada.svg *License*: Public Domain *Contributors*: User:SKopp

File:Flag of Panama.svg *Source*: http://bibliocm.bibliolabs.com/mwAnon/index.php?title=File:Flag_of_Panama.svg *License*: Public Domain *Contributors*: -xfi-, Addicted04, Duduziq, Fadi the philologer, Fry1989, Klemen Kocjancic, Liftarn, Mattes, Nightstallion, Ninane, Pumbaa80, Reisio, Rfc1394, Thomas81, ThomasPusch, Zscout370, Ö, Фёдор Гусляров, 17 anonymous edits

File:Flag of Italy.svg *Source*: http://bibliocm.bibliolabs.com/mwAnon/index.php?title=File:Flag_of_Italy.svg *License*: Public Domain *Contributors*: see below

File:Flag of Colombia.svg *Source*: http://bibliocm.bibliolabs.com/mwAnon/index.php?title=File:Flag_of_Colombia.svg *License*: Public Domain *Contributors*: User:SKopp

File:Flag of Uzbekistan.svg *Source*: http://bibliocm.bibliolabs.com/mwAnon/index.php?title=File:Flag_of_Uzbekistan.svg *License*: Public Domain *Contributors*: User:Zscout370

File:Flag of Brazil.svg *Source*: http://bibliocm.bibliolabs.com/mwAnon/index.php?title=File:Flag_of_Brazil.svg *License*: Public Domain *Contributors*: Brazilian Government

File:Flag of Cyprus.svg *Source*: http://bibliocm.bibliolabs.com/mwAnon/index.php?title=File:Flag_of_Cyprus.svg *License*: Public Domain *Contributors*: AnonMoos, Bukk, Consta, Dbenbenn, Denelson83, Duduziq, Er Komandanti, F. F. Fjodor, Fry1989, Homo lupus, Klemen Kocjancic, Krinkle, Mattes, NeoCy, Neq00, Nightstallion, Oleh Kernytskyi, Pumbaa80, Reisio, Telim tor, ThomasPusch, Ufo karadagli, Vzb83, 15 anonymous edits

File:Flag of Paraguay.svg *Source*: http://bibliocm.bibliolabs.com/mwAnon/index.php?title=File:Flag_of_Paraguay.svg *License*: Public Domain *Contributors*: Republica del Paraguay

File:Flag of Albania.svg *Source*: http://bibliocm.bibliolabs.com/mwAnon/index.php?title=File:Flag_of_Albania.svg *License*: Public Domain *Contributors*: User:Dbenbenn

File:Flag of Mexico.svg *Source*: http://bibliocm.bibliolabs.com/mwAnon/index.php?title=File:Flag_of_Mexico.svg *License*: Public Domain *Contributors*: User:AlexCovarrubias

File:Flag of Turkey.svg *Source*: http://bibliocm.bibliolabs.com/mwAnon/index.php?title=File:Flag_of_Turkey.svg *License*: Public Domain *Contributors*: User:Dbenbenn

File:Flag of Venezuela.svg *Source*: http://bibliocm.bibliolabs.com/mwAnon/index.php?title=File:Flag_of_Venezuela.svg *License*: Public Domain *Contributors*: Bastique, Denelson83, DerFussi, Fry1989, George McFinnigan, Herbythyme, Homo lupus, Huhsunqu, Infrogmation, Klemen Kocjancic, Ludger1961, Neq00, Nightstallion, Reisio, ThomasPusch, Vzb83, Wikisole, Zscout370, 12 anonymous edits

File:Flag of Saint Vincent and the Grenadines.svg *Source*: http://bibliocm.bibliolabs.com/mwAnon/index.php?title=File:Flag_of_Saint_Vincent_and_the_Grenadines.svg *License*: Public Domain *Contributors*: User:SKopp

File:Flag of Bahrain.svg *Source*: http://bibliocm.bibliolabs.com/mwAnon/index.php?title=File:Flag_of_Bahrain.svg *License*: Public Domain *Contributors*: User:SKopp, User:Zscout370

File:Flag of Greece.svg *Source*: http://bibliocm.bibliolabs.com/mwAnon/index.php?title=File:Flag_of_Greece.svg *License*: Public Domain *Contributors*: (of code) (talk)

File:Flag of Tajikistan.svg *Source*: http://bibliocm.bibliolabs.com/mwAnon/index.php?title=File:Flag_of_Tajikistan.svg *License*: Public Domain *Contributors*: Alex Spade, Anime Addict AA, Apatomerus, EugeneZelenko, Fry1989, Homo lupus, Johnny Rotten, Klemen Kocjancic, Mattes, Nameneko, Neq00, Nightstallion, Rinkio, Zscout370, Умед Джайхони, 3 anonymous edits

File:Flag of Armenia.svg *Source*: http://bibliocm.bibliolabs.com/mwAnon/index.php?title=File:Flag_of_Armenia.svg *License*: Public Domain *Contributors*: User:SKopp

File:Flag of Guatemala.svg *Source*: http://bibliocm.bibliolabs.com/mwAnon/index.php?title=File:Flag_of_Guatemala.svg *License*: Public Domain *Contributors*: User:Denelson83, User:Vzb83

File:Flag of Georgia.svg *Source*: http://bibliocm.bibliolabs.com/mwAnon/index.php?title=File:Flag_of_Georgia.svg *License*: Public Domain *Contributors*: User:SKopp

File:Flag of the Philippines.svg *Source*: http://bibliocm.bibliolabs.com/mwAnon/index.php?title=File:Flag_of_the_Philippines.svg *License*: Public Domain *Contributors*: Aira Cutamora

File:Flag of Kuwait.svg *Source*: http://bibliocm.bibliolabs.com/mwAnon/index.php?title=File:Flag_of_Kuwait.svg *License*: Public Domain *Contributors*: User:SKopp

File:Flag of the Dominican Republic.svg *Source*: http://bibliocm.bibliolabs.com/mwAnon/index.php?title=File:Flag_of_the_Dominican_Republic.svg *License*: Public Domain *Contributors*: User:Nightstallion

File:Flag of the Bahamas.svg *Source*: http://bibliocm.bibliolabs.com/mwAnon/index.php?title=File:Flag_of_the_Bahamas.svg *License*: Public Domain *Contributors*: Bahamas government

File:Flag of Peru.svg *Source*: http://bibliocm.bibliolabs.com/mwAnon/index.php?title=File:Flag_of_Peru.svg *License*: Public Domain *Contributors*: User:Dbenbenn

File:Flag of Sao Tome and Principe.svg *Source*: http://bibliocm.bibliolabs.com/mwAnon/index.php?title=File:Flag_of_Sao_Tome_and_Principe.svg *License*: Public Domain *Contributors*: User:Gabbe

File:Flag of Barbados.svg *Source*: http://bibliocm.bibliolabs.com/mwAnon/index.php?title=File:Flag_of_Barbados.svg *License*: Public Domain *Contributors*: User:Denelson83

File:Flag of Azerbaijan.svg *Source*: http://bibliocm.bibliolabs.com/mwAnon/index.php?title=File:Flag_of_Azerbaijan.svg *License*: Public Domain *Contributors*: User:SKopp

File:Flag of Maldives.svg *Source*: http://bibliocm.bibliolabs.com/mwAnon/index.php?title=File:Flag_of_Maldives.svg *License*: Public Domain *Contributors*: user:Nightstallion

File:Flag of Iran.svg *Source*: http://bibliocm.bibliolabs.com/mwAnon/index.php?title=File:Flag_of_Iran.svg *License*: unknown *Contributors*: Various

File:Flag of Jamaica.svg *Source*: http://bibliocm.bibliolabs.com/mwAnon/index.php?title=File:Flag_of_Jamaica.svg *License*: Public Domain *Contributors*: User:Madden

File:Flag of Syria.svg *Source*: http://bibliocm.bibliolabs.com/mwAnon/index.php?title=File:Flag_of_Syria.svg *License*: Public Domain *Contributors*: see below

Image Sources, Licenses and Contributors

File:Flag of Egypt.svg *Source*: http://bibliocm.bibliolabs.com/mwAnon/index.php?title=File:Flag_of_Egypt.svg *License*: Public Domain *Contributors*: Open Clip Art

File:Flag of Honduras.svg *Source*: http://bibliocm.bibliolabs.com/mwAnon/index.php?title=File:Flag_of_Honduras.svg *License*: Public Domain *Contributors*: D1990, Denelson83, ECanalla, Feydey, Fred J, Homo lupus, Klemen Kocjancic, Mattes, Matthew hk, Neq00, Oak27, Pumbaa80, Rocket000, RubiksMaster110, SKopp, ThomasPusch, Tocino, Vzb83, Yuval Madar, ZooFari, Zscout370, 10 anonymous edits

File:Flag of Jordan.svg *Source*: http://bibliocm.bibliolabs.com/mwAnon/index.php?title=File:Flag_of_Jordan.svg *License*: Public Domain *Contributors*: User:SKopp

File:Flag of Saint Kitts and Nevis.svg *Source*: http://bibliocm.bibliolabs.com/mwAnon/index.php?title=File:Flag_of_Saint_Kitts_and_Nevis.svg *License*: Public Domain *Contributors*: User:Pumbaa80

File:Flag of Antigua and Barbuda.svg *Source*: http://bibliocm.bibliolabs.com/mwAnon/index.php?title=File:Flag_of_Antigua_and_Barbuda.svg *License*: Public Domain *Contributors*: User:Dbenbenn

File:Flag of Haiti.svg *Source*: http://bibliocm.bibliolabs.com/mwAnon/index.php?title=File:Flag_of_Haiti.svg *License*: unknown *Contributors*: User:Chanheigeorge, User:Denelson83, User:Lokal_Profil, User:Madden, User:Nightstallion, User:Vzb83, User:Zscout370

The cover image herein is used under a Creative Commons License and may be reused or reproduced under that same license.

http://upload.wikimedia.org/wikipedia/commons/6/6e/Noeud_de_pendu_en_ficelle.JPG